Islands

GREAT LAKES' STORIES

Islands

GREAT LAKES STORIES

Gerry Volgenau

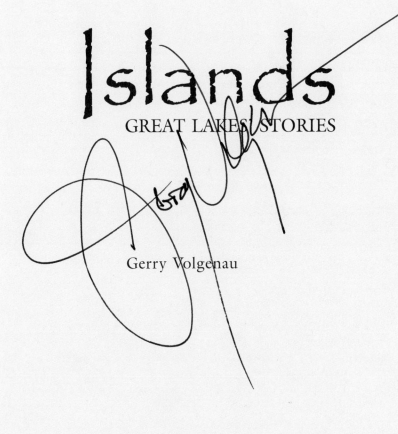

ANN ARBOR
MEDIA GROUP

All inquiries should be addressed to:
Ann Arbor Media Group LLC
2500 S. State Street
Ann Arbor, MI 48104

Printed and bound at Edwards Brothers, Inc., Ann Arbor, Michigan, USA
09 08 07 06 05 1   2   3   4   5

Library of Congress Cataloging-in-Publication Data

Volgenau, Gerry, 1940-
    Islands : Great Lakes' stories / Gerry Volgenau.
        p. cm.
    Includes bibliographical references.
    ISBN-13: 978-1-58726-128-2 (alk. paper)
    ISBN-10: 1-58726-128-6 (alk. paper)
  1. Great Lakes Region--History, Local--Anecdotes. 2. Islands--Great Lakes
Region--Anecdotes. 3. Great Lakes Region--Description and travel--Anecdotes.
4. Great Lakes Region--Guidebooks. I. Title.

    F551.V594 2005
    917.7--dc22

                                                        2005005537

ISBN-13: 978-1-58726-128-2
ISBN-10: 1-58726-128-6

To Christopher and Teresa

LAKE SUPERIOR

Sault Ste. Marie •

WISCONSIN

Green Bay •

LAKE MICHIGAN

MICHIGAN

IOWA

Chicago •

ILLINOIS

INDIANA

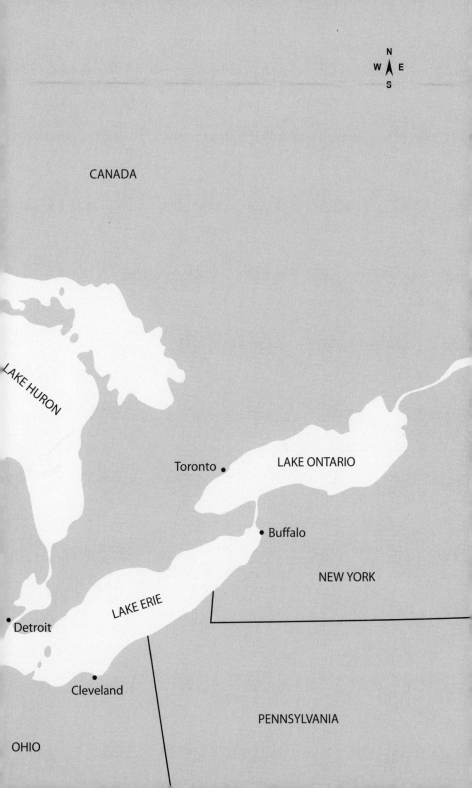

Contents

Lake Michigan

Lake Superior

Preface

In 1999, while I was the travel writer for the *Detroit Free Press,* my editor Kathy O'Gorman suggested an idea for the Sunday Travel front. Head on down to Lake Erie and do a story about Put-in-Bay and the Lake Erie islands.

That was the start—a smart editor with a smart idea. Once I got to the islands, I was captivated. Not only were the islands beautiful, but each one had a different personality. Each one had its own remarkable stories. Put-in-Bay was a sort of Key West of the North. Kelleys Island was laid back. Middle Island, at that point, was pulling day-trippers to its winery. And Johnson Island, one that I did not even know existed, had been a Civil War prison for Confederate officers. The Johnson Island story turned out to be the very stuff of movies with Confederate spies, piracy, and a plot to steal a Union war ship by drugging the crew in order to use the ship for a massive prison break.

As I wrote these stories, I realized that, with the single exception of Mackinac, I had never given much thought to Great Lakes islands as destinations for travelers. And when I looked into it, neither had anyone else.

I knew that just by their nature, these islands would be great places to visit and stay awhile—beautiful isolated places, beaches, water sports, fishing, maybe golf. Certainly they would be great places to just hang out. What's more, I thought that if the other islands were anything like the Lake Erie group, the stories of their past and present were likely to be wonderful—tales of bravery, ambition, dreams lost and found, and probably some downright silliness.

Little did I know. As I began writing *Free Press* stories on islands and then began looking toward doing this book, I discovered a storyteller's gold mine. I found island tales of Indian legends, murder mysteries, fierce battles, shipwrecks, heroic lighthouse keepers, a self-declared Mormon king, monsters that lurk in Lake Erie, harrowing escapes, islands that never existed yet were put on maps, and ghosts, lots of ghosts.

What I did not anticipate was that the stories of these islands, when taken together, would lie at the very heart of four hundred years of North America's history.

We, and I include myself, naturally have tended to think of islands as isolated places, enclaves that attracted little heed from the world at large.

But from the mid-1500s through the early twentieth century, the Great Lakes islands were at the heart of the North American story. During those centuries, roads were few, rough, and often dangerous. The easiest, fastest, safest way to get from one place to another was by water. The native people knew that. They had canoed the Great Lakes for eons. The Great Lakes were a natural highway, and, what's more, they provided direct passage to North America's greatest treasure trove of the era—beavers.

As for the islands, they were right in the middle of the Great Lakes' highway. They were the roadside stops where travelers pulled off for safety, rest, and supplies. Their harbors were protection from storms. They were the trade centers where beaver pelts were exchanged for blankets and musket balls. They were the equivalent of today's gas stations, where steamships loaded on lumber for fuel. Travelers got off for a drink and stayed the night. Island fishermen were near their jobs and could easily ship their catches. Farmers found the lake-moderated climate was good for crops. For years, the heart of America's wine industry lay in Lake Erie. Stores were set up, hotels were constructed, houses were built. People moved to these islands and stayed—not because they were isolated, but because they were at the heart of the action.

This era, of course, would pass with the coming of the first railroads and then cars and modern highways.

Tourism did take hold, however. It prospered in the late 1800s and early 1900s, only to wane and then revive in the later half of the twentieth century.

Given all the allure of the islands today and their remarkable stories, I also knew that this project needed limits. At the beginning, I could name only a few of the Great Lakes islands, but I knew there had to be lots and lots of them. It turned out that "lots and lots" was a remarkable underestimate. By some counts, the five lakes have some 35,000 islands. The count is quite vague since no one has really decided how big a chunk of rock must be to qualify as an island. As big as a football field? As big as a table top? No one really knows. I have seen official islands with actual names that barely can hold one house. At any rate, writing about them all would be impossible.

So to dramatically cut the list, I decided to include only those islands that people could get to without having to own a Chris-Craft or a seaplane.

People should be able to get to these islands for the price of a ferry ticket or a bridge toll. I, like the college admissions people, wanted diversity. That was no problem. Each island certainly had its own personality. The range went from the Toronto Islands, just a few minutes from one of North America's largest cities, to Isle Royale, a truly isolated wilderness where the wolves and moose are still in charge.

And finally, it got personal. I picked islands that just struck me as fascinating. I hope you agree.

Visit www.greatlakesstories.com for news, updates, and conversation on the Great Lakes' islands.

Acknowledgments

I'll never get an Academy Award. But I understand the actors' enthusiasm to thank so many people—no matter how boring it is to the rest of us. Like making a movie, writing a book of this sort can't be done by just sitting alone at a computer. As I traveled from island to island and then went on to do further research, many good-hearted people willingly gave up hours of their time and tapped their memories and expertise.

Frankly, like the superstars who often bore us with their shakily held lists at the Oscar ceremonies, I wish I could thank them all. I can't. But here are some of the major contributors.

Special thanks go to historians Gerard Altoff, former chief ranger at the Perry Victory and Peace Memorial, who patiently counseled me through the chapter on Oliver Harzard Perry and the Battle of Lake Erie; and Phil Porter, superintendent of Mackinac State Historical Parks, who at one point took me on a bike tour of the island's history. William Herd, of Sleeping Bear National Lakeshore and William Cashman, of the Beaver Island Historical Society and editor of the *Beaver Beacon*, double-checked my island stories. Rolf Peterson, leader of the Isle Royale Wolf and Moose Study and Michael Grosvenor, ferry boat captain for the Manitou Islands, are not official historians. But they offered some of the most profound knowledge about their islands that could have been found in no other place. All of these people not only shared their knowledge, but patiently read and corrected draft chapters of the book, saving me from some embarrassing errors.

It's still possible that errors exist in this book. But the fault is not theirs or anyone else's. I must claim sole responsibility for any goofs.

Thanks to the *Detroit Free Press*, where I was the travel writer and researched and wrote versions of these chapters that were published in the Sunday "Travel Section." At the newspaper I was helped by some first-rate print and photo editors. The *Detroit Free Press* has given permission to republish versions of my stories that now appear as the chapters on the Lake Erie islands, Drummond Island, North and South Manitou and Manitoulin islands, Les Cheneaux islands, as well as chapters on "The Mysterious Death of Danny Dodge," "It's Good to be King Strang," and "The Legend of Sleeping Bear."

Thanks also to Jeff Smith, editor of *Traverse: Northern Michigan's Magazine*, for his good counsel and to the magazine, which has published a version of "A Day with Rolf Peterson" and several photos.

There were others, of course. Many helped, on every island. Among the most stalwart were: on Toronto Island—Miriam McFarlane, resident, William Ward, whose ancestors were among the island's first residents, and Albert Fulton, the island archivist; Lake Erie islands—D. J. Parker, whose family goes back for generations on South Bass Island; Pelee Island—Irena Knezevic, of the Pelee Island Heritage Centre, and Mayor Bill Krestel; Birch and Grand La Cloche islands—Esther Osche, a modern storyteller and keeper of native traditions for the Whitefish River First Nation, and Linda Kelly, guardian of island memories at the Centennial Museum of Scheguiandah; Les Cheneaux Islands and Drummond Island—Glenn Lahti, a new Drummond islander but a passionate one, and Jessie Hadley, who brings the islands' ecology to life; Mackinac Island—Len Trankina, Mackinac's drollest resident and the former head of the visitors bureau, and from the Grand Hotel, President Dan Musser III, and the ebullient historian Bob Tagetz of the Grand Hotel; North Manitou Island—Rita Hadra Rusco, former island resident; Washington Island—Jeannie Hutchins, a local historian, fisherman Jake Ellefson, Laurie Veness, who keeps the Iceland horses, and Barbara Ellefson (no relation to Jake), the island archivist; Isle Royale—Bob Janke, former islander and expert on its flora, Pat Martin, a historian of the island's mining, Rolf Peterson's wife, Candy, and his sons, Jeremy and Trevor, and Paul Anderson, purser on the Ranger III ferry; Apostle Islands—Tom Nelson.

Historic photos were provided by the above groups and others who are given credit with individual photos. Contemporary pictures were taken by the author during his travels to the islands.

Lake Ontario

CANADA

Toronto

Toronto Island

Niagara Falls

LAKE ONTARIO

Rochester

NEW YORK

N
W E
S

Toronto Island

It's only natural to assume that Toronto Island was named for the city just across the bay. But it turns out that the opposite may be true.

It seems that Toronto is a Mississauga Indian word that means "a place with trees in the water," which is a pretty good definition of an island.

And other muddy definitions emerge about this cluster of islands. When you board the ferry at the foot of Bay Street, you may wonder whether you are going to Toronto Island (singular) or to the Toronto Islands (plural). It's the islanders' habit to say, "I live on Toronto Island." Mainlanders, with some attention to the map, are likely to say Toronto Islands with an *s*.

You can use either one and be understood. But since the islanders ought to be able to call their home whatever they want, we too should probably stick with the singular, Toronto Island.

It's illogical, of course. Of the fifteen to eighteen islands in the group, none of these islands is actually named Toronto.

And that brings me to another point. The actual count of islands can be frustratingly vague. The reason, as best I can tell, is that it depends on what bits of land sticking about the surface of Lake Ontario can actually be called islands. Most people count about fifteen, but island archivist Albert Fulton uses the official Toronto Harbour Commission map that includes some truly minuscule small bits of land. He counts eighteen.

And then there's Ward's Island, which is not an island at all. It is really part of Centre Island.

Historians might add yet another bit of perspective. Originally, Toronto Island was attached to the mainland. It was a peninsula. English-born gentry in horse-drawn carriages could simply drive out there from town. No need to take a ferry. That lasted until the mid-1800s, when a fierce gale slashed an opening at the island's east end. It opened a gap that soon became a major shipping channel and made the peninsula into actual islands.

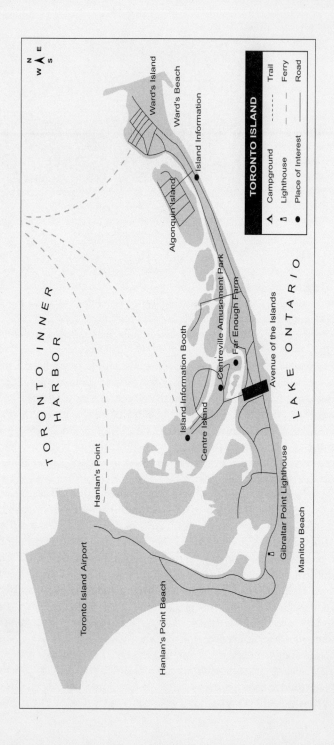

TORONTO ISLAND

Campground ⋀
Lighthouse
Place of Interest ●
Trail
Ferry
Road

N
W E
S

TORONTO INNER HARBOR

Ward's Island
Ward's Beach
Island Information ●
Algonquin Island
Centreville Amusement Park
Far Enough Farm
Avenue of the Islands
Island Information Booth ●
Centre Island ●
Hanlan's Point
Toronto Island Airport
Hanlan's Point Beach
Gibraltar Point Lighthouse ⋀
Manitou Beach
LAKE ONTARIO

Hey mom, are you looking? These giddy youngsters ride the antique windmill ferris wheel at Centreville Amusement Park on Toronto Island. Designed to delight smaller children, the park boasts a train, a log ride, an antique carousel, pony rides, and other fun stuff.

Walk on the Grass

But whatever you call them and whatever their number, Toronto Island is a wonderfully sweet place to spend a Saturday afternoon, a week, or, as the 650 year-round residents believe, years and years, even including the winters.

Each year, some 1.2 million visitors take the ferries across to the island, and a large portion of them are parents with young children. It's no wonder. This welcoming place actually has signs that read: "Walk on the Grass." Centre Island has a gentle amusement park called Centreville with gentle rides that run at speeds more suitable to Mr. Rogers than Roadrunner—a merry-go-round from 1908, a small Ferris wheel, and a log ride that does not kick up much of a wave. Also kids and their moms and dads can pet lambs and goats and ride Shetland ponies at Far Enough Farm, eat picnic lunches on broad lawns, chase each other through a maze of hedges, splash and build sand castles at the beaches, and paddle their own canoe on smooth protected waters.

On Toronto Island, everyone bicycles everywhere. Both visitors and residents. No cars are allowed. And it's no hardship, since the riding is flat and blissful. All day long you can see people pedaling by the amusement park or along the lagoons, swinging by a mysterious old lighthouse, circling the statue of Edward Hanlan, the world's greatest oarsman, skirting the beaches. A few of the immodest might stop at the Clothing Optional Beach on Hanlan's Point, which is popular with Toronto's gay community.

But best of all is to ride through and gawk at the island's munchkin-sized neighborhoods of cottages with gangly flower gardens that spill out over streets no wider than footpaths.

The island has 262 private homes. These houses are the last of what, at

No cars allowed on Toronto Island; everyone gets about on a bicycle— even the mailman. On this morning, he parked it for a few minutes while he walked a route.

one time, numbered in the many hundreds—some quite elegant. They were scattered from one end of the archipelago to the other. Now only these stubborn few remain. No McMansions here. These houses are tiny and squeezed into lots that could barely contain a suburban two-car garage. All are either on Ward's Island or nearby Algonquin Island, which is connected to Centre Island by a high-arched wooden footbridge.

The islanders themselves are a close-knit lot and more accepting of newcomers than many island communities where to be an islander means you must be born there.

"They can be considered an islander if they live here for five years, for chrissakes," says Bill Ward, a former city attorney and a fifth-generation islander.

Most of the locals commute by ferry each weekday to Toronto. Their jobs vary widely. They are teachers, nurses, lawyers, journalists, government workers, and so on. But it's the artists who truly seem to love island life. Some one hundred of the residents are working artists, says Albert Fulton, the island's archivist. That's almost one in six residents. They include painters, sculptors, photographers, costume and set designers, textile artists, and jewelry designers. And over the years, the island also has been home to numerous writers, editors, and radio and television personalities and executives.

Also contributing to the smell of oil paint and marble dust in the air is the island's Gibraltar Point Centre for the Arts, which opened in 1999. The centre, with its complex of buildings, has a residency program for artists, and studio and work space where they can work, think, and create undisturbed.

Impregnable Fortress of the British

As might be expected, Indians came first to Toronto Island. They fished and hunted, and some say the island served as a sort of native health spa, with fresh breezes off the lake and medicinal herbs growing among the trees. The earliest European settlers called their haunt Hiawatha's Island.

French fur trappers came next, but the British ultimately took over the Lake Ontario area in 1759 in the French and Indian War after the loss on the Plains of Abraham in the battle for Quebec. Life really began to change following the U.S. Revolutionary War. Some twenty thousand loyalists to the Crown (Americans called them Tories) fled north to what is now Ontario. At that point, the British regional capital was at present-day Niagara-on-the-Lake. Not good, reasoned John Graves Simcoe, lieutenant governor of the colony. Too close to the United States. Too indefensible.

So he moved the capital to what is now Toronto. The reason: any location for the capital would need a good harbor. Most travel and much troop movement were by ship. Toronto Island, then a five-mile spit of land running parallel to the shore, protected Toronto Bay and the town. And best of all, from a military standpoint, the harbor had only one entrance at the west end, which could be fortified.

Simcoe simply built two blockhouses and a guardhouse with cannons at the entrance and declared the passage impregnable—a virtual Gibraltar. Hence the name Gibraltar Point.

As it turned out, Gibraltar Point served as poor protection at the one time that it was important, during the War of 1812. In 1813, the Americans simply landed their troops on the mainland just west of the point fortifications, bypassed the guardhouse, and sacked the town, then called Fort York. On the way out a week later, they paused to demolish the Gibraltar Point blockhouses.

Lighthouse Ghost

Today's visitors love to bicycle out to the hexagon-shaped limestone lighthouse that stands back in the woods in a clearing at the west end of Centre Island. Completed in 1808, it was one of the earliest lighthouses on the Great Lakes. It now is Canada's oldest standing lighthouse and the oldest building in Toronto.

The original structure was fifty-two feet high with a wooden cage on top. Inside burned a lamp fueled by sperm whale oil. In 1832, the height was raised to its present eighty-two feet. And after thirty-one years, the light was fueled by coal oil, to be replaced in 1916 and 1917 with an electric light.

The lighthouse also was the scene of murder most foul in 1812, just four years after it was built.

Canada's oldest standing lighthouse rises up 82 feet high on Centre Island of Toronto Island. The structure was originally built in 1808 and then given extra height in 1832. Tales linger that a ghost still lurks in the old stone tower.

On January 2, lighthouse keeper J.P. Rademuller (also spelled Radan Muller) just disappeared. One day he was there; the next he was gone. Everyone suspected foul play.

The story goes that Rademuller did a little bootlegging on the side. And late on New Year's Day, two or three soldiers from Fort York dropped by for a whistle wetter. The keeper brought them a keg of beer. In a short time, the soldiers got roaring drunk. At that point, Rademuller refused to give them any more. His refusal led to a fight and, ultimately, his murder. People suspected that his body was buried somewhere west of the tower.

The story further goes, with no records to support it, that two soldiers were brought to trial, but got off since no body had been found.

Then this tale of murder takes a leap in time. Sixty-one years later, Joe Durman, the lighthouse keeper, had heard the murder story and went digging around. After some searching he discovered bits of a coffin with a man's jaw bone that had been buried about 350 feet west of the lighthouse. The nineteenth century had no DNA testing. But many believed Durman had found the remains of the ill-fated lighthouse keeper.

To this day, people report that when they stop by the lighthouse late at night, they hear the eerie sounds from inside. Hollow thumps and thuds. They think it is Rademuller's ghost. My own theory is that he's angry because people keep misspelling his name.

Islands for Real

Basically, Toronto Island has been a vacation getaway almost from the beginning. In the early 1800s, British officers stationed at Fort York would pack a picnic lunch in a buggy and go with their ladies out to the island. They would catch fresh lake breezes. The men would often go hunting. In 1833, the first hotel was built at the eastern end of the island, called the Retreat on the Peninsula. It was a rough-and-tumble place, for the most part filled by drinkers and gamblers. Two years later, a new owner renamed the hotel the Peninsula and tried to attract more genteel clientele. He put out ads calling it "a pleasant and healthy retreat for individuals and families desirous of changing the air of the city for the salubrious atmosphere of the island."

It's a shame that the term "salubrious atmosphere" has drifted out of today's travel advertising. But, in fact, the island was a good escape from the swampy town which was dubbed "Muddy York." Later named Toronto, York indeed was a breeding place for mosquitoes and some rather unpleasant diseases.

But important changes were in the works both for the island and for the hotel.

In 1852, a nasty storm ripped open a channel through a sandy spit that connected the peninsula to the mainland at its east end. A year later that watery cut had grown to 150 feet wide. Then in April 1858, another storm hit. This was a huge one. Lake water poured through the gap. And in the end, Torontonians found themselves separated from the island by 150 feet of water. The storm not only tore open this huge gap, but at the same time destroyed wharves, outbuildings, and the Peninsula Hotel, which was then owned by John Quinn.

The local newspaper quickly reported the obvious: "In the early hours of April 13, 1858, nature took matters in her own hands and in spectacular fashion created Toronto Island."

A new entrance had been cut into Toronto Harbor. A year later, the first steamship came through, the *Bowmanville*. By the mid-1860s, the channel was eight feet deep and three-quarters of a mile across. Today, it's twenty-seven feet deep and the main shipping channel.

A Hero: Sailors' Savior

Within a decade or so after Toronto Island officially became an island, two heroes emerged. They were contemporaries and friends, and both were sons of the island's earliest fishermen.

William Ward's destiny was set by a tragedy.

On a blustery day in 1862, fifteen-year-old William set out in a sailboat with five of his young sisters. It was going to be fun. He ignored warn-

Captain William Ward, son of a Toronto Island fisherman, was Toronto's greatest and most courageous lifesaver. He is credited with having saved 164 lives. On several occasions he went out in winter storms to save the crews of ships that had foundered off the island. Courtesy of the Toronto Island Archives.

ings about heavy winds and bad weather. But then the big winds came. They battered the small sailboat until it flipped over. Before help could arrive, all five of the girls had drowned. Only William remained alive.

Spurred by that day of horror, William went on to become the greatest and most courageous lifesaver in Toronto's history. He is credited with having saved 164 lives.

On one snowy, ferociously cold December day five years after the accident, Ward and his friend, Robert Berry, spotted the schooner *Jane Ann Marsh* foundering off the island. Ten crewmen had climbed into the rigging.

The two young men stripped to their underwear and started rowing a small skiff out to help. Three times huge waves overturned the boat, spitting the men into the frigid waters. Three times the young men righted the boat and set out again.

By the time they reached the schooner, the survivors were unable to move. They were literally frozen to the rigging by six inches of ice. With no other recourse, the rescuers took pieces of broken timber and pounded at the ice until the crewmen were freed. The whole process took seven hours in that storm. But they saved the entire crew.

Such stories were repeated again and again. Ward swam in freezing winter surf to carry a lifeline to another downed ship. He rowed out through a winter storm—when all others refused to leave the shore—and saved six men on a ship that broke up just after he pulled them onto his skiff.

Years later, Ward went on to build a hotel on Centre Island and then a bigger one close to what is now the Ward's Island dock. The island eventually was named for William and his family.

A Hero: The Boy in Blue

The story goes that Ned Hanlan was only five years old when he first rowed a boat between Toronto Island and the mainland.

True or not, Edward Hanlan, the son of a Toronto Island fisherman, did grow up to be the world's greatest competitive oarsman. As a sculler, he won more than 300 consecutive races, defeating the world's best oarsman at the time. A statue of Hanlan holding an oar stands near the west end of Toronto Island at Hanlan's Point.

It's hard to imagine the mass appeal of sculling in the late 1800s, especially because rowing events today get international attention only once every four years at the Olympics, and not much even then. But 130 years ago, rowing was hugely popular. Thousands of people thronged to the shore to watch sinewy young men streak across the water in their slender racing shells. Big money was bet. And Hanlan was a Canadian hero on the scale of today's hockey legend Wayne Gretzky.

He was young, lean, and handsome with a raffish moustache. Women adored him; men wanted to be him. He was an up-from-the-fish-docks success story. And his life story was the very stuff of movies filled with

Son of a Toronto Island fisherman, Ned Hanlan became the world's greatest competitive oarsman, winning some 300 consecutive races in the 1870s and 1880s. He was credited for being the first to use a sliding seat on his racing scull. This staged photo was taken about 1880. Courtesy of the National Archives of Canada.

brilliant skills, hairbreadth escapes, new technology, and sheer panache. So it's not surprising a film was made of his life, called *The Boy in Blue*. It starred a young Nicholas Cage.

Hanlan entered one of his first competitions in 1871 at the age of sixteen. It was a local race for Toronto fishermen. He came in second, behind his friend William Ward, who would become the legendary life saver.

But then his winning ways began. Two years later, he won the rowing championship on Toronto Bay, beating Canada's best. He got financial backing from a group of twenty Toronto businessmen, who were looking to win some big bucks gambling on the Hanlan races. Not only was his strength great, but he adopted a bit of new technology. It was a sliding seat that could increase his pull. Basically it is the same seat used on all racing sculls today.

But it was not a smooth ride to the top.

He ran into trouble with the law in 1876, just days before he was set to leave for the Centennial Regatta in Philadelphia. The competition was hugely important. America's best oarsmen would be there. And the prize was $800, a fortune in the 1870s. But it happened that the police discovered that Ned, as he was called, had been doing a little bootlegging on the side for his father's hotel. They put out a warrant for his arrest. Two days before he was to leave, the police spotted him at the Toronto Rowing Club. But, as the story goes, just as the cops came in the front door, Hanlan sneaked out the back. He jumped in a skiff and rowed, as only he could row, for a steamship headed out of the harbor. Making it to the ship, he climbed aboard using a rope ladder. Days later, he won the top prize in Philadelphia. So when Hanlan returned to Toronto, crowds cheered him as a conquering hero. The police, recognizing a bad idea when they saw one, discreetly dropped that little matter of bootlegging.

He became known as "the boy in blue" because he always wore blue racing togs and a red headband. In 1880, he won the championship in England and held the title for four years.

Many times Hanlan would streak off to such a commanding lead that he would literally stop rowing, lean on his oars for a while, and throw kisses to girls in the crowd.

Hanlan went on to become a city alderman in Toronto, and he opened a hotel and a huge amusement park on the island's west end, near where his statue is today.

Cottages, "Coney Island," Babe Ruth, and Conflict

During the second half of the nineteenth century and into the 1920s, more people came to the island and they were staying for longer times. Initially the island was a place of saloons and gambling. But summer homes cropped

No fancy summer mansions here. In the early part of the twentieth century, people set up tents on plots of land on Ward's Island, which is actually a part of Centre Island. It was an inexpensive way to get away from Toronto's steamy streets and enjoy Lake Ontario's waters and cool breezes. Courtesy of the City of Toronto Archives.

Hanlan's Point Amusement Park was "Canada's Coney Island," in the early 1900's. Thousands took ferries from Toronto to Centre Island. The attractions included the Big Scream roller coasters, the penny arcade, water shows, and baseball games. (Babe Ruth allegedly hit his first professional homerun here against the Toronto Maple Leafs.) The park even had a freak show with a fat lady and a South American wild girl. This photo was shot in 1917. Courtesy of the Toronto Island Archives.

up on Centre Island. First cottages, and then elegant Victorian mansions for Toronto's wealthiest families. A town of sorts developed, with a post office, grocery store, meat market, dance pavilion, and bowling alley.

At the turn of the twentieth century, a summer tent city started to grow on Ward's Island. People with modest incomes could afford a tent and a tiny plot of land. They escaped the city's swelter for beaches and cool breezes. In 1900, ten tents were set up on Ward's Island. In 1906, twenty-eight tents. And by 1912, the number grew to 685. Narrow muddy streets. Public water taps and toilets. No dogs allowed. In the 1930s, cottages replaced the tents.

None could have more than 840 square feet. After World War II, the summer cottages were insulated. Year-round living was possible.

Out on Hanlan's Point to the west, Ned Hanlan built his hotel in 1880 and constructed the beginnings of the era's greatest national amusement park. Scores of cottages were built. Twelve years later, the Toronto Ferry Company took over the hotel and park.

Crowds jammed the ferries to reach Canada's Coney Island. Disney could hardly have designed a more popular amusement park. The grounds blazed with lights. Rollicking music trilled and people laughed. A full day could be passed going to the penny arcade and the theater, riding the merry-go-round and a giant roller coaster called the Big Scream. Moreover, there were sculling races, a diving horse, shooting galleries, parades, and (something that would be considered politically incorrect today) a freak show with a fat lady from Africa, a South American Wild Girl, and a real-life Zulu with an Irish accent.

One of the biggest draws was Toronto's first professional baseball stadium. It was the home field for the Toronto Maple Leafs of the International League.

The story goes that on September 5, 1914, Babe Ruth hit his first home run as a professional in that stadium. At the time, Ruth was playing for Providence, a minor league farm team for the Boston Red Sox. "He hit the ball right out into the water," says Albert Fulton. "And I guess it's still there."

By the 1920s, the amusement park started to fall into decay, although it continued operating with modest success into the 1930s. But it came to a sudden end in 1938 when the land was taken over to build an airport. Lagoons for sculling races were filled in. Buildings were torn down. And a number of private cottages were picked up and transferred by boat to Sunfish Island, now called Algonquin Island. These original houses, often smaller than others on the island, now sit along Algonquin's shoreline.

But other private home owners would not get off so easily.

Time and local politics eventually created some big changes. In the late 1950s, the city of Toronto turned over possession of the island to the larger Metropolitan Toronto. And that body wanted to turn the island into a city park. Put in terms of New York City, Metro Toronto didn't want a Coney Island, it wanted a Central Park surrounded by water.

The Parks Department brought in backhoes and proceeded to tear down buildings, houses, cottages, and even the grand Victorian mansions. All the lands were stripped of structures on Hanlan's Point and Centre Island. By one estimate, 300 historic buildings were torn down.

But officialdom did not count on the people who lived in the 272 homes on Ward's Island and Algonquin Island. They dug in their heels and refused to go. It was a battle that continued in and out of the courts for almost forty

Backed with the family's distillery fortune, George Gooderham built the grandest summer house on Centre Island's Lakeshore Avenue. It was torn down in the 1950s, along with another 300 historic buildings on Toronto Island, when the city decided to turn the island into a city park. Courtesy of Fred Montague.

years. But finally a deal was cut in 1993 that allowed the islanders to own their homes and keep their land under ninety-nine-year leases.

Most visitors as they ride through the neighborhood probably have no understanding of the long battle for survival. They see cheery gardens, quaint homes, an island idyll within sight of the big city. And perhaps that's as it should be.

If You Go

Getting There: The three ferries to Toronto Island leave from the foot of Bay Street, just behind the Westin Harbour Castle Hotel. Most people take the ferry to Centre Island, where the docks are within an easy walk to the Centreville Amusement Park and Far Enough Farm (which have no admission fees), the maze, bubbling fountains, and the beach. A second ferry goes to Ward's Island at the east end of Toronto Island. The dock is an easy walk away from the communities on Ward's Island and Algonquin Island, to the sailing and canoe clubs, and a very nice beach. The third ferry goes to Hanlan's Point, which is close to tennis courts, baseball diamonds, the Gibraltar Point Lighthouse, and the clothing-optional beach.

For the ferry schedule, call 416-392-8193; www.city.toronto.on.ca/parks/island. Children ages twelve and younger ride free.

Transportation: The best way to see the island is on a bike. Bring your own, or you can rent them at the island docks or at the beach on Centre Island.

Food: Sandwich shops, pizza places, ice cream parlors, and other quick food spots can be found in Centreville, on the island's beaches, and at the Centre Island dock. The best public restaurant is the Rectory Café, which offers an interesting menu, a selection of wines, and, if the weather is good, patio dining. It's located on Centre Island close to the bridge to Algonquin Island. Call 416-203-2152. Generally reservations are not necessary.

Lodging: The island has no hotels. But it does have four bed-and-breakfasts in homes on Ward's Island and Algonquin Island. Check www.torontoisland.org.

Parking: If you need to leave your car before boarding the ferry, two open lots are just to the east of the Westin Harbour Castle Hotel.

Winter: Although most people visit the island in summer, winter also can be a good time. People skate on the lagoons, cross-country ski, and snowshoe.

Lake Erie

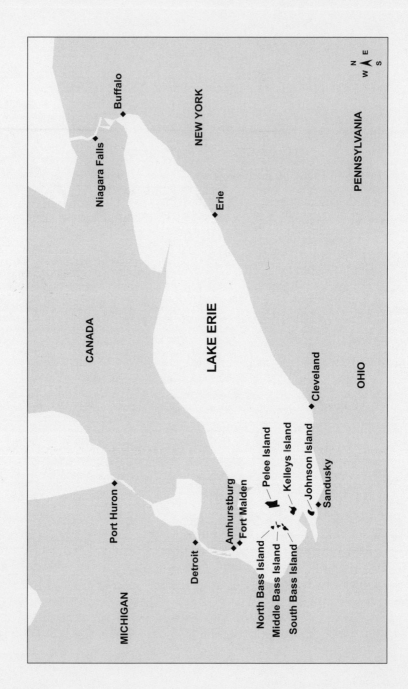

Lake Erie Islands

These are the wine islands.

In the green waters of western Lake Erie, these eleven glacier-scraped limestone islands—the bigger ones at least—all can boast a wine-growing pedigree that dates back more than one hundred years.

These Ohio islands, along with Ontario's Pelee Island, also are known for creating an avian bridge, where birds can fly from one island to another and work their way across Lake Erie during their spring and fall migrations. Not surprisingly, like the birds themselves, binocular-toting bird-watchers flock to the islands in just those seasons.

Once, long, long ago, these islands were much alike—with low-lying slabs of limestone and lots of trees, lying low as lily pads on the water. But these days, each one has evolved into a very different personality.

South Bass Island fancies itself the Key West of the North. In the village of Put-in-Bay on the marina, it's rum drinks, ribald songs, and dancing into the wee hours every warm night of the year, but especially on weekends.

Middle Bass Island is a sleepy little place with beautiful late nineteenth-century cottages owned by the rich from Toledo. If you can entertain yourself, you'll be fine. The long-famous Lonz Winery has been closed for several years, ending the usual wine-sippers' soirees from South Bass.

Kelleys Island is the G-rated island, good for kids and grandmas. If South Bass is Key West, then Kelleys is Low Key. Very homey and great for families who don't need a constant run of Disney World entertainment and for lovers who want to do little more than look into each other's eyes as the waves lap on the shore.

Johnson Island is a bit of water-bound suburbia that used to be a Devils Island for Confederate Army officers.

North Bass Island is basically a big vineyard. It is privately owned except for a couple of dozen undeveloped acres owned by Ohio's state parks system. About ten families live there, most of whom work at Meier's Vineyards.

The Erie archipelago also has a number of smaller, privately owned islands, some with amusing names like Mouse, Ballast, Starve, and Big Chicken.

As a result of the islands' variations, they have real appeal to a great variety of people.

You'll find plenty of twenty-somethings and thirty-somethings who think—as every generation before them did—that they are the first ones to discover the interesting potential for sex by combining Budweiser and loud music.

There are boaters who fish. Boaters who don't fish. And boaters who love to party, which is pretty much all boaters.

There are families looking for a good beach, a camping spot, or a glimpse of some wildlife; a merry-go-round with real wooden horses; and perhaps a pickup game of miniature golf.

History buffs delight in the Perry Victory and International Peace Memorial with its soaring tower and snazzy visitors' center. It was in Lake Erie, just off these islands, that Commodore Oliver Hazard Perry—with some very good luck on his side—knocked the bejesus out of the Brits in the War of 1812. It was there he filed his famous report: "We have met the enemy and they are ours."

The islands and two nearby counties boast two dozen eagle's nests, more than anywhere in Ohio.

Anglers generally can pull in something reasonably big and edible.

Snake fans (do such people exist?) can easily spot the increasingly rare Lake Erie water snake—a reptile likely to hit the endangered species list soon.

If you are really lucky, or perhaps are over-served at Put-in-Bay's Round House Bar, you also might catch a glimpse of South Bay Bessie, Lake Erie's very own monster.

Hammer-and-rock geology types can see stalactites and stalagmites in limestone caves, as well as what's touted as the world's largest geode. Or they can see huge, smooth rock grooves that run longer than a football field, scored by an Ice Age glacier.

Foodies find the island fare generally better than fair, but only in a few instances exceptional. Perch and walleye dinners are served up almost everywhere. The fish is fresh and delicious. Most of the rest is typical bar food—burgers, wings, spaghetti, pizza, steaks.

South Bass Island

One boater here told me that he has been coming to Put-in-Bay for 20 years. He usually comes by boat and has never, ever visited the tourist sights like Perry's Cave.

But, he said, speaking with the authority of two decades, "There are a lot of things to do if you want to party at the bars.

"In fact," he said, "if you can't have fun at the Bay, there probably are not many places where you will have fun."

That is Put-in-Bay's reputation, and in many respects its reality. On Friday and Saturday nights, the Chris-Craft and Wellcraft cruisers are quadruple parked in the marina, and the ferries from the mainland groan with overloads of the soon-to-be-loaded.

They come, they drink. They eat perch fried in batter. They tap their sandals to the rock 'n' roll blare. They talk loud, laugh loud, and dance like libertines.

They buy T-shirts that say "Real Fishermen don't need Viagra."

They rent golf carts—the most popular means of transportation—and drive them with all the care and deliberation of twelve-year-olds in carnival bumper cars.

These are the North Coast parrotheads, just Ohio good ole boys and party dolls trying to catch a little of Jimmy Buffett's Caribbean-style escapism. Never mind that instead of coral, Erie's reefs are covered in zebra mussels.

The island's hottest live music and beer-swilling spots are pretty much what they have been for years, all facing DeRivera Park along the booze run of Delaware and Hartford streets.

So much beer used to be spilled on the floor of the Round House that the owners feared patrons would slip and fall, recalls D. J. Parker, a member of one of the island's oldest families who worked for a time at the Round

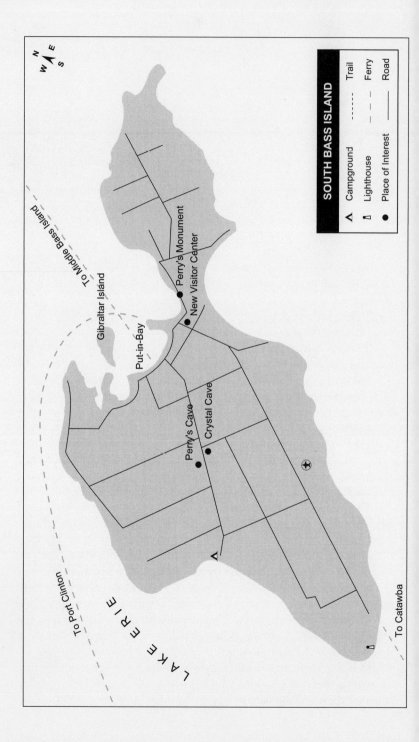

SOUTH BASS ISLAND

- ∧ Campground
- ⌂ Lighthouse
- ● Place of Interest
- ⋯ Trail
- -- Ferry
- — Road

Perry's Monument
New Visitor Center
Perry's Cave
Crystal Cave

Put-in-Bay
Gibraltar Island
To Middle Bass Island
To Port Clinton
To Catawba

LAKE ERIE

House. He said people had to be shooed out at about 4 or 5 PM, so the floors could be hosed down.

Other times, management went with the flow—turning the floor into a big sloppy beer slide. Customers competed to see who could glide the farthest. The bars have quieted down some since then, but boaters still get plenty of kicks.

If it seems like South Bass Island has fallen prey to some modern tourist debauchery, reconsider. For most of its human history, the island has been a tourist mecca.

In its earliest days, of course, Indians visited all the islands in the group. Then came French explorers.

Early maps showed the harbor as Pudding Bay, probably because it was shaped like a pudding sack. Some believe that was the origin of the name Put-in-Bay.

As white people moved onto the island, they used it for its natural resources. They chopped down the red cedars to feed the boilers of their steam ships, fished its waters, quarried limestone for construction, and, for a time, grew wheat, tobacco, rye, oats, hay, and clover. Some brought in pigs and sheep to feed on the island's plentiful hickory nuts and acorns.

By the 1850s, that sort of rural diversity was gone. Most farmers turned to grapes, and they stayed at it for decades. The island's climate was good because of the lake's moderating effect. It got 200 frost-free days a year. The grapes were Catawba, which some say produced high-quality wines that rivaled France's best. By 1880, almost half the island's 1,300 acres were planted in grapes. It had twelve wineries and five brandy distilleries.

By the century's turn, it was down to half a dozen wineries, but winemaking was still going.

An early morning stroll on the marina at Put-in-Bay, South Bass Island. Put-in-Bay attracts huge numbers of boaters on summer weekends, who come to loll on their sunny decks, drink beer, and laugh a lot.

Nope, not for golf. These carts lined up at the Heinneman Brewery are the major mode of transportation on South Bass Island and Put-in-Bay.

The island's biggest tourist boom came in the 1890s and early 1900s when it was one of biggest tourist destinations in the United States. At that point, 1,100 people lived permanently on the island, more than double the present 500. And steam ships carrying 1,500 passengers regularly came to Put-in-Bay.

The Great Lakes' Grandest Hotel
The island's really big draw was one of the world's biggest hotels—the Hotel Victory. Opened in 1892, it was a palatial, four-story wooden hotel with 625 rooms. Presidents dropped in to spend a night or two. Almost one thousand people could eat at once in the dining room. It had bowling alleys, a barbershop, and an ice cream parlor.

And the hotel's outdoor swimming pool broke all precedents. It was the first in the country where men and women were allowed to swim together. By 1919, it was all over. On August 14, the mega-hotel burned to

For more than 80 years, starting in the 1850s, South Bass Island was at the center of America's wine industry— awash in vineyards and wineries. Half the island's acreage was given over to Catawba grapes. At its height in the 1880s, the island had 12 wineries and five brandy distilleries. By the turn of the century, the island was down to half a dozen wineries. Then in the 1920s, national prohibition slammed the wine business hard. Now just one winery remains, Heineman's, which gives daily tours. Courtesy of Jeff Bykowski.

Put-in-Bay on South Bass Island has long been a tourist destination. In the years surrounding the turn of the twentieth century, it had a scream-and-gasp roller coaster located near the corner of Toledo and Delaware streets. The village also had a big toboggan slide and later, in the 1930s, a diving horse. Courtesy of Jeff Bykowski.

the ground. The flames could be seen as far away as the Detroit River.

Today, some of the hotel's original foundations still jut from the ground at the island's state campground.

What really slammed the island's tourist trade and the wine industry was Prohibition. From 1918 to 1933, tourists stayed away in droves, island-ers left, and the grape lands went to seed.

Now don't misunderstand, the island did not go out of the booze busi-ness during Prohibition, at least not entirely.

Just as birds have used these islands to get back and forth between the United States and Canada, so did the bootleggers of the 1920s. While long-

Built in 1892, the Hotel Victory at Put-in-Bay was one of the world's largest and grandest. A four-story structure with 625 rooms, it had a fancy dining room, bowling alleys, a barber shop, and a swimming pool where men and women actually swam together. Quite racy at the time. The hotel helped make Put-in-Bay one of the country's great tourist destinations. It was destroyed by fire on August 14, 1919. Courtesy of the Put-in-Bay Gazette, Jeff and Kendra Koehler.

Trollies in Put-in-Bay head for the island's most lavish destination, the Hotel Victory. Courtesy of the Put-in-Bay Gazette, Jeff and Kendra Koehler.

Crowds gather to watch the cornerstone being set for the Perry Victory Memorial on July 4, 1913. The monument was later renamed the Perry Victory and International Peace Memorial. The monument finished as a Greek Doric column towering 352 feet high over the tourist village of Put-in-Bay. Courtesy of Jeff Bykowski.

time residents still are reluctant to talk about those days, you can rest assured that lots of Canadian hooch came south via South Bass Island. Some of the few historical records show that one operator towed the same scow load of coal (with booze hidden beneath) many times between South Bass Island and Pelee Island, which was just across the international border. In winter, bootleggers would fill up trucks with illegal whiskey and drive them across the ice to thirsty U.S. buyers.

In fact, driving on the ice has been a longtime winter entertainment on the island, even without booze in the trunk. Young bucks, in particular, would skitter across the ice to other islands or to the mainland. This, of course, was well before the lakes began feeling the effects of global warming.

The drivers, Parker said, used to take old junkers and cut off the doors so if the car hit a soft spot and broke through the ice, they could jump out.

The island's wine industry never really recovered from Prohibition. Today, it has a few dozen acres given over to grapes. And only one winery remains, the venerable Heineman's, which gives tours and, of course, lets you take multiple sips in its tasting room. Grape juice for the kids.

But these days, visitors still can find much to do without a beer mug or a wine glass in one hand.

In early mornings, it's a fine time for a bike ride or a walk along the marina as the crisp lake light melts to butter. You can hear the clink-a-clink of sailboat riggings and the hum and chatter as families come by on their golf carts on their way to play miniature golf or visit some of the sights.

Perry's Monument

One architectural feature dominates the entire island. You can see it from miles out in the lake. It is Perry's Victory and International Peace Memorial, a 352-foot Greek Doric column. It is the United States' third tallest monument, after the St. Louis Arch and the Washington Monument. If

A pleasure boat, the steamship Chippewa *carried passengers from Sandusky to the Lake Erie islands and also did excursions from Detroit, Toledo, and Cleveland. This photo was taken in 1935. The* Chippewa *sailed on the lakes between 1923 and 1938. Courtesy of Russell Matso.*

the thought appeals to you, you can see Detroit from the top. It honors Oliver Hazard Perry's War of 1812 defeat of the British fleet in the Battle of Lake Erie. It was built in 1915 and originally called Perry's Victory Monument, but later a sensitivity to Canadian feelings arose and the words "and International Peace Memorial" were added.

The monument has a first-rate visitors' center with movie theater, a model of the battle, and Ohio's oldest statue of Perry, who looks quite dashing.

Perry's Cave

This drippy limestone cave lies fifty-two feet underground and has its own little pond, called a lake, that rises and falls with the waters in Lake Erie. It was said that Perry's crew used this cave for storage before the big battle in 1813. But little evidence supports that romantic notion.

However, John Gangwish, known as the Little Old Man of the Cave, used to lead tours with a lantern in the years before he died in 1929. He'd come to the island originally as a well driller in 1882, but found guiding to be easier and more profitable.

Down underground, Gangwish told the old stories and often would feign surprise as he "discovered" an old shoe, which of course he previously dropped there himself. "Oh," he would say, "it must have been left by one of Perry's men." And then he'd sell it to the highest bidder.

Crystal Cave

Crystal Cave, located at Heineman's Winery, has what is reputed to be the world's largest geode. It's thirty feet in diameter and encrusted with fifty tons of bluish-white celestite crystals. (A geode, in case you missed that class, is a stone with a hole in it that's lined with crystals or minerals.)

Other island diversions include panning for crystals in the sluice, watching the flutter at the Butterfly Museum, and playing miniature golf, all at Perry's Cave; visiting Stonehenge Estate with a classic stone farmhouse and wine-press cottage from the mid-1800s; taking a ride on Kimberly's Carousel, built in 1917, with all hand-carved wooden animals; or catching a glimpse of South Bass Island's history at the Lake Erie Islands Historical Center by the town hall on Catawba Avenue.

If You Go

Getting There: South Bass Island and the village of Put-in-Bay can be reached by regular Miller Boat Line (800-500-2421, www.millerferry.com) car and passenger ferries from Catawba Island (actually a peninsula) and by Jet Express (800-245-1538; www.jet-express.com) passenger ferries from Port Clinton.

Transportation: Cars are transported on the Miller Ferry, but most visitors prefer to ride about in golf carts or on bikes that can be rented at the docks or elsewhere on the island.

Dining: You can find fresh walleye and perch on all the islands. The finest dining on South Bass seems to move from restaurant to restaurant with the chefs; it is best to check with the locals.

Information: For details on hotels, motels, campgrounds, and other attractions, call the Ottawa County Visitors Bureau at 800-441-1271; www.lake-erie.com.

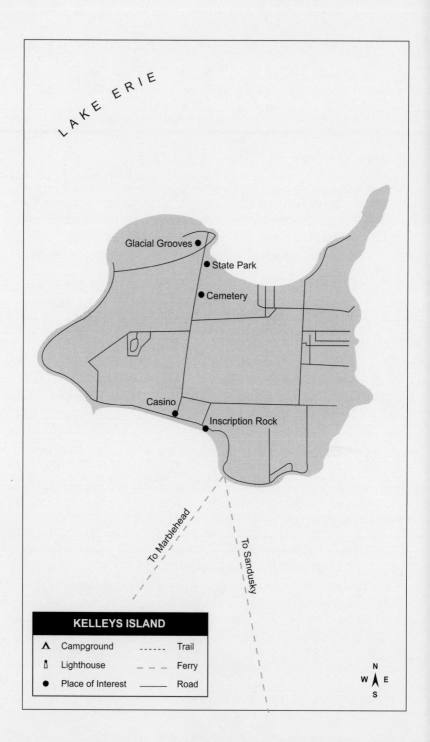

Kelleys Island

You get the sense on Kelleys Island that it didn't look much different forty-five years ago. And that is its charm.

Downtown—if two blocks can be called a downtown—is a collection of decades-old frame buildings. If you don't look too closely, you get the sense that you have dropped into a period movie and that a stout Babe Ruth might come strolling along. Also the island has a marina, a few bar-restaurants by the docks, churches, a grade school for about twenty-six students, and many well-kept homes, most owned by summer cottage people. Like many islands, it's a slow-going, small-town kind of place where everybody knows everybody else's secrets.

No neon flash, no glitz. To alight from the ferry on Kelleys Island is to feel your pulse rate drop.

There is no hotel. Visitors rent cottages, stay at bed-and-breakfasts, or stake out their tents at Kelleys Island State Park right by the island's one public beach. On weekends, the yachts do raft up at the marina and boaters stop motoring on liquids and start drinking them. But this is not a patch on Put-in-Bay's boozy weekend days and nights.

From Rock Pictures to Days of Wine and Limestone

Back in the sixteenth century, Indians had at least two villages on the island. These ancient people were wiped out by the Iroquois in the 1660s. It's believed that either the prehistoric people or wandering bands of Iroquois left their handiwork, the drawings carved into Inscription Rock, that is located near the ferry dock. On a massive piece of limestone, this petroglyph is considered one of the finest pieces of aboriginal art in the Great Lakes region.

No one is sure what the drawings of men and animals mean. But some

The carved figures now are faint on Inscription Rock on Kelleys Island. Ancient Indians made carvings in this slab of limestone some 400 years ago. Researchers believe the inscriptions might have been messages left by one group of Indians for another, telling of where they had been, how the hunting had gone, and where they were going. Pre–1900 postcard courtesy of Russell Matso.

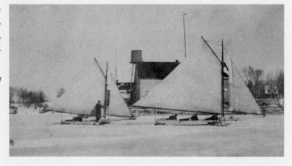

Ice boating was a great way to take the curse off the long winter of 1912–1913 on Kelleys Island. Courtesy of Russell Matso.

researchers suspect that the stone was used to convey messages, and that the now-faded drawings indicate where the artists had been hunting and fishing and where they were going next.

No one knows what the Indians called Kelleys Island. In fact, the Kelley name did not show up until decades after a French man named Cunningham, the first white settler, showed up in 1810.

So it was on Cunningham's Island that wood was cut to fuel passing steamships and two passenger-cargo ships were built, one a sailboat, the other a steamship. For a time, it was even called Island No. 6.

But the name changed permanently after the Kelley brothers, Datus and Irad, showed up in 1833 and developed the island industries—fishing, quarrying the limestone which was a favored building material from New York to Chicago, and, of course, growing grapes.

The Kelleys Island Wine Company, founded just after the Civil War in 1866, eventually dominated wine production on the island. In 1872, the island produced 126,000 gallons, made from grapes picked from 650 acres.

The 30,000-year-old glacial grooves on Kelleys Island are some of the world's most famous. Great glaciers, a mile thick, scraped these grooves in the soft limestone during the Ice Age. The grooves are 400 feet long, 30 feet wide, and just as deep. The Glacial Groove State Memorial is at the north end of Kelleys Island.

The North Shore Loop Trail is one of the prettiest and most interesting hikes on Kelleys Island. It passes through the woods, by the remains of the 1888 loader building where limestone was piled into railway cars, and then skirts along the water. Don't worry about the gray Lake Erie water snakes, they aren't poisonous.

Almost half were pressed by the Kelleys' company, the remainder by twenty-five independent cellars.

Over time, the wine industry tailed off on the island. Prices dropped, Prohibition hit, and eventually people began to prefer California wines. Today, the Kelleys Island Wine Company still exists. It sells wine made from grapes, at least some of which are grown on the island. They have names like Coyote White and Long Sweet Red. As for quarrying, that, along with tourism, is still a major source of island income.

Speaking of history, Kelleys Islanders can pridefully show off some really old stuff—30,000-year-old glacial grooves cut into the limestone on the north side of the island. During the Ice Age, a mile-thick glacier foot-dragged its way south across what is now the Great Lakes region. These grooves, which locals claim are the world's most famous, run 400 feet long, 30 feet wide, and just about as deep.

Hiking is among the fine things to do on Kelleys Island. Most trails are relatively short.

In the early morning, you can stroll down the boardwalk at the estuary, where you may spot great blue herons, snowy egrets, and wood ducks. The trailhead is on the north side of Ward Road, west of the 4-H Camp.

Or take East Quarry Trail, which, as you might expect, goes around a limestone quarry. The trailhead is near the S turn on Ward Road, east of the 4-H Camp.

But my favorite hike is the North Shore Loop. It runs about a mile but takes in some island history and an extraordinarily pretty woodland walk. You pass the site of the old Kelleys Island Lime and Transport Company. The almost palatial walls and some of the guts still remain from the 1888 loader building, where crushed limestone was dumped into railroad cars to be hauled to the dock or lime kilns.

Farther back in the woods, near the old quarry, is a brick dynamite shed. The powder's gone, so sparks aren't a problem. And besides, the door is locked. Walking along this shady trail that skirts the rocky shoreline, you also are likely to see a deer or two, and an example of the state tree, the Ohio buckeye. And you'll catch a glimpse across the water to the north of Ontario's Middle Island, and beyond it Pelee Island.

For a little bit of critter contact without a walk, many people stop by to see the flutterings at the Sweeny Valley Trading Post and Butterfly Kingdom.

For something a bit more social with grandma and the kids, drop by Caddy Shack Square downtown. Play nine holes on an old-fashioned miniature golf course, complete with a windmill.

Pick up a quarter pound of fudge. Oh, better make that half a pound. Check out the shops for tropical skirts, antiques, an island T-shirt, or the inevitable nautical crafts. And for a big finish, try a waffle cone with peach ice cream.

If You Go

Getting There: Kelleys Island can be reached on the Kelleys Island Ferry Boat Line for cars and boats (419-798-9763) from Marblehead. Jet Express (800-245-1538) has a continuation of its South Bass Island run from Port Clinton that goes to Kelleys Island.

Transportation: Transport your car on the ferry or rent a golf cart or bike. Golf carts are available at the ferry dock.

Dining: Kelleys Island has two restaurants with interesting menus. One is Kelleys Island Wine Company at 418 Woodford (419-746-2678) and the Island House on Division Street in the village (888-597-3003). Fresh fish and bar food are good at the restaurants by the marina.

Information: For Kelleys Island, call the Sandusky/Erie County Visitors and Convention Bureau at 800-255-3743; www.sanduskyohiocedarpoint.com or www.kelleysisland.com.

Middle Bass Island

If you are looking for quiet, Middle Bass is close to comatose. Quiet country roads, quiet marinas, soft-spoken people. The island has only thirty or so year-round residents, summer cottages for perhaps 300, cottages and condos to rent, two airstrips (one grass, one paved), a grocery store, a gift shop, two restaurants, an old red, one-room schoolhouse built in the 1860s, and the buildings from the abandoned Lonz Winery at the ferry dock. And that's pretty much it.

Starting in the late 1800s, grapes and wineries offered a pretty good living on Middle Bass. But all that is pretty much gone now.

The Ohio state park system has bought 124 acres of the 758-acre island. This acreage includes the old Lonz Winery property, about a mile of beaches, and a marina that the agency plans to improve and expand. The grape fields have gone to seed.

In the later part of the nineteenth century, rich businessmen and politicians, mostly from Toledo, who liked to get away for fishing vacations, started the Middle Bass Club. They built summer cottages in the grand style. None, curiously, had kitchens; it seems everyone ate at the clubhouse. That same clubhouse also managed to serve booze right through the Great Depression. After a time, the club fell on hard times and folded. But many of the grand old summer homes have been purchased and rehabilitated.

If You Go

Getting There: Middle Bass Island can be reached by Miller ferries from Catawba Island and by the *Sonny S* (419-285-8774) ferry from the downtown Put-in-Bay marina.

Transportation: If you've taken your car to Middle Bass Island, you're fine. But most visitors prefer to ride about in golf carts or on bikes that can be rented at the docks or elsewhere on the islands.

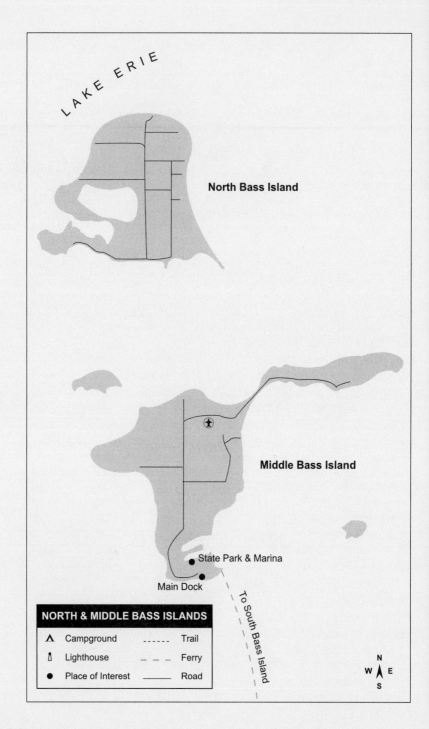

LAKE ERIE

North Bass Island

Middle Bass Island

State Park & Marina

Main Dock

To South Bass Island

NORTH & MIDDLE BASS ISLANDS

⋀	Campground	------	Trail
⌂	Lighthouse	-- --	Ferry
●	Place of Interest	——	Road

N
W ⭡ E
S

For years, Lonz Winery was the big attraction on Middle Bass Island, filling ferry boats with festive people out to have a good time and sip a glass or two of island vino in the sunshine. The winery has been closed for many years.

Food: You can get fresh walleye and perch on all the islands. Bar food generally is plentiful and well made.

On Middle Bass, you have two choices of bar food. The locals prefer J. F. Walleyes Eatery and Brewery near the ferry dock. The other place is Hazard Brewery & Restaurant.

Information: For further details on hotels, motels, bed-and-breakfasts, rental cottages, campgrounds, restaurants, and attractions:

For Middle Bass Island, call the Ottawa County Visitors Bureau at 800-441-1271; www.lake-erie.com.

"We Have Met the Enemy . . ."

Oliver Hazard Perry did not really seem to have the makings of a naval hero.

As a child, he had been sickly and a little pudgy. By age twenty-seven with thirteen years in the U.S. Navy, he had done little to distinguish himself from all the other young officers, the glory hounds who were mad to go to war in ships and rise through the ranks.

Looking at his portrait today, historians remark that Perry, with his massive sideburns, looks a bit like Elvis.

Perry had no real battle experience. He was not a crack naval tactician. And he was rash, a potentially dangerous trait in a military leader.

But by 1813 when Perry was named commander of the Navy's Lake Erie fleet, he had something that would be difficult to display on a résumé.

He was hitting a major lucky streak.

And with that perfectly timed luck—plus hard work and sheer unadulterated courage under fire—Perry achieved every bit of glory that he might ever have dreamed about.

He became a national hero after winning a historic battle against the British navy in Lake Erie. That battle would become one of the most important and well-remembered battles of the War of 1812.

Even today, almost 200 years after that epic battle, many schoolchildren still memorize his words of victory: "We have met the enemy and they are ours."

But it was no easy victory.

In the early afternoon of September 10, 1813, Perry neither seemed lucky nor much like a winner as he stood on deck on his flagship in the midst of gun smoke, flying splinters, broken masts, and a blood-spattered crew.

Oliver Hazard Perry, the hero of the Battle of Lake Erie in the War of 1812. Perry's message to his commander has been memorized by school children for almost 200 years. "We have met the enemy and they are ours..." Today's viewers of this painting, however, often comment, "Doesn't he look a bit like Elvis?" Courtesy of U.S. Naval Academy Museum. Portrait by John Wesley Jarvis.

British shot had pummeled the *Lawrence*. Shot after shot reduced the newly built American brig to a defenseless hulk that was barely floating. The hull had been splintered. The cannons could no longer be fired. The decks flowed with blood. Eighty-three of Perry's 106-member active crew were either dead or wounded.

This was Perry's make-or-break moment, says Gerard T. Altoff, a leading expert on the battle and longtime chief ranger at Perry's Victory & International Peace Memorial on South Bass Island. The monument is about half a dozen miles from the battle site.

Clearly the battle had not gone as Perry had planned. When Perry's *Lawrence* charged into the fray, a second American brig, the *Niagara*, was supposed to join in. But inexplicably the *Niagara* held back, sitting safely out of cannon range. As a result the *Lawrence* was forced to stand alone while three British warships pounded it into submission.

Perry now found himself on a helpless ship, with a deck running redder than an amputee's operating table. He had two choices, Altoff said. "One, he could surrender. Or two, he could get really mad.

"Well, there was no way Perry was going to surrender."

In that pivotal moment, Perry decided to leave the floating wreck of his flagship and resume the battle from on board the unscathed *Niagara*. He grabbed the *Lawrence*'s battle flag and, with British shot splashing all around him, he set off in a rowboat to reach the *Niagara,* which was about one-third of a mile away.

History does not record what Perry was thinking at the time. Perhaps he felt humiliated because he had had to pull the colors and flee his ship. Perhaps he was fuming in anger at the captain of the *Niagara,* standing back while his comrades were shot to pieces.

But history does note that Perry took fierce resolve from the large, navy-blue battle flag he held bundled under his arm.

The flag read: "Don't Give Up the Ship."

In Altoff's words, "At that moment, Perry had only one thing on his mind. That was to win. He did give up the ship, but he was not going to give up the battle."

Nothing Like High School History Books

Many historians agree that the War of 1812 had been a dumb idea from the outset.

"It was the first war that the new United States of America declared, and arguably the most senseless," wrote historian Bil Gilbert in *Smithsonian* magazine.

"We were ill prepared for it. It was ill conceived and often ill conducted. During its course our capital was put to the torch. It ended in stalemate. Large sections of the country were against it; some New England states, their trade cut off by [a British] embargo and their ships rotting in harbor, actually threatened to secede."

What's more, we lost the majority of the battles. And, today's historians agree, while we may not have lost the war, we certainly did not win it. None of our objectives were achieved.

Altoff said simply, "The U.S. Congress was incredibly stupid to start this war."

Now this is not the story most of us were taught in high school American history classes. We were told—if we were told much of anything at all—about a plucky new nation that stood up for its rights against the evil British empire.

We were told that this was a moral war, one filled with high purpose. It was all about free trade and the rights of American sailors.

Our history books said the United States entered the war to stop the British from interfering with our men and ships on the high seas. True enough. The British, who were fighting the French at that time, felt that it was perfectly fine for them to stop U.S. ships and dragoon sailors for its own ships.

But what many U.S. history books fail to mention is that the United States had other, arguably less admirable ambitions for this war.

It was casting greedy eyes north to Canada.

American war hawks, mostly from the American South and what is now the Midwest, coveted a big chunk of Canada—specifically a huge swath of fertile farmland in what is today central and western Ontario. The hawks' slogan was "On to Canada."

The war hawks figured that it would be a snap to grab off a big chunk of Canada. After all, they reasoned, half of the settlers in what is now Ontario were American born. They figured that the Canadians would greet our forces with open arms, maybe even throw flowers.

Were they worried about the vaunted British navy? No. It was far away on the high seas and up to its scuppers in the conflict with the French.

Thomas Jefferson figured that it would take "a mere matter of marching" north for Canada to throw up its hands in surrender. Henry Clay opined that the Kentucky militia could do the job all by itself.

Timidity, Incompetence, Poor Intelligence: Lost U.S. Territory

What they didn't figure on were quick losses in battle due to a small, largely untrained, and often unwilling U.S. militia, colossal screwups, timid and hugely inept American generals, and some of America's earliest examples of failed military intelligence.

Instead of storming through Canada after war was declared in June of 1812, the Americans quickly suffered one embarrassing defeat after another. Not only did they not capture Canadian land; they lost some of their own.

The Americans planned to overwhelm Canada with a three-pronged attack. Instead of three prongs it turned out more like Larry, Moe, and Shemp with dinner forks.

In October, Stephen Van Rensselaer, a patrician landowner with no military background, tried to lead a U.S. Army of largely untrained militia across the Niagara River. They got clobbered by a much smaller British force.

In November, Major General Henry Dearborn's American troops were supposed to cross the St. Lawrence River for an attack on Montreal. But after arriving at the river, most of his troops refused to cross into Canada. Those few who did cross were so confused that they apparently inflicted as much damage on themselves as on the British.

The third prong was led by General William Hull. War was declared in June of 1812. In July, he took 2,500 soldiers from Dayton, crossed the Detroit River, and proceeded toward Amherstburg and Fort Malden, a principal British military base on Lake Erie.

But en route, Hull got the bad news that Fort Mackinac had fallen, along with a bit of disturbing military intelligence. Well, actually, the intelligence was more of a rumor. He was told that 5,000 pro-British Indians were paddling his way from Lake Huron.

Terrified, Hull skedaddled back to Detroit.

In fact, no Indian attack force was coming. And if Hull had soldiered on, his troops could have easily taken Fort Malden, which was manned by only 500 British regulars and poorly armed, ill-trained Canadians, plus about 400 Indian warriors.

Once he was back in Detroit, Hull's timidity apparently deteriorated into panic.

Over the next few weeks, British soldiers and Indian warriors made two raids on Hull's supply lines to the south. Hull crumbled under the threat of the British and the so-called red menace. On August 16, the American general did the unthinkable. Without a shot being fired, he surrendered Detroit and his entire army to British Major General Isaac Brock.

Later, Hull was court-martialed and sentenced to execution by firing squad. He had the distinction of being the only general officer in the history of the U.S. Army to get such a sentence. President James Madison later pardoned him, but of course his reputation was ruined forever.

The brash young Americans were in trouble. Detroit had fallen. British troops had grabbed Fort Mackinac and Fort Dearborn (Chicago). And Indian raiders were running rampant, terrorizing villages and posts across what are now the Great Lakes states.

Tactically, the British now had a lock on the upper Great Lakes. Lake Erie was a British pond, providing a clear unimpeded path to run supplies to British troops and Indian warriors anywhere in the upper lakes.

The key was Lake Erie. If the Americans were ever to mount a counteroffensive and restart their invasion of Canada, they had to recapture that lake.

General William Henry Harrison began getting ready for a counterattack south of Lake Erie, eventually mustering an American army of 8,000. Harrison was no wimpy Hull. He already was a national hero for thrashing Indian warriors at the Tippecanoe River in 1811. Later, he would successfully run for president with the slogan "Tippecanoe and Tyler too." (Unfortunately his presidential term would last only one month. He caught a cold at his inauguration speech in March and died of pneumonia less than a month later.)

But Harrison knew that he could not move his army until the Americans regained control of Lake Erie. Marching to Detroit around the west end of the lake was nearly impossible. The way was blocked by massive swamps and Indian raiders. He needed ships to carry his troops to the battle in Canada. And he needed the British supply lines blocked and his own to be opened up and running. That was a job for the Navy.

Perry and the American Thrust

Unfortunately the Americans had no ships in Lake Erie. That's why the twenty-seven-year-old Perry was sent there—to oversee the construction of a fleet.

The job was big and difficult: chop down trees to make decks and masts, bring in supplies over terrible roads from Pittsburgh, and, from keels to crow's nests, build an American fleet that could whip the British.

Perry wanted this job badly. He was hoping for action. So he lobbied hard with the Navy Department in Washington and also with the U.S. Navy commander for the Great Lakes, Isaac Chauncey, who was an old acquaintance.

He was not an obvious choice. At that point, Perry's naval record showed competence but no real brilliance. He first served as a midshipman on the twenty-eight-gun *General Greene,* which was captained by his father, Christopher Raymond Perry. He sailed with the Navy against the French in the West Indies, then in the Mediterranean in the war against Tripoli. He spent two years in charge of building American gunboats—basically rowboats with single cannons—in Rhode Island and Connecticut.

But what he lacked in battle and command experience, he made up for with the start in his string of good luck. He had chosen the right friends. Chauncey picked him for the job, which was basically to build the fleet, but not to command it. Chauncey figured that being commander was his job.

Perry went to Erie, Pennsylvania, where, with the direction of a master builder, the Americans started from scratch building two 260-ton brigs and four 50-to-65-ton gunboats.

The construction site at Erie was picked, in part, because it is protected by the Presque Isle Peninsula, which is basically a set of sandbars that parallel the shore for about five miles with a very narrow, very shallow entrance at one end.

This single, shallow entrance kept the British from coming in. That was good. But it also created a problem for the Americans. Once their ships were completed in late July of 1813, that shallow passage was their only way out. And the British squadron, under the command of Robert Barclay, was just sitting out there waiting for them.

The escape logistics were complicated, and tough. Perry's newly built warships had a draft of nine feet. The gap across the sandbar normally had six feet of water, too shallow for a crossing. To make it tougher still, the water level recently had dropped by a foot or perhaps two.

But the Americans improvised. They could manage to get their newly built warships—the *Lawrence* and the *Niagara*—across the gap by lifting them over the shallows using barges, called camels, on each side of the ship.

It was a good plan. But they could not manage the job when the ships were loaded down with heavy cannons and other supplies. The big guns had to be taken off first. As a result, the emerging ships would be helpless against the waiting British squadron.

Perry had worked hard, shown zeal and fortitude getting the fleet built. Now he needed luck. And it would come.

The Americans waited. The standoff continued until Sunday, August 1. That morning, the surprised Americans awoke to see no British ships out in Lake Erie. Why had they gone? The Americans wondered. Could they finally get the American ships out? Was it a British trap?

Perry decided to go for it. He sent the smaller ships out first. Then he unloaded the cannons from the brigs and within three days managed to get the *Lawrence* out and the *Niagara* to the gap in the sand bar.

But then on the morning of August 4, Barclay sailed back to resume his blockade.

Since the *Lawrence* had no cannons, Perry was in trouble. With almost no other option at hand, he decided to run a bluff. He put his small ships into formation and sailed out as if for battle. Barclay, unaware that the *Lawrence* was unarmed, thought he might be facing the entire American fleet. He turned and fled to the west end of the lake.

For Perry, "it was just guts and dumb luck," Altoff said.

With the British ships out of the way, the *Niagara* was moved on to the lake and both American warships were rearmed with twenty guns each.

Looking back, some historians contend that while Perry deserved high praise for the famous naval victory that would come later, his greatest accomplishment was in building the fleet and actually getting it onto the lake.

Perry's escape had hinged on Barclay's odd disappearance at just the right moment in history. What happened is still a matter of some debate. But by one account, Barclay simply got bored with the blockade, so he took a couple of days off. Some say he went off to visit an attractive widow in Port Dover.

Altoff contends this view is unfair. He cites evidence that Barclay's ship, the *Queen Charlotte*, had suffered damage and needed repairs. Also, the British fleet needed to replenish supplies. But Barclay was a young man; during the stop in Port Dover, Altoff admits, the British commander probably did pop by for a visit with the widow.

Now the stage was being set for the final battle.

Barclay returned to Fort Malden. There he would pick up the nineteen-gun *Detroit*, a fighting ship whose construction was just being completed.

Barclay would have six ships—the *Detroit*, the *Queen Charlotte* with seventeen cannons, the *Lady Prevost* with thirteen, the *Hunter* with ten, plus three small, one-to-three-gun ships. In terms of armament, the British had the advantage of cannons that could shoot long range, up to a mile. So they could sit back in relative safety and pick off opposing ships at a distance.

Perry would have ten ships—the twenty-gun *Lawrence,* the twenty-gun *Niagara* under the command of Master Commandant Jesse Elliott, and eight other small, lightly armed ships. Their warships' guns were carronades or "smashers." They were powerful but accurate only at a range of about 300 yards, about half the distance the British guns could fire.

So Perry instructed his captains to quickly sail in close to the enemy.

Perry first sailed his new fleet west to Kelleys Island, then finally anchored at Put-in-Bay on South Bass Island, near Sandusky. There he waited for the British to join the battle.

"We Have Met the Enemy . . ."

That moment of battle came on the morning of September 10.

As the British squadron approached, Americans said they could hear a band aboard the *Detroit,* playing "Rule Britannia." The weather was not helpful. The southwest wind was against Perry's ships—definitely a disadvantage for a ship sailing into battle. To move ahead, Perry had to tack (or zigzag) against the breeze. He tried again and again for more than two hours, not really making much headway.

Perry's frustration grew worse and worse. But just before he made the rash decision to turn around and charge into battle even with the wind against him, the breeze shifted. Now it was coming from the southwest. It was a light breeze, but finally it was behind him.

Another stroke of Perry's luck.

But the first round went badly for the *Lawrence,* which was basically fighting alone. With his ship defenseless and dead in the water, the determined Perry chose to be rowed back to the undamaged *Niagara* and its recalcitrant captain.

This was a dicey move. The British knew Perry was in the rowboat. Six British ships concentrated fire on him. Cannons fired. British sharpshooters popped off shots from high in the masts. But the British shots did little more than splash the American commander's uniform jacket.

Perry's luck was holding.

It was never clear why Elliott, the commander of the *Niagara*, did not follow orders and sail into the attack with Perry. Gilbert wrote, "There has been speculation that Elliott was jealously waiting until Perry was beaten so he could become the American hero—or was simply terrified."

Altoff said flatly, "There was no excuse for Elliott to sit and watch his shipmates get killed while he kept fifty percent of the American firepower out of the battle."

When Perry finally clambered aboard the *Niagara*, one account reports, the two American officers had a short and very odd exchange.

"How goes the day?" Elliott asked.

"Badly enough," Perry answered.

Elliott then volunteered to go to the rear and bring up the lagging American schooners. Perry took command of the *Niagara* and hoisted his own "Don't Give Up The Ship" battle flag to the topmast.

At this point, Altoff said, the British too were suffering. Their ships were damaged. Guns on their port side were out of commission. All the British ship commanders were either dead or wounded. And so were their first officers. The renewed battle would have to be fought by junior officers who had virtually no command experience.

As the *Niagara* bore down on them, the British ships *Detroit* and *Queen Charlotte* simultaneously turned to face the oncoming American ship. At that critical moment, the *Queen Charlotte* rammed into the stern of the *Detroit* and the riggings of the two ships got entangled. They were immobilized and helpless.

Perry's luck was at a high.

He sailed into the British line with guns blazing left and right. The powerful smashers devastated the two entangled ships as well as the other British ships.

The *Queen Charlotte* surrendered first, followed by the five others.

Perry returned to the *Lawrence,* which had never actually been boarded by the British, and sent his famous dispatch to Harrison.

"We have met the enemy and they are ours. Two ships, two brigs, one schooner, one sloop."

Perry, an impetuous young man who dreamed of glory, had won it.

Now the American ground troops could go on the attack.

Perry's ships ferried Harrison's soldiers across Lake Erie. The British by then had abandoned Detroit, and the Americans quickly took Fort Malden. From there, they chased British troops and the Indians up the Thames River past Chatham, eventually winning the day and killing Tecumseh himself.

Perry, still eager for battle, joined Harrison as his aide during the Battle of the Thames.

The Americans held Fort Malden and a nearby section of Canadian land until the end of the war.

Perry's bravery and tenacity, of course, carried the day on Lake Erie. He was a national hero.

His financial reward would amount to $12,140 for taking the British prizes, a huge amount of money at the time. Members of his crew got $214.89 each.

The effects of the Battle of Lake Erie were several, according to Altoff.

With Lake Erie under U.S. control, the Americans were able to transport Harrison's troops to Canada, ultimately overrunning a small piece of Canadian territory.

The American supply lines were open and safe. The British supply lines to the upper lakes were cut off.

After one humiliating defeat after another, the Lake Erie victory was a huge morale booster for the American public.

Finally, and most important, the captured Canadian land gave the Americans an important bargaining chip during the peace negotiations that resulted in the Treaty of Ghent, which was signed on Christmas Eve of the following year.

Did the Americans win the war, or achieve any of their goals? Not really.

The quest for Canadian land was foiled, completely. Under the treaty, the original border between the United States and Canada would remain unchanged.

The Americans would get out of Canada entirely. The British would give back Mackinac Island and Chicago.

The Americans wanted the British to stop harassing American ships on the high seas and impressing U.S. sailors. That did not happen until the British and French finally ended their ongoing war.

Yes, Andrew Jackson won the Battle of New Orleans. But that victory actually came *after* the war was officially over—a needless last battle for an ill-conceived war.

Two Final Notes About Oliver Hazard Perry

His nearly equally famous younger brother. Perry had a younger brother, Matthew Calbraith Perry. Forty years after the great battle of Lake Erie, Matthew Perry led an American squadron into Japan's Tokyo bay. The island nation had basically sealed itself off from most outside contact for two centuries. The arrival in 1853 of Perry's steamships—smoky monsters that the Japanese had never seen before—convinced the nation's leaders to open their doors to international trade.

An almost unknown fact about Oliver Hazard Perry. Yes, Perry was brave. He rightly stands listed among the most courageous of America's naval heroes. But, at least according to one source, he was not totally without fear. One thing terrorized him—cows. He apparently was so phobic that he would walk great distances to avoid any field with a cow. Even the sound of mooing panicked him. Wisely he chose a naval career with blazing cannons, but very few cows.

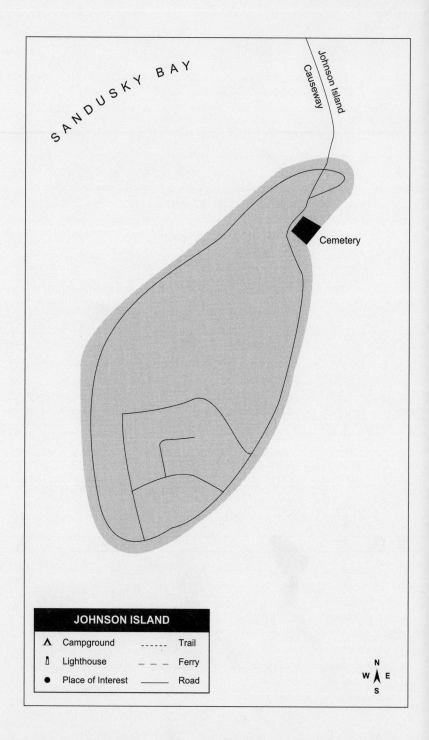

S A N D U S K Y   B A Y

Johnson Island
Causeway

Cemetery

JOHNSON ISLAND

Λ Campground   ------ Trail
Å Lighthouse   — — — Ferry
● Place of Interest   ——— Road

N
W E
S

Johnson Island

Charles Cole had a certain dash. He turned heads with his fine suits and the perfumed smoke of his expensive cigars.

He said he was an oilman from Pennsylvania. He introduced people to his wife, Annie, who was equally stylish. He bought drinks. He made friends.

In fact Charles Cole was no oilman. He was a spy, a Confederate spy.

And the couple had skulduggery in mind when they arrived in Sandusky, Ohio, in August of 1864, in the waning months of the Civil War, a time late in the war when every battle seemed to go badly for the South.

Cole and a cabal of Southern sympathizers hoped to pull off one of the most elaborate and daring attacks of that war.

Their plot involved drugging the crew and then capturing the *Michigan,* the Union's only gunship on Lake Erie. The *Michigan* was a fierce battleship. Some 163 feet long, it was one of the world's first ironclad ships and could run under brigantine sail or steam power. Once the ship was in Confederate hands, Cole and his compatriots planned to use it first to stage a massive prison break at Johnson Island, which held some 3,000 Confederate officers, and then to sail about terrorizing port cities around the Great Lakes.

The idea was to create a Northern front that would draw Union attention away from the crumbling Confederate armies in the South.

The Island

Today a visit to Johnson Island gives little hint of its dramatic prison history or this wild-eyed scheme. All that remains is a small, tree-shaded cemetery with 206 graves of Confederate soldiers. Nearby stands a bronze statue of a Confederate soldier, erected in 1910.

But for the most part the island seems like a suburban neighborhood of pleasant homes, well-trimmed lawns, and good-sized lots.

So it's hard to imagine that this Lake Erie island, a place so close to the

The Civil War prison camp for Confederate officers on Johnson Island was spread across 16.5 acres and contained 13 blocks—12 as prisoner housing units and one as a hospital. This view was sketched by Edward Gould. Courtesy of the Put-in-Bay Gazette, Jeff and Kendra Koehler.

Prisoner barracks at the Civil War prison camp for Confederate officers on Johnson Island. The camp had a capacity of more than 3,000. During its three years of existence, more than 10,000 prisoners spent time on the island. Most were officers, but the rebel prisoners also included enlisted men. Courtesy of the Put-in-Bay Gazette, Jeff and Kendra Koehler.

Canadian border, might have played any role at all in the Civil War clashes so far to the south.

But from April of 1862 until its closing in September of 1865, a stockade on Johnson Island held some 10,000 Confederate soldiers. Most of the prisoners were officers, but there were a few privates who apparently had confused paperwork.

At any one time, the prison could hold more than 3,000 men. For much of its three-year history, the prison was a relatively easy place to be a prisoner, nothing like the South's infamous, disease-wracked Andersonville in Georgia.

On the island, prisoners usually just sat around and were bored. Some played baseball, read books from the 600-volume library, put on theatrical productions, or simply anted up again and again to lose incredible amounts of Confederate money in endless poker games.

Typically food was as plentiful and at least as good as what the Union soldiers got. But in 1864, that changed. The South started losing badly. They could not feed their own soldiers, much less prisoners of war. The

This grassy cemetery with its 206 stones is all that remains of the Civil War prison camp for Confederate officers that was on Johnson Island in Lake Erie. Between 1862 and 1865, this prison was designed to hold some 3,000 men far from the battlefields to the south.

Union soon got word of the starvation and horrible conditions in places like Andersonville.

In retribution, U.S. Secretary of War Edwin Stanton ordered all Confederate prisoners' rations cut in half. Prisoners on Johnson Island came close to starvation, close enough that they began what became known as "The Great Rat Hunts of '64."

So the cabal had yet one more reason to break these soldiers out of prison.

The Not-So Great Escape

The plot was hatched by Confederate commander Jacob Thompson, who was based in Toronto, according to an article in the February–March 1987 issue of *Blue & Gray* magazine. Joining him on the plan were, in the magazine's words, "Confederate prison escapees, refugees, Kentucky cavalrymen, rapscallions, and a few Union deserters and spies."

Cole was a pivotal member in their scheme. With him were John Yates Beall, a Confederate privateer from Chesapeake Bay and Bennet G. Burleigh, a Scot who had joined Beall on the bay.

Cole's role was to worm his way into the confidence of the *Michigan's* captain and then drug the crew so the Confederate pirates could storm aboard and take the ship with ease.

Cole did his part. He charmed the captain, who in turn gave him a detailed tour of the ship. Many, many thanks, he told the captain. But you must let me repay you by treating the entire crew to a champagne dinner. And no, Cole would not take no as an answer. He planned to lace the champagne with knockout drops.

In the meantime, Beall and Burleigh headed off to Windsor to pull off

their part of the plot. Their job was to steal a ship and then use it to help capture the *Michigan*. They settled on the *Philo Parsons*, a ferryboat that made daily runs between Detroit and Sandusky.

The two pirates, along with seventeen other men, boarded the *Parsons* as passengers in Detroit. Somewhere off Marblehead Point, about ten miles north of Sandusky, the Confederates pulled their guns and hijacked the ferry. Then things started to get a bit complicated.

The pirates quickly discovered that the *Parsons* was low on fuel. They needed wood, so they headed back to Middle Bass Island to take on wood. But while they were there, up steamed a second ferry, the *Island Queen*. Since the *Parsons* was in its dock space, the *Queen* simply tied up to the *Parsons*. They were blocked in.

Faced with no other choice, the pirates then captured the *Queen*, which included among its passengers twenty-five Union soldiers who were on leave. Perhaps applying the theory that many hands make light work, the pirates waved their guns and ordered island locals and the soldiers to help load wood on the *Parsons*.

At this point, the Confederate pirates needed to get rid of one boat and a whole bunch of passengers. So they made the soldiers and other passengers swear they would not fight against the South and put them ashore. As for the *Queen*, they towed it out into Lake Erie and sunk it. Then the band sailed off in the *Parsons* toward a rendezvous with the battleship *Michigan*.

Soon Beall, Burleigh, and the others pulled the ferry within sight of the *Michigan*. There they waited for Cole's signal that the crew was drugged, and that they could come aboard.

Little did the pirates know that minutes after they left Detroit, a spy had telegraphed a warning about the plot to the *Michigan's* Captain Carter. Then a second telegraph arrived telling of Cole's role in the plot.

Cole was quickly arrested and soon confessed everything, including spilling the beans about seven other plotters who were to arrive in Sandusky by train. They too were captured.

Meanwhile every sailor aboard the *Michigan* was ready to take action when the *Philo Parsons* sailed up.

Unaware that the plot had been exposed, the rebels aboard the *Parsons* continued to wait for Cole's signal. They waited and waited. And the longer they waited, the more nervous they got.

Finally—in what was probably a rare democratic moment for pirates—the rebels took a vote on whether to attack the *Michigan* without a signal.

Two—Beall and Burleigh—voted yes; the other seventeen voted no.

Beall called them a bunch of cowards. But still, they turned tail and ran for Detroit.

The pirates dropped most of the crew and passengers at Fighting Island on the Canadian side of the Detroit River channel and then docked at Sandwich, Ontario. From there, they left the *Parsons* to sink and began walking to Windsor.

Then What?

The Confederate plot was foiled. The *Michigan* remained in Union hands. The Confederate prisoners remained on Johnson Island.

Beall was arrested near Niagara Falls. He was charged with piracy and spying and was hanged on February 14, 1865.

Burleigh was arrested and jailed in Port Clinton, Ohio. But he managed to escape and returned to Scotland.

The *Philo Parsons* was refloated; it sailed for many years but then was burned to the waterline in the Great Chicago Fire of 1871.

The *Island Queen* also was raised. It was put back into ferry service, but ended its days as a cargo carrier.

Cole went to prison.

And Annie, his supposed wife, turned out to have been hired for the charade. She was actually a hooker from Buffalo.

If You Go

Getting There: From Interstate 80-90 through Ohio, take U.S. 53 north. Go past Port Clinton heading west. Where U.S. 53 turns north again toward Catawba Island, continue straight on Ohio highway 163 toward Marblehead and then follow the signs to Johnson Island, which can be reached by a causeway. Once you are on the island, signs mark the way to the Civil War cemetery.

Food and Lodging: Johnson Island has none.

South Bay Bessie and Other Lake Monsters

Charter boat Captain John Liles truly believes he saw it.

And if the "it" was not a lake monster, well, he did see *something*.

He and his wife, Holly, were about two miles off Kelleys Island when they spotted a giant, snakelike creature about two hundred feet away.

"The thing is huge," he told the *Wall Street Journal* in 1993. It was dark-colored, he said, and looked to be about fifteen to twenty-five feet long. And its body moved up and down, not side to side like a snake.

Adding to the credibility of Liles's sighting: just nine days before, a fisherman—also near Kelleys Island—reported seeing a serpent that was thirty to forty feet long.

Be there monsters in Lake Erie?

For that matter, could there be some in the other Great Lakes?

It's unlikely. But that hasn't stopped reported sightings that date back nearly two hundred years. And if nothing else, word of monsters has spurred a lot of galloping good humor among the locals along Ohio's Lake Erie shore—including a $100,000 reward for the monster's live capture and a bemused scientist who—tongue firmly in cheek—investigated the number of possible monster pairs in the lake, their diet of walleye, and why they could swim faster than any speedboat ever built.

In the early 1990s, the *Ottawa County Beacon* in Port Clinton ran a few sea serpent stories for yuks and then dubbed their monster South Bay Bessie. Just to the east of Sandusky, the town of Huron passed a resolution naming itself the National Live Capture and Control Center for the Lake Erie Monster. They dubbed it L.E.M., for Lake Erie Monster.

It's been more than a decade since the last flurry of Lake Erie monster sightings in 1993.

Some of the reports, like those of Liles, seemed almost credible. But at the same time came other serpent sightings that can only be described as

In August 1993, the grocery store tabloid Weekly World News *ran this picture of a 200-ton serpent crushing a 38-foot sailboat in Lake Erie. Supposedly the photo was shot by a fellow flying over in an airplane. (American Media, Inc. Reprinted with permission.)*

laughable. One sighting even cropped up in a national newspaper. O.K., it was the *Weekly World News,* the grocery store tabloid. But it was national.

First a local yarn.

In the early 1990s, three teenage boys said they were out in a small boat when their anchor line got wrapped around the neck of the Lake Erie Monster. They said the mega-beastie towed them for five miles. The monster then broke loose, they said, by biting the anchor rope in two.

"It pulled us through the water like a water skier. The thing was so big, it looked like a mountain. I thought we were all going to die," one of the boys was quoted as saying.

As their story went, the boys' boat drifted for hours. For the whole time, the boys said, they feared that either the monster would come back or they might never be rescued.

The three lads said a freighter eventually passed, saw the drifting boat, and radioed to the U.S. Coast Guard for help.

One suspects that when their dad discovered his boat was missing, he did not buy the story either.

Sailboat Killer

In August of 1993, the front page of *Weekly World News* showed a photograph of a giant serpent, weighing an estimated two hundred tons, that had coiled itself around a hapless sailboat and then crushed it "like an eggshell."

The headline: "LAKE ERIE MONSTER SINKS SAILBOAT. Photograph taken seconds before 38-foot craft was snapped in half. 3-Page Special Report!"

The tabloid's story stated that, as luck would have it, an airplane was passing overhead when a passenger spotted the action and snapped the picture just before the monster turned the sailboat into splinters. Yeah, right. The monster did sink the boat right after it fathered a love child with Roseanne Barr.

Reports of monster sightings in Lake Erie go back at least as far as 1793, when the captain of the sloop *Felicity* contended he saw a seventeen-foot snakelike creature while duck hunting near Middle Bass Island.

He said the monster, which apparently was taking a nap on shore, rose up out of the grass and chased him for more than a hundred yards.

Almost all of the scores of reports describe a snakelike creature, varying in length from twelve to forty feet. The color is typically dark, ranging from dark brown to black. Although one did have Elvis-like spangles. Ontario residents in Port Dover claimed they had been bitten by the monster.

And while booze seems to have heavily flavored some of these reports, others came from reputable citizens—respected fishermen, boat captains, police officers, park rangers, and so on.

As it turns out, monsters have been spotted in the other Great Lakes as well.

Other Lakes, Other Monsters

In Lake Michigan, nineteenth-century fishermen reported seeing a serpentine creature at various places from near Evanston, to a mile and a half off Chicago's Hyde Park, to the bay at Milwaukee.

In Lake Ontario, accounts of serpents date back to the early 1800s. One near Kingston, Ontario, was dubbed Kingstie. In August of 1931, two physicians sailing from Alexandria Bay to Kingston Yacht club said they saw a thirty-foot cyclops with "one eye in the middle of his head as well as two antler-like horns."

In Lake Superior, an ancient Chippewa legend tells of a giant sturgeon that could swallow a whole ship. And French voyageurs in 1782 said they saw a merman (as opposed to a mermaid) near Thunder Bay, Ontario. Its upper body appeared to be human with the head of a seven- or eight-year-old child.

Natives on the north Superior shore also said they knew of the merman, whom they called Manitous Niba Nibais, the god of the water and lakes.

More recently, people on Lake Superior reported seeing a monster they called Pressie (because it was spotted near the Presque Isle River). It apparently is seventy-five feet long, with the head of a horse and the tail of a whale.

Which, when you think of it, is a whale of tale.

If Not Monsters, What Are They?

The question remains: if no monster actually lives in the lakes, what are people seeing? One common suggestion is a sturgeon, a fish that can grow to six or seven feet. Satellites have spotted snakelike things in the water, but they are likely to be mud slicks caused by a ship leaving a shallow harbor.

Ohio State University professor Charles Herdendorf also came up with another interesting notion. Carp often go up small streams from the lake to spawn. Sometimes they get trapped by a sandbar. They gather, waiting to get out. When a storm comes along and creates a small hole, they file out in a "long, sinuous pattern" that might be mistaken for a giant snake.

Monstrously Good Fun

As for the early 1990s hoopla over the Lake Erie Monster, much can be laid at the impressively large feet of Tom Solberg, who runs the Huron Lagoons Marina in the lakeside village of Huron, Ohio.

Solberg, it turns out, has been the Lake Erie Monster's biggest publicist—at least from a physical perspective. Solberg is 6-foot-7 and weighs 350 pounds with a Shaq-sized mass of good humor.

As Solberg tells it, the idea of monster publicity came up in the early 1990s. A recession was on. And he and some pals were sitting around the bar at the marina trying to think of promotion ideas that might fill his empty slips with boats.

In a eureka moment, they came up with the idea of having the marina offer a reward for the capture of the beast. The first offer was $10,000. Within days, the happy monster mongers realized this offer was too low, so they hoisted the prize to over $100,000 with some insurance backing from Lloyd's of London.

To add an aura of legitimacy, Solberg called for help from Charles Edward Herdendorf, professor emeritus of geological and biological sciences at Ohio State University and a man who immediately saw hilarious possibilities in the plan.

Herdendorf set the criteria for a proper prizewinner. It must be at least thirty feet long, weigh 1,000 pounds or more, and be a heretofore unknown aquatic species. Also, it had to be captured unharmed.

Announcement of the reward hit the news wires, and within three days Solberg was getting calls from news media from as far away as Japan.

Folks in Huron played it for all it was worth. The city passed the resolution naming itself the Live Capture and Control Center for the Lake Erie Monster. Solberg put up a sign by a newly dug pond on his property: "Future Home of the Lake Erie Monster." The joke was that it was a dredging pond to hold the scrapings from the bottom of his marina. It looked big, but it was only one and a half feet deep.

Professor Herdendorf, who was equally caught up in the monster fun fest, came up with some near-scientific explanations to explain the monster and its lifestyle.

Classifying it in a proper scientific way, Herdendorf declared that the monster was of the phylum *Chordata* (vertebrates) and of the class *Ichthyo-reptilia* (link between fish and snakes). Its proper name: *Obscura eriensis huronii* (which loosely translates as "rarely seen Lake Erie monster indigenous to the waters off Huron, Ohio").

Further, he calculated in a seven-page paper the approximate number of such monsters in Lake Erie based on how much they would need to eat and how fast they could swim.

Herdendorf posited that each monster was thirty-five feet long, weighed two thousand kilograms (two metric tons), and would need to eat ten kilograms of fish for every kilogram of weight. Then he figured that based on the lake size of 10,000 square miles, with 25,000 tons of fish available, the lake could support 125 monsters, assuming they ate 10 percent of the "harvestable fish."

As for speed, he noted that science has already determined that adult fish can reach speeds dependent on their body length and form. Cruising speed (sustained swimming) is from one to three body lengths per second. Burst speed (for a short duration to escape danger) is about ten body lengths per second.

Given—or rather speculated—that the monster is ten meters long, it should be able to cruise at ten meters per second or twenty-two mph. Burst speed pumped that time up to 100 meters per second or an astounding 220 mph. As a comparison, you might think of the monster as able to hit speeds that are 50 percent faster than the roaring turbo-powered hydroplanes that race each July on the Detroit River in the Thunderfest.

Certainly one would be a sight to see.

But when asked when he thought the next monster might be sighted, Solberg grinned and said, "Well, not till Jack Daniels goes on sale."

Pelee Island

The temptation is to describe Lake Erie's Pelee Island as Mayberry RFD with beaches.

And that's a compliment.

It's not that this Canadian island doesn't have all the tourist-attracting qualities of a sweet Lake Erie retreat. It does. It offers a wonderfully laid-back, almost sleepy feel, with quiet roads for bicycling, good restaurants offering fresh fish or fancy cuisine, Canada's second oldest lighthouse, some of the Great Lakes' best bird-watching, and pheasant hunting in fall and winter.

The island's history is filled with tumultuous stories—including a sneak attack by Americans, rum running during Prohibition, a day when Robert E. Lee turned snake killer, a rich men's fishing club that started with tents but soon attracted presidents, a legend of an Indian girl's lost love, and one of the lake's most amazing escape stories.

But the island's rural roots are embedded—that's the Mayberry part. And it's not just a matter of history. Today, actual farmers still plow actual fields on 80 percent of the acreage. And these aren't hobby farms. They are growing soybeans, winter wheat, and seed corn, and the islanders have given some acreage to wine grapes. This island has historically been a great wine producer, along with North, South, and Middle Bass Islands and Kelleys Island on the American side of Lake Erie. The point here is that Pelee maintains, at least for me, a certain authenticity, a down-to-earth sensibility that separates it from some islands now entirely given over to summer cottages, beachwear shops, and miniature golf courses.

By Any Other Name . . .

On some of the earliest maps, Pelee Island was marked only as part of the Lake Erie archipelago called *Iles des Serpens Sonnettes*, the rattlesnake is-

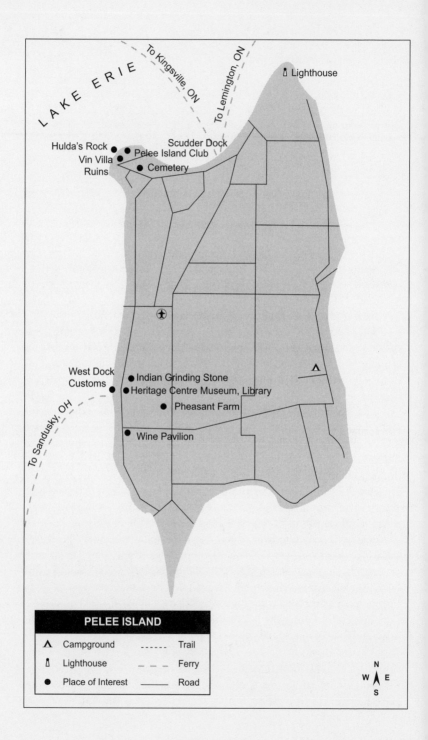

LAKE ERIE

To Kingsville, ON

To Lemington, ON

🏮 Lighthouse

Hulda's Rock ●
Vin Villa ●
Ruins
● Pelee Island Club
Scudder Dock
● Cemetery

⊕

West Dock
Customs ●
● Indian Grinding Stone
● Heritage Centre Museum, Library
● Pheasant Farm

Λ

● Wine Pavilion

To Sandusky, OH

PELEE ISLAND

Λ Campground   ------ Trail

🏮 Lighthouse   - - - Ferry

● Place of Interest   —— Road

N
W ✦ E
S

lands. Clearly that was an era before the Chamber of Commerce showed up. Later it was named Point au Pelée Island, after the nearby spike of land sticking south from Ontario. *Pelée* is French for barren or rocky. Still not a PR man in sight. Actually, in those early days, much of the island was swampland. After that, the name was whittled down to just Pelee Island.

If promotional types had been around, they might have gone for a classier origin of the name, created by a Capuchin friar named Ladislaus Segers. In the early 1900s, Segers wrote in a poem that the island was named for Peleus, a prince in Greek mythology who married a water nymph. Their child was Achilles, hero of the Trojan War. Because of this marriage, the name Pelee is often used for the sea and watery places.

Pelee Island is nine miles long and three and a half miles wide, and it sits as low as a freshwater Amsterdam in Lake Erie's brown-green waters. Regularly scheduled ferries connect it to both the Ontario and Ohio mainlands. The island has a year-round population of 190, meaning those who stay right through the winter. The population jumps to 275 if you add those who bail out for Florida in the coldest months and return for the other three seasons.

Pelee also holds a distinctive place in Canada's geography. It lies farther south than any other populated place in Canada. Clearly this does not mean that the island is balmy in the Florida sense. But as a result of its latitude and the moderating effects of Lake Erie, it might be mistaken for a place much farther south where farmers can grow tobacco, which they have done. At this point, it should be noted that one other Canadian island sits farther south than Pelee. But it has no people. It is tiny Middle Island, three miles away and yet still north of the U.S.–Canada border. It once was a haunt for bootleggers, gamblers, and Detroit's Purple Gang. But now tiny Middle Island is populated exclusively by hundreds of cormorants that, sadly enough, treat it like a mid-lake toilet.

Three Bushels of Corn and Hulda's Rock

Thomas McKee's wonderful deal might be a good starting point for Pelee's story.

Back in the early 1800s, McKee was a half-breed trader who was very well liked by both the Indians and the British. During the War of 1812, he joined the British forces and fought with the Indians and British regulars at the Battle of the Thames. The Indians liked him so much they gave him Pelee Island for 999 years. The price: three bushels of Indian corn to be paid each year to the local chiefs of the Chippewa and Ottawa tribes, "if demanded." As one might guess, not many demands for corn have been made for the last 150 years or so. And you thought $24 in beads for Manhattan was a good deal.

Of course, native people were the first to come to Pelee Island. Researchers have found Indian mounds and many artifacts, including a projectile point that dates back to 7500 B.C.

One legend from the Indians' years—which has been embellished over time—is the tale of Hulda's Rock.

You can see her rock to this day. It lies just off Sheridan Point on Pelee Island's northwest corner. Frankly, it does not look like much; it's just one of several small rocks sticking out above the water. It used to be the size of a refrigerator, locals say. But over time Lake Erie's waves broke it down.

The story begins with a white European woman—some say German, others French—who was kidnapped by the Indians and brought to Pelee Island. Her name was Gertrude. She adapted well and eventually married a tribal chief. They had a daughter named Hulda.

Hulda was a beauty with fair skin and long, straight black hair. And when a young Englishman came by the island, he fell in love with her. Soon they married and started a small trading post in a tent on the island. All was blissful until one day the Englishman got a letter saying that his mother was dying. Promising he would return soon, he left the island for England with the damp stain of Hulda's tears still on his lapel. He did not know that she was pregnant.

Each day afterward, Hulda walked out to the northwest point of Pelee Island and climbed up onto the rock in hopes of seeing her husband return. Weeks went by, and then months. Eventually it became clear, even to Hulda, that he would never come back. Faced with sadness and desperation born of lost love, one evening Hulda went to the rock and never returned. She threw herself into the lake.

The Lighthouse and Robert E. Lee's Snake

Thomas McKee never really got very involved with Pelee Island, and ultimately it was sold in 1823 to William McCormick for 500 pounds. McCormick and his family would become a major force on the island. He set up lumber operations cutting red cedar, commercial fishing, and farms. His limestone quarries eventually supplied some of the rock to build the Welland Canal between lakes Ontario and Erie. McCormick also was Pelee Island's first lighthouse keeper, a job that first brought him and his family to the island in 1834.

The lighthouse—rehabilitated in 1999 and 2000—is now one of the island's principal tourist attractions. Sixty feet tall, it is one of the oldest on the Great Lakes. Originally built in 1833, it is a classic stone, conical-shaped lighthouse with buttresses.

One story goes that Robert E. Lee, the famed Confederate general, came to Pelee Island in the summer of 1835, soon after he graduated from

The Pelee Island lighthouse, at the north end of the island, was originally built in 1833 as an aid to boats passing through the dangerous Pelee passage. It went out of service in 1909. The lighthouse has recently been refurbished.

West Point. He was surveying the boundary between Michigan Territory and the state of Ohio.

Arriving in hopes of climbing up for a good view of the lakes, Lee found the tower dirty and in disrepair. And as he entered the door, Lee wrote in a letter that his group found the keeper to be "irascible and full of venom. An altercation ensued," he wrote, "which resulted in his death."

Could Lee, who became such a revered leader, actually have killed an innocent, though bad-tempered, lighthouse keeper? Apparently scholars debated this for some time. But later in the letter Lee explains the slaying, although a bit obliquely.

"I hope that it will be considered that we have not lopped from the government a useful member [meaning the keeper], but on the contrary, to have done it some service as the situation [keeper's job] may now be more efficiently filled & we advise the new minister the choice of a better subject than a d__d Canadian snake."

Actually finding a snake in the lighthouse probably would come as no surprise to anyone who knew the island's history. After all, it was once part of the *Iles des Serpens Sonnettes*.

Americans Attack
On February 26, 1838, Pelee Island was invaded. A group of five hundred heavily armed but ragtag Americans stormed onto the island after walking

across the ice from Sandusky, Ohio. Their plan: mayhem, looting, and pillaging. Their motivation was only loosely connected to a recent uprising in Canada.

In the preceding year, William Lyon McKenzie had launched a revolt aimed at upsetting the crown's authority in Canada and deposing the privileged upper classes. He wanted an American-style democracy. The revolt did not work out all that well. Soon McKenzie was exiled to the United States with a price on his head. But he swore to fight on and began a series of raids on Ontario towns and border islands. For those on the Canadian side of the border who were still smarting from the War of 1812, McKenzie's rebellion started to look like an easy excuse for American attacks.

The so-called Patriot Army from Sandusky swept across Pelee. The island's ten families had no chance. Acting like the worst sort of thugs, the Americans burned houses and barns, looted silver services, smashed the plates and dishes, slaughtered the pigs, and made a wreck of the lighthouse.

But word soon reached the British army command at nearby Fort Malden. Troops were assembled from British regulars, Canadian militiamen, and some Indians. Arms were issued, including a couple of small cannons. And finally some four hundred men set out on March 3.

The next day, the British split their forces into a pincer attack. The main force would hit the north end of the island and the other soldiers would head south to stop the so-called patriots from fleeing.

The Americans should have had the advantage. They had advance warning of the British arrival; they were dug in; and they outnumbered the split British force by three to one. But not long after the first shots were fired, the Americans cut and ran.

It was a rousing victory for the Canadian loyalists. Eleven Americans were killed, forty wounded, and twenty taken prisoner. Others fled to the south, although some fell through the ice and drowned. Five of the British forces were killed and eleven wounded.

In time, McKenzie and his family returned to their home and to the lighthouse.

The Great Escape

The aftermath of the American attack on Pelee Island would swoon sweep up American Jake Hay into a saga that's hard to imagine.

Hay was a carpenter on Kelleys Island, some miles to the south and across the border in U.S. territory. He was a carpenter for all needs, making oxen yokes, sleighs, wagons, cupboards, gates, and coffins. In the mid-1830s he bought some land on Pelee Island and planted it with grain that was harvested by a local farmer.

In August of 1838, just half a year after the Americans raided Pelee

Island, Hay stopped by the island to check on his property. His timing could not have been worse. The islanders, still smarting from the Americans' raid, accused Hay of being part of the Patriots group. They confiscated his rowboat and threatened to hang him.

Hay fled. Walking and running he made his way to the south end of the island, where he eventually ran out of land. Not daring to stop, he swam for his life, splashing three miles to Middle Island. There he was safe, but stuck. But then Hay found a canoe that had been abandoned a year before. One end of the canoe was split. But, being a carpenter, he simply sawed off that end and nailed a board over it. He figured the still leaky boat would do in a pinch, especially if he kept bailing. He then set out for home on Kelleys Island, using a board as a paddle and an old nail keg to bail out the water.

At this point, Hay's story of escape turns into a true saga.

After he had paddled for several hours and had less than a mile to go to Kelleys Island, a nasty storm marched in from the west. Hay's canoe was almost uncontrollable in the gale. With all the responsiveness of a stick being carried downstream, his canoe blew past Kelleys Island and on down the lake. Huge waves and winds constantly threatened to turn the canoe sideways and sink it. To get some control, Hay broke off the canoe's thwarts, hammered them together into a makeshift mast, and then used his shirt for a sail. The piece of board that was his paddle became a rudder.

The storm lasted all day and through the night. When the sky cleared the next morning, he could see no land. He continued to paddle. By evening, he could see the Ohio shore. He was approaching Avon Point to the west of Cleveland. But the shore was so rocky, he dared not attempt a landing. The huge waves crashing ashore would have splintered his boat and probably killed him. Frustrated, dispirited, and savagely hungry, he once again steered into the open water of the lake.

Another day passed and another long, sleepless night. But by the next morning, Hay had reached Dover Bay. There he was finally able to pull ashore, where a local farm family helped him out. But Hay still had to get home. So from there, he walked to Cleveland and caught a boat headed toward Sandusky. At this point, his adventure should have been over. But it wasn't.

It turned out both the captain and the crew were drunk. The ship soon strayed off course and was in danger of foundering. So Hay and a young woman passenger, whose husband also was drunk, wrested command from the captain and managed to get the ship to the Huron River. From there, Hay once again started to walk, eventually reaching Sandusky, where he caught a boat back to Kelleys Island.

By this time, he had been gone for two weeks. Lake travel was dicey in good weather, but a storm had blasted through. So when Hay walked in the door, his friends and family were amazed. They had thought that Hay was surely dead. In fact, he was a sort of Lake Erie Odysseus.

Grapes, Dikes, and Rich Guys with Fishing Poles

In 1867, a few years after the American Civil War, two brothers and a friend from Kentucky came to Pelee Island with wine on their minds. They had seen how well wine grapes were growing on Kelleys Island, so they pooled funds and bought some land for vineyards on Pelee Island. The Canadian land was just as good, and what's more it was cheaper.

In 1868, the brothers D. J. and Thomas Williams and their friend Thaddeus Smith built a hefty stone building that would become an architectural icon on the island. It was a winery, the first estate winery in all Canada. It was constructed over a wine cellar that was twelve feet deep, sixty feet long, and forty feet wide. This is especially impressive since it was dug out of solid rock. The Kentuckians called it Vin Villa. Visitors can still see it, or what's left of it. School kids apparently burned it as a prank several decades ago, but you can see the elegant ruins out in an overgrown field at Sheridan Point.

The wine business blossomed on the island. By the end of the 1860s, a dozen or more people were growing Catawba and other wine grapes. The weather was mild, with the lake's warmth lengthening the growing season. The soil was right. And Pelee Island Wines would become the best-selling in all Canada. But then, after the turn of the century, the wine industry

Leaders of the Pelee Island wine industry line up for a formal photo in front of J. S. Hamilton & Company. In the 1870s, Hamilton & Company not only made wine but sold grapes to other wine makers on the island. Courtesy of Pelee Island Heritage Centre.

began to wither. Prohibition cut sales in the United States; then came the Great Depression; and later people developed a preference for California wines. Today, the island has one winery. It is the Pelee Island Wine Company, which draws many of its grapes from three hundred acres on the island.

It was around the time of grape growing that swampy Pelee Island got drained. By the 1880s, some fifty years after the first white people moved to the island, about half of the acreage was still marshy. That changed in 1888 and 1889 when Lemuel Brown, nephew of the renowned abolitionist John Brown, and Dr. John Scudder, of Cincinnati, saw potential rich farmlands beneath the ooze. So they dug canals and assembled steam dredges to suck out the water. They had one pumping station. In the 1890s, two more pumping stations were added with the backing of the Municipal Drainage Act of Ontario. Today people driving or bicycling on the island will notice that most of the roads are set on embankments well above the surrounding farmland. The embankments, of course, were dikes set up during the days when the island swamps were sucked dry.

In the 1890s, with the vineyards closing, farmers turned to growing tobacco. By the 1920s, Pelee growers shipped 1.5 million pounds of tobacco leaves a year. Then came the Great Depression. Tobacco sales dropped. And in 1935, farmers switched crops again, this time to soybeans. In 1944, the Pioneer Hi-bred Seed Company began growing seed corn on the island. Today the breakdown of island crop acreage is about 90 percent soybeans and 10 percent corn and winter wheat.

Commercial fishing, as on most Great Lakes islands, was a big moneymaker for a long time. Today, the island has just one commercial fishing boat. It sails out of Scudder Harbor.

An American Getaway

Pelee Island has long had its share of famous visitors. In recent times, one of the regulars has been Margaret Atwood, one of Canada's foremost novelists.

But one place above all has attracted the famous and powerful—the Pelee Island Club. It opened in 1883 and continues operating to this day. The club was formed by a group of twenty-five extremely rich, extremely influential American men who wanted a getaway where the black bass fishing was good, the booze flowed, and they could sit around and talk guy talk.

For a time, the Pelee Island Club was one of the most exclusive in all North America. The membership and guest lists read like a Who's Who of the late nineteenth and early twentieth centuries—Robert Todd Lincoln, the son of the president; George Pullman, inventor of the sleeper car; lumber baron Marshall Field; U.S. Presidents Chester Arthur, Grover Cleve-

The venerable Pelee Island Club dates back to 1853. Still operating, it was started by 25 very rich men who loved to fish for black bass in Lake Erie. Members have included George Pullman, inventor of the railroad sleeper car, Marshall Field, the lumber baron, and Presidents Grover Cleveland and Chester Arthur.

land, Rutherford Hayes, and Howard Taft. Another guest was General Philip Sheridan—hence the name of the club's location: Sheridan's Point.

In the late 1870s, the first members came by boat, slept in tents, and spent their days fishing. But one day in 1879, a storm blew in and flattened their tents, and they were forced to seek shelter in Vin Villa. At that point, they agreed a clubhouse was needed.

They settled on a prefab building. Wood was planed and made ready at Pullman's mills and then shipped to the island. In 1883, they had a clubhouse with a big dining room, hotel-style rooms for members and guests, handsome fireplaces, a billiard room, a two-lane bowling alley, and boathouses.

In *Pelee Club: Our First 100 Years—1883–1983,* authors Dr. John Test and Dr. David Henning wrote: "Just like 100 years ago, we belong to the Pelee Club for the specific reasons of satisfying some of man's most basic urges—fishing, drinking, eating, and talking, in that order."

The club had good years and not-so-good years. It still operates with a limit of fifty members. They still come and stay in the old building, catch fish on the lake, sit on the screened-in front porch and watch the waters, eat superbly cooked meals, and, yes, drink a toddy or two.

But the clubhouse today seems less like the grand place it once was. The building, still beautiful from the outside, is less than convenient by today's standards. Hallways are drafty. Bathrooms are down the hall. And the rooms are tiny, with no closets. In the late 1800s, clothes were hung on the wall on hooks. But it's still a guys' place. Members still love it. As for their wives and girlfriends, some have been known to sigh and take on that long-suffering look.

Booze, Gangsters, and Middle Island

Few people are willing to talk about the Prohibition era on Pelee Island or, in fact, on any of the islands of the Lake Erie archipelago. The reason: lots of relatives were involved, relatives who well understood the economic advantages of geography.

The Lake Erie islands, including Pelee, are stepping-stones between the United States and Canada. Birds have long known it. So have Monarch butterflies. They use these islands in their annual migrations to get across the lake. And during Prohibition—that great American experiment that ran from 1920 to 1933—the islands also proved to be perfect stepping-stones for smuggling booze.

By some accounts, fifteen to twenty bootleggers regularly ran between South Bass Island in Ohio and Pelee and Middle islands just across the line in Canada. Money was good. A Pelee Island fisherman could make $100 a trip.

Middle Island was a hot spot. Joe Roscoe, who was reputedly connected to the Toledo underworld, opened a seven-room hotel on tiny Middle Island. He had a casino in the basement, and, some say, a little prostitution was going on. Many believed that Roscoe was connected to the notorious Purple Gang that ran speakeasies and blind pigs (after-hours drinking places) in Detroit. Also talked about were connections to Al Capone. So the guests included gangsters, who would drop by or even hide out for a while. Wealthy Americans steered their yachts to Middle Island for a glass or two of that

The Middle Island Clubhouse was a haven for rum runners, gangsters on the lam, politicians on the take, cops who could avert an eye, and, during Prohibition, American yacht people who'd stop by for a sip of Canadian whiskey. Middle Island, south of Pelee, was safe from the U.S. cops because it was just over the Canadian line. The clubhouse was a seven-room hotel with a casino in the basement. It was built in 1930 by Joe Roscoe, who reportedly had connections with the Toledo underworld and Detroit's famed Purple Gang. Al Capone is said to have visited. This picture was taken before the clubhouse burned down in 1982. Courtesy of Pelee Island Heritage Centre.

smooth Canadian whiskey. Their wives and girlfriends were known to play the slot machines while wearing their white gloves. And even the cops would drop by for a drink or two as well.

Booze was big business. In 1920, Canadian whiskey sales hit $219 million. Ontario alone boasted twenty-nine breweries and six distilleries.

The old Middle Island hotel burned down a number of years ago. The island had a lighthouse, built in 1871. Now only the foundation remains. Today the island is a roosting place for cormorants. And as time goes on, their guano is killing every tree and bush.

Tomorrows

Historically, Pelee Island has been a getaway for Americans. Most of the visitors and most of the tourists were from the States. The Pelee Island Club's membership, for example, is exclusively American. Today Mayor Bill Krestel says about 75 percent of the cottage owners are American, 25 percent Canadian. But when it comes to tourists, those who come for a day or a weekend or more, Krestel thinks the numbers are reversed—75 percent Canadians and 25 percent Americans.

In terms of island economy, he says that tourism ranks first followed by agriculture and the winery. His hope is to expand tourism. Negotiations are underway to put in an 18-hole golf course with condominiums on the south part of the island.

Glasses, crystal, bottles, lamps, souvenir whatnots, gewgaws, frippery, and whatchamacallits jam the windows and cram the tables to overflowing at the Pelee Island Trading Post just steps from the ferry dock.

Places to See

Getting off the ferry at the West Dock, stop by Pelee Island Heritage Center, which is a better-than-average local museum. While there, you can pick up "A Bicycle Guide to Pelee Island," a first-rate guidebook even if you are driving a car. It is loaded with historical detail on the island. Just to the north of the museum is a small park that you're likely to walk past without noticing. In the park is a large rock known as the Indian Grinding Stone. Look closely and you'll see oval-shaped depressions. It was here that Indians ground their food, probably including acorns. How long ago is unclear.

A block or so south, you can take the tour at the Pelee Island Wine Pavilion. Take the tour, sample some wine, stay for lunch.

Then head north on West Shore Drive. When you reach Sheridan Point Road, make a hard left; it will take you past the old cemetery and then, just at the point where the road makes a hard right, stop and park. You'll see a path back into the woods. You can walk back in to see the stony skeleton of Vin Villa and walk across the field to the shore to see the remains of what was Hulda's Rock. The Pelee Island Club is nearby, but it is private.

Get back on the road (North Shore Road) heading east; if you stop at Scudder Dock, you might spot the island's only commercial fishing boat at the marina. Then continue in a westerly direction toward Lighthouse Point. Here are trails through a wetlands, leading to the Pelee Island Lighthouse. You'll find a good swimming beach here.

About 10 percent of the island has been given over to conservation and natural areas. Other hikes can be found at the south end of the island at Fish Point Nature Reserve and at Stone Road Alvar, where unique plants grow on limestone bedrock. As might be expected, the trailhead is off Stone Road. Also at the island's south end is a spot where you can see grooves left by the glaciers some 15,000 years ago. They are on Mill Point at the southeast corner, just off Cooper Road. Interestingly, these grooves do not run north and south, but rather east and west, following the length of the lake.

Another fascinating stop is the island's Pheasant Farm on Center Dike Road, north of East-West Road. Here keepers raise twenty thousand baby pheasants for fall and winter pheasant hunts. These have been a tradition since 1932. The hunts are substantial moneymakers for the island. Look around the farm, whose cages hold exotic kinds of pheasants from around the world. Also you'll see that the chicks all wear little plastic blindfolds. That's to keep these aggressive birds from attacking and killing each other.

If You Go

Getting There: The Pelee Island Transportation Co. has passenger/vehicle ferries that run from Leamington and Kingsville in Ontario and, less frequently, from Sandusky, Ohio. Call 800-661-2220 or go to www.peleeisland.ca. The island also has an airport with a 330-foot paved runway.

Transportation: Bring a car or a bike, or both. Roads are pleasant and traffic is almost nonexistent, but only about one-third of the fifty-five miles of roads are paved. Bikes can be rented at the West Dock. Don't rely on walking. The island is too big and the sights are too far apart.

Dining: The island has a number of good restaurants. For a quick breakfast, you might stop by the Alles Gute Bake Shop & Delicatessen on North Shore Road. For lunches and dinners, you can get good bar food at Scudder Beach Bar & Grill at the north end of the island and at the Westview Tavern or the Pelee Island Hotel & Pub at the West Dock. For dinners, locals love the meals at the Anchor and Wheel Inn and the Island Restaurant at the island's north end, just where West Shore Drive meets North Shore Road. For fancy cuisine, try the Tin Goose Inn (519-724-2223 for reservations) near the east end of East-West Road.

Lodging: The island has about twenty different places to stay, including hotels, inns, bed-and-breakfasts, and cottages. The East Park Campground is located off East Shore Road. For details, contact the township offices at 519-724-2931 or www.pelee.org.

Off Season: Pelee Islanders have tried to make the island attractive in other seasons besides summer. Fall and winter draw pheasant hunters. Birdwatching in the fall and spring is a very big deal. This island is part of a principal north-south migration corridor. So birders come from all over the United States, Canada, and the world with their binoculars and notebooks.

Beaches: Basically, the island has four public beaches—at Lighthouse Point to the north, Fish Point to the South, Sunset Beach (north of the West Dock) to the east, and East Park to the east.

Oddest Store: Stop by the Pelee Island Trading Post, a gift and curio and glassware shop just north of the West Dock. It is a ramshackle place that dates back to 1888. Dick Holl, the owner, is incapable of throwing out anything. So everything is there, with shelves and tables so thickly massed you're in constant fear of knocking something to the floor.

Information: For details, contact the township offices at 519-724-2931 or www.pelee.org.

Lake Huron

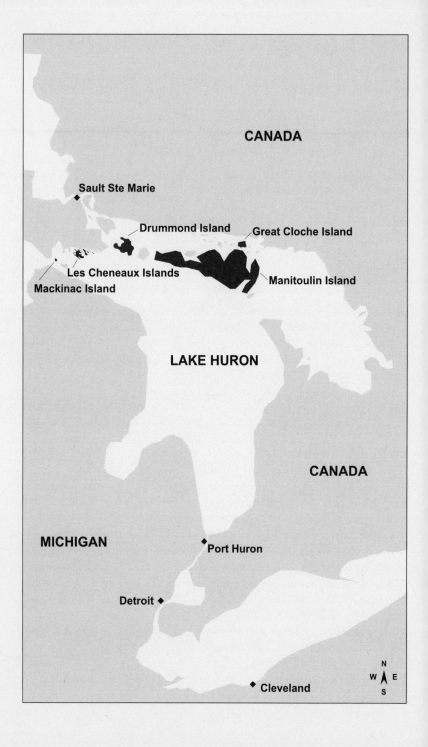

Mackinac Island

The Indian legend of Mackinac Island begins with the great flood. Waters covered all the land.

The god Manitou asked the Great Turtle, Michilimackinac, to retrieve a grain of sand from deep in the lake bottom.

Manitou blew on the grain until it was dry and it expanded into an island.

Manitou then placed the first man here. And the first woman. Then, as the world dried and land emerged, their children and their children's children and their many descendants eventually spread throughout the whole world.

The legend has several variations. But in all of them Mackinac Island serves as Eden for many native people. The world began here. And because of the island's high, rounded bluffs in the shape of a turtle's back, they named it Michilimackinac. In the mid-nineteenth century the name would be shortened to Mackinac, which is pronounced *MAC-in-aw*, not *Mac-in-ack*.

Today, Mackinac Island may not be a perfect, pre-snake Eden. But most visitors agree that it's still a little slice of wonderful.

Almost no one who's been there doesn't love this island. Travelers, both from in the state and elsewhere, rate it as their favorite Michigan destination. The island is a must stop for virtually all cruise ships, which now once again ply the waters of the Great Lakes. Skipping Mackinac would be like going to Pisa and not seeing the Leaning Tower; or to Orlando and bypassing Disney World. Unthinkable.

Set in the ink-blue waters within sight of the five-mile-long Mackinac Bridge, the island evokes a time that seems simpler, sweeter and perhaps more American than our own.

Visitors can easily imagine they've been dropped into some dreamy, long-ago America where a brass band oompahs in the gazebo, apple pies

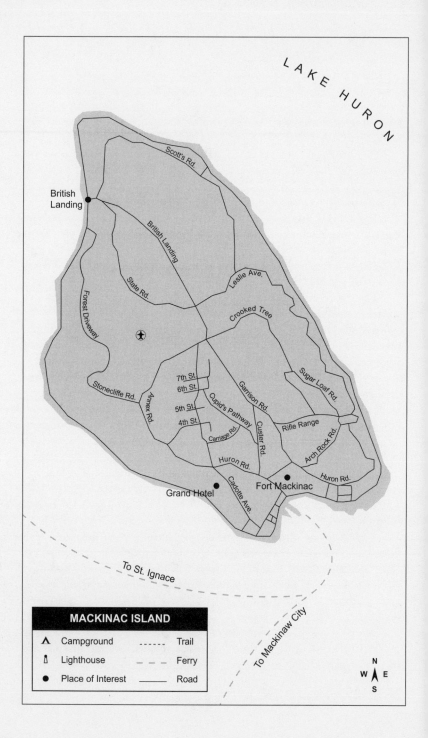

LAKE HURON

Scott's Rd.

British Landing

British Landing

State Rd.

Leslie Ave.

Forest Driveway

Crooked Tree

Stonecliffe Rd.

Annex Rd.

7th St.
6th St.

5th St.
4th St.

Cupid's Pathway

Garrison Rd.

Sugar Loaf Rd.

Carriage Rd.

Custer Rd.

Rifle Range

Arch Rock Rd.

Huron Rd.

Cadotte Ave.

Grand Hotel

Fort Mackinac

Huron Rd.

To St. Ignace

To Mackinaw City

MACKINAC ISLAND

⋀ Campground   ······ Trail

⌂ Lighthouse   ---- Ferry

● Place of Interest   —— Road

N
W ✦ E
S

cool on the window sill, and romance—the hand-holding innocent sort of romance—wafts on every breeze.

It is no wonder that *Somewhere in Time,* one of the gooiest of romantic movies, was set in the Grand Hotel on this island. And when the movie's fans—and there are thousands of them—come to visit the island, they usually find what they expect—a place with a sense of romance from a time gone by.

The island is a historic place, in fact the most historic place in Michigan. The houses, hotels, and public buildings are a hundred and even more than two hundred years old. A two-hundred-year-old, British-built fort, starched and white as an Eton collar, sits high on a bluff above the village.

Automobiles, the very symbol of modernity, are not allowed on the island. They've been banned for more than a hundred years. So no hooting horns. No heavy-treaded eighteen-wheelers. No stereos with bass-line booms that can rock the suspension of an Oldsmobile. And as a result, the streets are still narrow, basically as they were two hundred years ago—with room enough for two carriages to pass. And barns are still barns, not garages.

Here the street sounds are still turn-of-the-twentieth century street sounds. People talking and laughing. The clip-clop of big-hooved horses. The whir of bicycle tires. The taxis are horse-drawn carriages. Golfers even ride to the first tee in carriages. Everything that must be moved on the island—lumber, furniture, groceries, and suitcases—is moved by horses pulling flatbed carts. In fact, Mackinac is the one place in America where you actually can rent a horse-drawn carriage—one with a fringe on the top—and drive it yourself. "Chicks and ducks and geese better scurry." But most personal transportation is by bicycle. Young people and old ride. They pedal

A horse-drawn freight wagon clip-clops out onto the docks on Mackinac Island.

Once a horse-and-buggy town, always a horse-and-buggy town. Even in this old photo, the village on Mackinac Island is instantly recognizable with the fort on the hill and many of the buildings remain. Courtesy of the Burton Historical Collection, Detroit Public Library.

practical bikes, not the skinny-tired Lance Armstrong sort. Island bikes have fat tires, fenders, and big baskets that hang from the handlebars to carry home a few days' worth of groceries.

And along with the horses, the bikes, and the hundred-year-old buildings, the island also boasts one of the most elegant hostelries of days gone by: the Grand, one of America's last great wood-framed hotels from the Victorian era. Here men and women actually dress for dinner and go for evening strolls on the hotel's long front porch. No one dresses in historical costumes on the streets of Mackinac. But you almost expect a Gibson girl to step out of a Main Street shop with her tiny corseted waist and hair piled high. Or perhaps a young dandy with a straw skimmer cocked over one eye.

To be sure, Mackinac Island is a modern tourist place with all the modern tourist stuff. Hotels, in antique buildings, are everywhere. So are bed-and-breakfasts and condos. Shop windows are stuffed with T-shirts that say Mackinac, snow globes, carved wooden seagulls, and Indian-appearing things. Butterfly houses. The island may be small, but it has two butterfly houses. Fudge sellers abound. Fudge is the island's signature sweet. Possibly no other place is as famous for its sweets, with the exception of Atlantic City and its saltwater taffy. Eateries also sell ice cream, cappuccino, burgers, estate-bottled wines, and fine planked whitefish. All of this draws thousands of people who keep not one but three ferry lines churning the waters between the island and Mackinaw City and St. Ignace.

But make no mistake. Mackinac is no Disneyesque creation. It is real, as real today as its remarkable history was in the past.

Mackinac's story is the classic among those of the Great Lakes islands, starting with the Indian visitors who have been coming to the island for

Dawn at Mackinac Straits. Looking out past the Round Island Lighthouse to the five-mile long Mackinac Bridge that spans the straits between lakes Huron and Michigan.

centuries. Researchers have found bits of pottery, fish hooks, and spearheads that date back a thousand years. Typically the Indians did not stay year round. They lived farther south, in what is now southern Michigan and near Saginaw Bay. They journeyed up to the Mackinac Straits for summer fishing. The island was a sacred place. Native people still come to Mackinac Island each year, and some even participate in sunrise worship ceremonies, says Phil Porter, historian of the Mackinac State Historic Park.

The first Europeans to come to the island were the black-frocked priests and French voyageurs. The priests brought Catholicism. The voyageurs brought trinkets, blankets, steel knives, and guns to trade for beaver skins. Soldiers came too. They brought five-foot-long muskets and six-pound cannons to protect the fur trade. And fierce battles broke out here as the British and Americans fought it out in the War of 1812. The island fort changed hands four times.

Fishermen, mostly Irish, were the heart of the island's economy for the better part of a century. In the beginning, they went out into the lakes in open boats and hauled heavy cotton nets to bring in the whitefish.

Then, starting in the years following the Civil War, tourism increasingly became the island's economic mainstay. As an added way to bring visitors and to maintain the old fort, Mackinac Island was named America's second national park, right after Yellowstone. It now is a Michigan state park.

In recent decades, the island has reached some of the highest levels of popularity ever, but what draws the people is what has always drawn visitors to the island: fresh lake breezes, woodland beauty, fascinating history, a certain sense of high Victorian fashion, and, of course, the fudge.

In the Center of the Road

Mackinac Island long has been a key location in the Great Lakes, Porter says. Until just over a century ago, most travelers got around by water—first in canoes, then in sailboats, followed by steam and diesel-powered boats. It was the easiest way to travel. Faster and safer than walking or riding through forests and swamps, thick with wild animals and perhaps unfriendly Indians.

So as explorers, voyageurs, fur traders, and then settlers moved west, they found, in Porter's words, that "Mackinac Island was right in the center of the road and in the center of three lakes—Michigan, Huron and Superior." For a few centuries, it was the Great Lakes equivalent of Rome—all roads led there.

It was the perfect location for trade in pelts, which were being brought across Lake Michigan from as far as the Mississippi River and across Lake Superior from the northern reaches of what is now Ontario. Fur traders found it handy to maintain connections and alliances with Indian tribes. In terms of military needs, it was key to controlling the Upper Lakes and all that lay beyond. What's more, Mackinac had a fine, deep natural harbor and huge cliffs for positioning guns.

One of the first Europeans to come was Father Jacques Marquette in 1671. He settled in with a group of Huron Indians, whom he'd brought back from western Lake Superior because they were being harassed by the Sioux. They stayed on the island a year, found the ground too rocky to farm and so moved to St. Ignace on the north shore of the Mackinac Straits. A year later, Marquette and French explorer Louis Joliet, hearing word of the Great River, went on to explore the upper reaches of the Mississippi River.

Back at St. Ignace, the people and the fur trade stayed for more than forty years, but then moved across the straits to what is now Mackinaw City for better farmland. There the French built Fort Michilimackinac in 1714. All this time, the French and the English were jockeying for control of the lucrative fur trade.

Eventually the French and English went to war, fighting what's called either the Seven Years' War or the French and Indian War. In the end, the British won and peacefully took over Fort Michilimackinac in 1761. But taking the fort and holding it were two different things. The British did not get along well with the Indians, certainly not as well as the French had. The British were arrogant. They ignored gift-giving traditions. The Indians—Ojibwa and Sac—wanted them out, and they were clever about it. Two years later, the Indians staged a lacrosse game in front of the fort. Everyone came out to watch. Then at one point, the players tossed the ball over the stockade wall. When the stockade gate was swung open to retrieve it, the Indians stormed in, took the fort, and killed twenty-one British soldiers.

Skull Cave

The English soldiers and traders who survived were held captive, except for one man—Alexander Henry. Fortunately Henry was a friend of an Ojibwa chief, who managed to sneak him away and then hide him in a cave in the center of Mackinac Island. The cave, while decent shelter, had an unnerving aspect. It was filled with old bones and skulls.

Today, visitors can visit Skull Cave, which is on Garrison Road not far from the fort. The skulls are long gone.

A year later, the British returned. They improved their relations with the Indians, and, because war seemed to be brewing with the Americans, they paid additional heed to the vulnerabilities of their fort.

They decided it would be far easier to defend Mackinac Island, with its high bluffs, than Mackinaw City.

They then bought the island from the Ojibwas for the equivalent of five thousand British pounds, paid in the form of canoe loads of goods and merchandise. They built the fort on the island's south side, just above the harbor. And to make sure that the largely Roman Catholic villagers made the move, the British waited for winter, dismantled St. Anne's Church, and used oxen to haul it from the mainland to the island, where it was reassembled. The present St. Anne's Church on Main Street across from the city marina was built much later, in 1874.

Fort with a Flaw

The British troops moved into the new fort on May 12, 1781. Fort Mackinac had many good military qualities. It was on high ground, an important advantage in a fight. Unfortunately the ground was not quite high enough. Yes, if they approached from the harbor side, any attackers would face a steep hill climb over open ground before having to cope with the fort's high walls. The fort's failing lay on its rear or north side. There yet another hill rises up behind the fort, giving would-be attackers the advantage of high ground.

Even so, the British settled in, perhaps planning a long stay. It was not to be. The Revolutionary War ran its bloody course, and in 1783 the two sides signed the Treaty of Paris. Under that pact, Mackinac Island would be part of the United States. The redcoats managed to hang around for another thirteen years, but finally in 1796 they marched out and the Americans moved in.

But the British did not leave entirely. Not about to relinquish their hold on the fur trade, they set up another fort on St. Joseph Island, just around the corner of the eastern Upper Peninsula on the approach to Sault Ste. Marie and Lake Superior. Tensions between the two countries continued.

Surprise Attack, at Least to Some

Like the British, the Americans also thought they'd hold the fort forever. But like their predecessors, they too were wrong.

On June 18, 1812, the United States declared war on the British, starting the War of 1812. You'd think someone would have warned the troops at Fort Mackinac. But no one did.

Word, however, did reach Charles Roberts, the British commander at St. Joseph Island. He quickly began adding to his force of 50 British regulars, bringing in 400 Indians and about 150 French-Canadian and Métis (French-Indian) voyageurs.

Back at the fort, American Lieutenant Porter Hanks did notice some unusual movements by the Indians. So on July 16, he asked a local trader named Michael Dousman to paddle his canoe over to St. Joseph Island, have a look, and report back. As it turned out, Dousman made it only fifteen miles before running into the British armada. He was taken captive. But Dousman knew Roberts. So as the British force approached Mackinac Island, Dousman cut a deal.

Roberts agreed that the trader could sneak in ahead of the attack, warn the villagers, and take them to safety on condition that he would not alert the men in the fort. Dousman did what he had agreed to do. Roberts then landed his force on the north side of the island, at a place now called British Landing. From there, they swept across the island and silently took command of the high ground behind the fort. The next morning, Lieutenant Hanks was shocked to hear a warning shot coming from a British cannon mounted on the hill above him.

The Americans were outnumbered ten to one. The British held the high ground. And if a battle ensued, the Indians would likely wreak havoc. Lieutenant Hanks sensibly surrendered. No drop of blood was spilled on either side.

The British were back in charge.

Thus ended the first engagement of the War of 1812. It was a humiliating defeat. But even worse for the Americans, it was just the beginning of a series of humiliating defeats. Detroit fell soon after. And Chicago did too.

No Surprise, No Victory

With the taking of Fort Mackinac, the British held control of the upper Great Lakes. And understandably, the Americans wanted it back.

But they were stalled until the next year, when Oliver Hazard Perry managed to trounce the British fleet in the Battle of Lake Erie. After that, the way was open for the Americans to move north.

The winter passed, and in July of 1814, the powerful American fleet showed up off the shores of Mackinac Island. The five ships were the stuff of legend, all veterans of the Battle of Lake Erie. The brig *Lawrence* was Perry's flagship and had been badly battered in the early stages of the Lake Erie fight. The brig *Niagara* was the ship with which Perry finally won the battle. And along with the two battleships came the small brig *Caledonia,* the schooner *Scorpion,* and a little gunboat called the *Tigress.*

Unfortunately the American battleships weren't quite prepared to attack a hilltop bastion like Fort Mackinac. As they approached the harbor, the ships' masters realized that they could not elevate their canons high enough to do any damage to the fort's walls.

Frustrated, American Lieutenant Colonel George Croghan decided to attack by land, repeating the British tactic of putting ashore on the north end of the island and then sweeping south to the hill that overlooked the fort.

Not surprisingly, the British were ready for that move. Under the command of Lieutenant Colonel Robert McDouall, the British fortified the hilltop and named it Fort George. They also set up a battle line on a ridge that overlooked the farm owned by Michael Dousman, the same man who had warned the villagers of the British attack two years earlier.

Once again, the British held the high ground. They looked down across the open fields where the Americans would come. And 350 Indians, sympathetic to the British, covered their flanks in the woodlands.

Today, you can see exactly where the battle was fought. If you stand at the first tee at Wawashkamo Golf Course, you'll be exactly where the British dug in. Look north down the fairway, and you can almost imagine the American troops emerging from those trees.

The British let loose with cannons. Their muskets flared. And, in the words of Phil Porter, the Americans "got creamed."

The Americans, led by Major Andrew Hunter Holmes, tried a quick flanking maneuver through the woods to the British left. They ran headlong into a band of Menominee Indians. One of the first shots fired came from a six-foot-two brave named L'Espangnol. It killed Major Holmes. The warriors then proceeded to kill another ten soldiers. Ultimately the Americans retreated back to the ships.

The American ships *Lawrence* and *Caledonia* carried the wounded to Detroit, soon followed by the *Niagara.* The small gunships *Scorpion* and *Tigress* remained as a blockade to stop food and supplies from reaching the fort. That might have worked, but the Americans were in for another nasty surprise. In a stealthy night maneuver, the British managed to sneak up and capture both ships. The blockade was broken. The Americans, having lost the fort originally, now had suffered a second defeat which was described as "mortifying." And the British maintained control of the northern lakes.

Back in the U.S.A.

As it turned out, what American forces could not accomplish, American politicians could. The Treaty of Ghent that was signed on Christmas Eve of 1814 not only ended the war but also reinstated all the original borders. Fort Mackinac once again was American. The British marched out on July 18, 1815. The Stars and Stripes once again flew over the fort. The returning American troops renamed the fort Holmes after the fallen officer. But the name Fort Mackinac stuck, and the Holmes name was given to the fort on the hilltop.

Lieutenant Colonel McDouall took his troops to Drummond Island, where they built another fort. The Americans had burned the redcoats' original fort on St. Joseph Island.

From that point on Fort Mackinac remained in American hands. But over time, it became less and less important. For some years, it protected the American fur trade and the interests of John Jacob Astor's American Fur Company. The fur trade finally faded from the scene in the 1830s and 1840s. It was replaced by commercial fishing as an economic mainstay of the island.

Eventually, the fort became a military backwater. The country had no fears of being attacked by Canada. So those soldiers who found themselves stationed there typically were on call to be shipped off to more serious battlegrounds when the need arose. They went to the Second Seminole War (1837–40), the Mexican War (1848), the Santee Indian Uprising (1857–58), and to the Civil War.

The fort once again became important when Mackinac Island became the nation's second national park; President Ulysses S. Grant made it official with his signature on March 3, 1875. The fort was part of the attraction. And the soldiers stationed there were expected to look after the park. The park later was redesignated a Michigan state park in 1895 and now covers 82 percent of the island.

Fudgies

Mackinac Island is renowned for several things. But certainly one of them is fudge, the nationally known Mackinac Island fudge. Wander through the village and it seems as though almost every other storefront is selling fudge. Chocolate fudge, vanilla fudge, maple fudge. White-aproned fudge chefs stand in windows, swirling the goo with paddles. The air is redolent with fudge smells, which is probably fortunate given the number of horses passing by.

No visitor, it seems, can spend more than a few hours on the island without picking up a stone-heavy box of the stuff. "Let's see now. Two for us, one for Aunt Martha, one for grandpa . . ."

It's little wonder tourists have been dubbed "fudgies," a term that has spread throughout northern Michigan and far beyond.

Selling sweets began even as island tourism started to first hit its stride following the Civil War. Merchants would sell all kinds of sweets, including maple sugar that was put in Indian-style birch-bark containers called "mokuks." Fudge first showed up on the island when the Murdick family opened Murdick's Candy Kitchen in 1889. They made fudge in the back of the store, using marble slabs. The marble gave the fudge a unique flavor and also was a great show for the buyers. Over the years, candy shop ownerships changed and others joined in the candy business. Times were bad during the Great Depression and during World War II, when few people traveled and sugar was hard to get.

But the fudge business really started to take off in 1960, when Harry Ryba showed up. He'd learned to make fudge from the Murdicks. But he brought pizzazz. He took fudge making out of the back and put it in the front window. Throngs would gather to watch the show. He used the Murdicks' trick of using fans to blow the sweet smells into the street. He ran radio commercials. He put up billboards. He added flavors. By 1965, Ryba bragged that he offered ten flavors, twice as many as his competitors. He put his fudge in distinctive pink boxes that everyone would notice. And he also gave customers handy shopping bags with handles and, importantly, his logo.

Ryba even credited himself with inventing the term "fudgie" for tourists. With every purchase, Ryba gave away a pin that read "Ryba's Mackinac Island Fudgie."

The rising tide of island fudge sales not only lifted Ryba's boat, but also the boats of all the other sellers. Today, five marble-slab fudge makers operate fifteen shops on the island. The operators are Ryba's, Joann's, Kilwin's, May's, and, the granddaddy of them all, Murdick's.

The Grand Hotel

The Grand Hotel, white as a wedding cake, perches on the bluffs west of the village—it is one of America's great hotels.

One-time guests are known to announce for years afterward, "Oh yes, I stayed at the Grand." From the beginning, staying at the Grand has meant doing something quite stylish and sophisticated. Yes, the old stairs are a little off plumb. Pipes extend down from the ceilings. But that's character for a historic place with every amenity.

For more than one hundred years, the wealthy and powerful have vacationed here. As they did in the hotel's yesterdays, couples today must still dress up for dinner. Meals are superb. An orchestra plays. People dance waltzes and fox trots. They sip martinis, because isn't that what sophisti-

The impressive Grand Hotel dominates this view of Mackinac Island. The porch is big enough to hold 100 rocking chairs.

cates do? Days can be spent by the pool where Esther Williams swam, on the two manicured hotel golf courses, or simply sitting on the 660-foot long porch, looking out toward the Mackinac bridge and counting the shades of blue in water and sky.

A Grand Hotel publicist once declared that the hotel had the world's longest porch. Maybe it was true, maybe it wasn't. Either way, the Grand Hotel made it into Ripley's Believe It or Not.

The Grand certainly is among the last of a class of vintage hotels that includes the Hotel del Coronado in San Diego. Bob Tagatz, the hotel's historian, notes that in 1900, America had 1,200 such large, wood-frame hotels. Today there are only twelve. And the Grand is the last one to be privately owned.

Not bad for a hotel that was built in 1887 in just ninety-three days.

The Grand was built at a time when railroads were extending north from Detroit and Chicago, and steamship lines were plying the waters with pleasure passengers. What people needed was a place to go. So the Michigan Central Railroad, the Grand Rapids and Indiana Railroad, and the Cleveland Steamship Navigation Company put their money together.

A lumber mill was set up in St. Ignace. Some 1.5 million feet of lumber were hauled across the ice in March. And 600 laborers were brought to the island, where they lived in tents.

As Tagatz tells it, the men knew it was an important rush job, so they tried to hold out for more money—triple wages to be exact. The builder refused. What's more, he said, if you don't work, you'll get no food, no money, and no transportation off the island. And this was in the heart of winter.

The Grand Hotel's front porch stretches for 660 feet. Ripley's Believe It or Not once said it was the world's longest. And maybe it is. Either way, today it offers a wonderful view of the Mackinac Bridge and the Straits of Mackinac. The hotel was built in just 93 days in 1887. Courtesy of Burton Historical Collection, Detroit Public Library.

The men agreed to double wages. Ultimately the hotel costs were $250,000 for the construction and another $62,000 for the furniture.

The hotel was an immediate hit. It became the most fashionable place to go in the Midwest. People would come and stay for days, weeks, or even months. The impact on the surrounding area was immediate. People had already begun building summer cottages on the bluffs where the hotel was located, and also on the eastern bluffs. But once the Grand opened, they began building mansions. Many smaller places were torn down or got additions that permitted a more elegant summer life filled with balls and parties.

Mackinac Island, of course, had other hotels. The Island Hotel, in fact, is Mackinac's oldest operating hotel. And many more followed.

But despite the applause and fancy guests, the Grand Hotel had to struggle financially not just for years, but for decades. In fact, Tagatz says that the hotel made money for the first time in 1951—a full sixty-four years after it opened.

Unlike hotels that stay open year round, the Grand always had to make whatever money it could during the warm months. The rest of the year it was closed, and still is. Some years most rooms would be filled; in other years most would be empty. In bad times, repairs were neglected, furniture became frayed and broken, and the place looked pretty dowdy. Occasionally owners debated closing it down altogether. In the early years, hotel managers used gimmicks to bring the customers—greased pole races and dog races in the water.

During prohibition, Tagatz said, the Grand never had a dry day. Booze was brought down from Canada. Deliveries came on Wednesday and Thurs-

Even in the 1920s when golfing women wore cloche hats, the Grand Hotel looked much the same as it does today. The hotel also was the setting for the romantic movie Somewhere in Time, *with Jane Seymour and Christopher Reeve. Courtesy of Burton Historical Collection, Detroit Public Library.*

day. Law enforcement was wired. The Coast Guard actually helped load the booze. And periodically, for appearances' sake, a police raid would be arranged—but only after all the high-profile guests had been whisked away. Announcements of the raids would hit the papers down as far as Detroit, and they ultimately brought in more guests, all looking for a bit of fun and a drink.

The hotel had a series of owners, some better than others. But things improved dramatically and the modern era of success began under the guidance of Dan Musser, who started as a waiter in 1951, advanced through the ranks, and eventually took over in 1960. Rooms were upgraded and enlarged. Bright colors were added. Whole wings were added. Each year improvements continued to be made. This tradition was followed by his son, Dan Musser III, who took over in 1986.

One of the interesting events at the hotel each year hinges on the movie *Somewhere in Time,* starring Christopher Reeve and Jane Seymour. The film became such a favorite that Somewhere In Time Clubs developed all over the country.

Now in October just before the hotel closes, romantics who loved the movie gather at the hotel. They dine. They go to places portrayed in the movie, including along the shore where the lovers first met. They have a grand ball where everyone dresses in Victorian finery.

The movie may have been a bit sugary for some, but its concept fit the scenery. The Grand Hotel and Mackinac Island are very romantic places.

Places to See

A highlight of visiting Mackinac Island is a bike ride around it, following the shore. The road is smooth, paved, pretty, breezy, and an actual Michigan highway, M-185. Locals joke it's the only highway in Michigan never to have had an auto accident.

Along the way, you find great views of Lake Huron and the Mackinac Bridge, places to stop for a picnic, trailheads for hiking, British Landing, where His Majesty's troops came ashore in 1812, and a hole in a cliffside known as the Devil's Kitchen.

In the town, look on Market Street, one block in from Main, to find many of the village's oldest buildings, some dating back to the fur trading days. Here is the old fur warehouse used by John Jacob Astor's American Fur Company and, near the corner of Fort Street, the old company store that dates back to 1822. It was here that a young voyageur was shot in the stomach at close range. He lived, but the hole remained in his stomach. As a result, Dr. William Beaumont, the fort's physician, conducted experiments by dropping in pieces of meat to see the effect of gastric juices. Although they seem crude today, Beaumont's experiments led to a groundbreaking understanding of the digestive process. The Dr. Beaumont Museum is in this building.

At Fort Mackinac, just up a steep hill above the city marina, you'll find men in uniform and see them fire muskets and cannons. Behind the fort, you can take Huron Road west a short distance and pick up Garrison Road, which leads through the middle of the island to the north. It ends at British Landing. Along the way, you pass Skull Cave on the right. This is where an Ojibwa chief hid one of the English traders, following the attack on Fort Michilimackinac in 1763. If you choose, you can turn right on Rifle Range Road, and up on the left you'll find stairs leading up to Fort Holmes, which has bunker walls and a fine view out over Lake Huron. Continuing north on Garrison Road, you pass the Catholic Ste. Anne's Cemetery, the military cemetery, and the Protestant Mackinac Island Cemetery.

Just past Mackinac Island Cemetery is Fort Holmes Road on the right. You can take this road if you'd like to ride your bike up to the old hilltop fort. Continuing straight, Garrison Road changes its name to British Landing Road. You pass the island airfield on the left and then come to Wawashkamo Golf Course. This is a classic links golf course. Built in 1898, it is one of Michigan's oldest continuously operating golf courses. If you stand at the first tee, not far from the clubhouse, you can get pretty much the same view that the British had when the Americans attacked in 1814—a long, broad field of fire. Today it's fairways and greens. Then it was Michael Dousman's farm. The golf course's name came from an Ojibwa Indian who lived nearby and watched golfers zigzag along, as they followed their shots. "Wawashkamo" means "the trail is crooked."

Back up behind the fort, another option is to take Huron Road east and turn left on Arch Rock Road. This will take you to a cliff top overlook and to Arch Rock, one of the island's famous sights. Also at Arch Rock, you can pick up a very pretty hiking trail called Tranquil Bluff Trail. The island is laced with fine hiking trails, but this one has pretty vistas of the water as it runs atop the bluffs on the east side of the island. If you decide to continue bicycling, head north from Arch Rock picking up Crooked Tree Road; this will lead to Sugar Loaf, another famous site on the island. This is a seventy-five-foot tall limestone stack, left over from the era when all but the center of Mackinac Island was covered with water. Sugar Loaf was then a small, eroding island.

Back in town and heading east along Main Street, which becomes Huron Street as it passes the city marina, you will see the statue of Father Marquette in front of the fort and an Indian-style bark lodge like the one Marquette used for a chapel. Moving on, you pass the 1838 Indian Dormitory, which under a treaty was built so the Indians would have a place to stay when they were dealing with the government; Island House, dating from 1852, the island's oldest operating hotel; Ste. Anne's Church; the 1829 Mission Church, where the Protestants worked with the Indians; the Mission House, which was a Protestant school for Indians; and finally the Mission Point Resort. It was originally built in the 1950s and 1960s by the International Moral Re-Armament Association, a group dedicated to moral and spiritual reawakening in order to achieve racial justice, world peace, and free and democratic societies.

To reach the Grand Hotel, walk away from the fort on Market Street and at Cadotte Avenue turn right. It leads right to the hotel. Visitors—that is, those people who are not guests—must pay an admission fee to go into the hotel. Over the years, the hotel managers found that so many visitors were roaming around the long, long porch, through the lobby, and around the sitting areas, that paying guests were constantly being blocked and bumped.

If You Go

Getting There: Most people get to Mackinac Island by ferry, either from Mackinaw City at the northern tip of Michigan's Lower Peninsula or just across the Mackinac Straits at St. Ignace. Three ferries serve the island— Arnold, Shepler's, and Star. Parking in the ferry lots is free.

A word of caution: even on the sunniest summer days, the crossings can be chilly for those wearing just a T-shirt. You may be more comfortable if you bring a jacket or ride inside.

Ferries can and do regularly carry people's bikes across for a small fee. It's certainly cheaper than renting. Also you can fly from St. Ignace. Contact Great Lakes Air at 906-643-7165; www.greatlakesair.com.

Transportation: Well, you can forget about your car. Most people—both islanders and visitors—ride their bicycles everywhere. You can bring your own bike or rent one at the ferry docks. Horse-drawn taxis can be hired. Also, you can go to Jack's Livery and rent a carriage with fringe on the top that you can drive yourself. Riding horses also can be rented on the island.

Many people take horse-drawn carriage tours that will give you a good sense of the island and a feel for the history. These are run by Mackinac Island Carriage Tours, Inc., and Arrowhead Private Carriage Tours.

If you are staying overnight, most hotels and bed-and-breakfasts will make arrangements to pick up your luggage. The Grand Hotel, which is a long walk from the village, runs carriages to carry people back and forth from the ferry docks.

Dining: You can eat well on Mackinac Island. The Grand Hotel's dining rooms have superb menus. Locals love the Village Inn, a casual place with good breakfasts and, later in the day, wonderful planked whitefish. Chefs, of course, come and go. But good grades have been earned at the French Outpost, the Pub & Oyster Bar, the Yankee Rebel Tavern, and the Ice House at the Island House Inn.

Fudge: Which one should you pick? You're on your own there.

Lodging: Of course, there's the Grand Hotel. But despite good value for the money, the price can be a bit stiff. Special rates and packages are available. Contact at: 800-33GRAND (800-334-7263); www.grandhotel.com. Mission Point Resort is the island's other big hotel, with a pool and other amenities, including a good restaurant. Call 800-833-7711; www.missionpoint.com. Island hotels, bed-and-breakfasts, and condos cover the full price range. Some are wallet stunners; others are quite economical. Accommodations range from a bed-and-breakfast that's like staying at grandma's house to lodgings with superb, large rooms and stunning decorations. Some are in nineteenth-century homes; others are quite modern. All, with a couple of exceptions, are either in the village or within walking distance.

Swimming: Yes, you can swim from almost any shore of the island. But remember, the water is chilly. And because the lake bottom is rocky, put on some kind of footwear—sandals, old tennis shoes, or water shoes. No lifeguards.

Winter: Mackinac is partially open during the winter. And frankly, it's a treat to have the island almost all to yourself. You'll love cross-country ski trips out to the Rock Arch and through the woodland trails.

Getting to the island takes a bit of extra effort. If the ferries are not running because of the ice, you may have to catch a flight from the St. Ignace airport. Contact Great Lakes Air at 906-643-7165, www.greatlakesair.com. All but a few stores are closed. For lodging, Mission Point Peninsula Resort and several inns are open. Meals and drinks are still served at the Village Inn and the Mustang Lounge.

Information: For details on lodging, restaurants, special events, and most other aspects dealing with the island, contact the tourism bureau at 800-454–5277; www.mackinacisland.org. Or stop by the information booth when you get to the island. It is across from the Arnold Ferry dock.

Ghosts of Mackinac

A lot of eerie stuff is going on around Mackinac Island.

Ghosts are doing some serious lurking. They talk. They walk about. One even plays the piano.

All this spookiness must seem unlikely to most summer visitors who spend their days taking carriage tours, pedaling a rental bike along the shore, and perhaps buying a not-quite-gooey slab of fudge at one of the shops on Mackinac's turn-of-the-century Main Street.

It's all very cheery.

But Mackinac Island is an old, old place. Its history dates back to when histories were not written but told in stories that were passed from generation to generation of native people. Old places like Mackinac have seen many lives, and perhaps not a few afterlives.

"Before the white men, Indians came here to Mackinac to bury their dead," said Ron Dufina, owner of the popular Village Inn Restaurant, whose family history on the island goes back to the mid-1800s.

"Downtown is a total burial ground. Wherever you dig, you find bones."

Indian bones may indeed be rattling. But most of the island's ghost stories, at least those that islanders are willing to tell, have more to do with the Europeans who came, settled, and died on the island.

Searching for Her Lost Husband
One story is told by Phillip Porter, the superintendent of Fort Mackinac and the Mackinac State Historic Parks, which cover land and historic buildings both on the island and at Mackinaw City on the Michigan mainland just to the south.

Porter and his wife, Valerie, lived in the old Hospital Stewards' Quarters next to the fort, where historically the assistants to the fort physician used to live.

The Porters had three small children—two boys and their baby daughter Suzanna. Very late one night in the summer of 1985, Valerie heard Susanna crying in the next room and went to see her.

Valerie said that as she walked into the baby's room, "I briefly caught sight of a woman in the corner who was dressed in late nineteenth-century work clothes, which included a wrap-around apron that was pinned in the back.

"I only saw her briefly from behind," Valerie said. "It appeared as if she was working on something with her hands.

"The image quickly disappeared."

Valerie would have none of that. "I left the room and returned with a small bottle of holy water. When I sprinkled the water in the location of the image," she said, "it created a distinctive hissing sound."

Later the Porters learned some interesting details about the people who lived in the Hospital Stewards' Quarters, which were built in 1887.

One of the earliest residents was a hospital steward, Judson Rogers. He lived with his wife Anna Rogers, a hospital matron, and their two children, one of whom was six-year-old Leon.

One day in the late spring of 1887, Judson Rogers and Leon sailed off to Milwaukee so the father could get some dental work done. On the way back, on June 17, their steamer, the *Champlain,* sank near Charlevoix.

Judson Rogers' body was discovered almost immediately. In his pocket, searchers found a note that read: "If anything happens to me, contact Mrs. J.J. Rogers, Fort Mackinac, Mich." Seven days after the wreck, young Leon's body was found. Both were buried on the south side of the Post Cemetery.

Today, some speculate that Anna's ghost may have stayed to prepare the rooms for her lost husband and son.

After the sprinkling of holy water, the ghostly image never returned.

Late for His Own Funeral

Porter also tells a story connected to the Geary House on Market Street, just next door to the Beaumont Memorial house.

In the 1870s, Matthew Geary, the town's fish inspector, lived in that house. He was a prominent figure on the island, overseeing its most important industry.

He was old, so few people were surprised on the day he died. They gathered at his house for the wake. Later in the day, Geary's coffin was loaded in a horse-drawn hearse to be taken up to the Catholic Cemetery. To this day, you can still find his gravestone in that cemetery behind the fort.

It was a sad occasion, but all seemed normal. Then, just as the hearse was setting out, one woman realized that she had left her gloves back in the house. It was a cold day, so she turned back to get them. As she came through the front door, she looked up the stairs and there he was—old man Geary.

He was coming down the stairs, one step at a time.

Porter smiles as he tells this story.

"We lived in that house for eighteen seasons," he said, "and we never saw any manifestations."

Perhaps, one might suggest, old man Geary was trying to catch up to his own hearse.

Little Girl Sad

"Did you see what I saw last night?"

This is a question often repeated in the morning by guests staying at two turn-of-the-century bed-and-breakfast inns on Mackinac's Bogan Lane, Pine Cottage, and Chateau Lorraine.

What these guests have seen is the ghost of a sad little girl with long hair.

The frail little girl often weeps.

Guests ask her: "What do you want?"

"Mommy," she sobs. "I want to go home."

She also has been seen and heard playing the piano in the parlor of the Chateau Lorraine. Sitting below a ceiling painted with angels, the girl picks out melancholy tunes with her childish fingers on the Steinway baby grand.

The piano has its own story. It was purchased from the Grand Hotel in the mid-1990s, and it had been used in the movie *Somewhere in Time*, made in the late 1970s. The film tells the romantic story of a young man, played by Christopher Reeve, who checks into the Grand Hotel and then finds a way to go back in time to meet his true love, played by Jane Seymour.

When guests speak of the spirit, they say they never feel afraid. After all, they say, she is just a little girl.

Shamus' Message

The year was 1990, or thereabouts. A guest, who was suffering with a hiatal hernia, stood at the window of her room in Mackinac Island's century-old, clapboard McNally Cottage Bed-and-Breakfast on Main Street.

Worried and in pain, she stared vacantly through the night toward the Round Island Lighthouse, just offshore.

She thought she was alone. But then she felt a soft hand on her shoulder. Not at all frightened, she turned to see a wizened little old man standing behind her.

It was not until the next morning when she came down to breakfast that she spotted an old portrait hanging on the wall. It was the same old man. The picture showed Shamus Mary McNally, the son of Michael

McNally, who built the house in 1889. Shamus lived there as a boy until 1904, when he went off to college at the University of Detroit.

"Oooohh," said the woman, her voice trembling as she stared at the old photo, "that was him."

What's more, she said that Shamus spoke to her. In a voice that was as soft as his touch, he told her, "Everything will be all right."

And as it turned out, everything was all right. Not long afterwards, she recovered completely.

Les Cheneaux Islands

These islands look like a giant black bear clawed them out of the eastern shore of the Upper Peninsula.

One huge swipe, slashing down and to the right. Land shredded, rock unearthed, splintered trees sent flying. And in the moments that followed, Lake Huron's waters rushed in to fill the gouges.

Where once the land lay solid, thirty-six islands were formed, lank and linear.

It's no wonder the French-English dictionary translates "les cheneaux" (pronounced lay sheh-NOH) as "the gutters." Most locals prefer the less exact but more genial translation "the channels."

Of course it was the claws of an Ice Age glacier that formed the islands, not those of a bear. And this geographic violence produced one of the most fascinating and varied places in the Great Lakes, a place with protected waters that were perfect for small boats and the sheer enjoyment of the outdoors.

The Nature Conservancy, a leader in natural land conservation, calls Les Cheneaux "one of the last great places" in the United States where natural systems are still unsullied.

The Conservancy also points out that this area of limestone bedrock has plant species found almost nowhere else in the world—dwarf lake iris, Houghton's goldenrod, and pitcher's thistle.

In the spring, its trees draw birds migrating north from South and Central America. These include a number of warblers—black-throated greens, blacks, whites, and magnolias.

To the visitor, the Les Cheneaux Islands (with the sound alike nickname, "the snows") are a place of cerulean waters plaited with island strips that are dark with pine and cedar. Human fishers stalk the waters. And so do airborne fishers—eagles that loaf in the updrafts, ospreys, ring-billed gulls, and the birds that islanders despise, the cormorants.

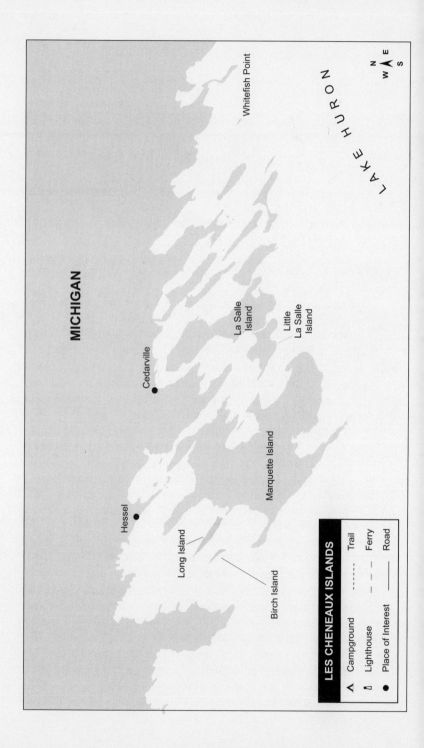

MICHIGAN

Whitefish Point

LAKE HURON

N
W E
S

Cedarville

La Salle
Island

Little
La Salle
Island

Marquette Island

Hessel

Long Island

Birch Island

LES CHENEAUX ISLANDS

∧ Campground   ········· Trail

⌂ Lighthouse   ‒ ‒ ‒ Ferry

● Place of Interest   ——— Road

One Island, one house. A perfect fit. Dollar Island, between the mainland and Marquette Island, in the Les Cheneaux Islands is just the right size for this house, a boat house, and of course, a gazebo.

Low waters here at Les Cheneaux Islands and in all of Lakes Huron and Michigan. In part, the sinking waterline was due to years of low snow falls in the north. But a permanent one-foot loss has come because dredging and erosion in the St. Clair River near Detroit has, in effect, reamed out the plug that held the waters to their original height.

The Les Cheneaux Islands are peopled places—but not like Traverse City and Charlevoix, thick with chain hotels, chain restaurants, and chain retail stores. They are more like Michigan of times gone by.

The islands have has mom-and-pop places where families stay in individual cabins with kitchens. Restaurants are called Cheryl's and Pammi Jean's after their owners, who actually work in the kitchens. Forget Burger King and Starbucks.

There are summer cottages, lots of them dotting the shore. These are owned by people who came, saw, and decided to sink some roots.

A Haven for Wooden Boats

People who work with their hands can still be found here.

Men like Bruce Patrick, whose family dates back to the late 1870s, can

A tired old boat house at Hessel in the Apostle Islands.

Boat houses on the Les Cheneaux Islands range from very old and weather-beaten to palatial. An afternoon can be whiled away boating around the islands viewing all manner of architectural styles.

actually build wooden boats, beautiful boats with lines that have a ballerina-like grace.

Steaming wood and then bending it to just the right shape, Patrick can build a boat from scratch or reconstruct a family's backyard embarrassment into a floating heirloom.

Les Cheneaux may be one of the few places in the world where people tour around to look at garages—garages for boats that is. This is a boater's world, where transportation means Chris-Crafts, sailboats, skiffs, runabouts, and any other water craft you can imagine. Houses for boats, basically buildings with watery floors, are so varied and architecturally interesting that people collect their photographs like baseball cards.

But really, these islands always have been about boating.

The nation's very first Chris-Craft dealership opened its doors in 1925 in Hessel. The story goes that it was a supply-and-demand situation. Rumrunners needed boats to smuggle liquor here during Prohibition.

At any rate, E. J. Mertaugh Boat Works is still operating in Hessel, but now it is under the ownership of Bruce Glupker.

Hundreds of classic boat lovers gather on the docks in Hessel on the second Saturday of August each year for the Les Cheneaux Islands Antique Boat Show. Photo by Carl Ter Haar. Courtesy of Les Cheneaux Historical Association Archives.

The Mackinaw boat seen here in Les Cheneaux Islands was the ultra-practical workhorse of the Great Lakes. With a prow on both ends and a removable rudder, it could be sailed or rowed. Its masts could be lifted out and used as rollers to pull it ashore. Starting in the 1830s and for the next 80 years, it was used by fishermen, fur traders, mail carriers, settlers, lake travelers, and anyone who needed to get cargo across the water. It was wide at the waterline and narrow at the bottom, making it fast when it was empty and stable when it was loaded. Courtesy of Les Cheneaux Historical Association Archives.

For people who love traditional boats, the best time of year to visit the islands is the second Saturday in August for the Annual Wooden Boat Show and Festival of Arts. Typically as many as 10,000 people show up in Hessel to ogle and touch 150 or more wooden boats.

Almost any other time of the year, boat lovers can get a quick antique boat fix by stopping by the Les Cheneaux Maritime Museum, just east of Cedarville on M-134. You can check out everything from a birch bark canoe to a 1936 L-Class sailboat to a collection of old outboard motors.

The islands' boating history necessarily goes back to the Indians, and later the voyageurs who came by canoe. Then logging schooners appeared, and double-ended Mackinac fishing boats. These came with clever detachable masts that also could serve as rollers so fishermen could pull their boats up on the shore.

Since the area had no roads in the late 1800s and early 1900s, real estate agents necessarily used boats to show their clients the island lots.

In the 1920s and 1930s, summer people—up from Chicago, Detroit, and Cincinnati—gamboled about in sleek mahogany resort boats made by Chris-Craft. Later came durable yachts of fiberglass and aluminum with big engines and lots of rear deck space for sipping cocktails in the late afternoon.

Most recently, kayakers have appeared. To a degree, this is sort of retro watercraft since island boating started with people and paddles. The modern paddlers skim along the protected waters in boats as thin and bright as Crayolas straight from the box.

Indians, Voyageurs, and a Man with a Hole in his Stomach

The first people on the islands were, of course, Indians. For centuries, they would stop over on the islands. For them, Les Cheneaux were a sort of interstate highway pullout where they could rest, get something to eat— like a mess of perch—and then move on.

Later came the voyageurs, who followed the watery paths of the Indians. Beaver pelts were gold in that era. And French paddlers were chosen if they had short legs that would not take up space in the canoe that could be filled with pelts.

Les Cheneaux were on their highway to riches. Their route was from Montreal, up the Ottawa River. Then, emerging from the French River at the northeast corner of Lake Huron, they paddled across the North Channel to Les Cheneaux and from there on to Lake Michigan, to trading posts at St. Ignace or Mackinac Island, or often on to Lake Superior and Fort William, near what is now Thunder Bay, Ontario.

The history of Les Cheneaux was chronicled by Phillip Pittman, an author, a former English professor at Marshall University in Huntington, West Virginia, and a resident of Marquette Island, Les Cheneaux's largest island.

Pittman, in *The Cheneaux Chronicles*, tells the story of one of the islands' most famous residents, a nineteen-year-old French-Canadian voyageur and trapper named Alexis St. Martin.

One day in 1822, St. Martin was accidentally shot in the stomach while he was on Mackinac Island, about 18 miles from Les Cheneaux.

Dr. William Beaumont, a surgeon at the Mackinac fort, could not know it at the time, but St. Martin's wound would eventually bring him international fame.

St. Martin's wound was huge, the size of a man's hand. And while Beaumont could bring St. Martin back to health and strength, he could not get the wound to close. It had to be covered so that St. Martin could eat and drink.

With this condition, St. Martin could no longer endure the rough life of a voyageur, so Beaumont hired him as a handyman to chop wood and mow fields.

Two years later, in August of 1825, Beaumont had moved to Fort Niagara. St. Martin followed him there, and it was at this time that the doctor began his experimental studies of gastric juices.

He would take half-ounce pieces of meat, tie them to a silk string, and then lower them through the hole into St. Martin's stomach. Thus Beaumont became the first person to see the human digestive system as it actually worked in the human body.

Over the years, Beaumont did a series of experiments with St. Martin, later dropping in bits of sausage, pieces of mutton, and even raw oysters.

While it all sounds rather ghoulish, St. Martin lived to the age of eighty-six, dying on June 24, 1880.

And Beaumont became world-famous for his studies. Near Detroit, William Beaumont Hospital is named for him.

Big but Spartan Hotels and Cottages

By the 1850s, according to Pittman, white people began to show up in substantial numbers. They included lumbermen, homesteaders, and parties of sportsmen. In this case, the sportsmen were mostly military men stationed at Fort Mackinac, who left their wives and children, to fish among the islands.

Life got busier by the 1880s. Railroad companies were laying tracks farther and farther north. Steamships were bringing vacationers up through the Great Lakes. To give the visitors an attractive destination and a place to stay—and spend money—investors built the Grand Hotel on Mackinac Island in 1886.

Completion of the Grand kick-started summer recreation in the nearby Les Cheneaux Islands. Arnold Lines, now best known for its ferries that transport people to Mackinac Island from Mackinaw City and St. Ignace, ran a ferry from Mackinac island to Hessel.

Over the years, big hotels were built on the islands and on the adjacent mainland—Patrick's Landing, the Muscalonge, The Les Cheneaux Club, Elliot House, The Lakeside, and the grand Islington. For the most part, these hotels were used by real estate salespeople to house potential clients. But vacationers stayed there too, in what were rather spartan rooms.

Like Mackinac Island and much of Michigan's north country, Les

Vacationers celebrate the 4th of July on the dock outside the Elliot House Hotel, one of the many hotels that blossomed in the Les Cheneaux Islands in the late 1800s and the opening decades of the 20th century. In that era, the hotel rooms were typically spartan. Guests were tourists and very often prospective clients brought in by local real estate salesmen. Courtesy of Les Cheneaux Historical Association Archives.

Cheneaux every year drew summer people who came to escape the heat, humidity, and foul air of the big Midwestern cities.

World War II ended the growth. Money was tight. Travel was restricted. The men went off to fight. And after the war, America found its addiction to the open road. Gas rationing had ended; people had cars and they wanted to drive them. It was a new attitude. Forget spartan hotel rooms. Many people wanted to buy property, places to build a cottage. Over time, the islands' big hotels disappeared, never to be replaced.

Fishers Love It, So Do Cormorants

Today, people still come to Les Cheneaux.

It's a quieter place than, say Traverse City. It's a fine family place. The visitors, who quadruple the local population of 2,200 in the summer, come to boat, to stay in cottages and at resorts, and to fish in the calm, protected waters.

Fishing has long been one of the islands' big draws. But of late, it has created quite a controversy. Not fishing by people, but fishing by birds.

The cormorant population has grown exponentially over the last dozen years. And visitors and locals alike are complaining that these birds, once rare in the Great Lakes, are decimating the perch fishery.

"I've seen 3,000 to 5,000 cormorants in a closed bay," said Brian Harrison, head of the local chamber of commerce and owner of the Great Outdoors, which sells fishing and hunting gear.

"They moved across the bay like a combine. Each one can eat up to one and a half pounds of fish a day. That's six or seven perch."

Despite that, Harrison added, the local perch fishing has been making a comeback. Fishers in Les Cheneaux also continue to pull in salmon, lake trout, pike, and other lake fish from the islands' blue channels.

Sport fishermen just back from trolling the waters among the Les Cheneaux Islands show off their catch in this postcard from the 1920s. Courtesy of Les Cheneaux Historical Association Archives.

Visitors fall in love with these islands. They come back year after year. It's a feeling that well may go back to the Indians who were here originally.

Pittman suggests that the islands' name came not from the French word for gutters, but from a French translation of the Indian term for the islands. They called the islands "our home." In French that translates as *chez nous*, which sounds very like *cheneaux*.

If You Go

Getting There: Go up Interstate 75, cross the Mackinac Bridge, continue about 10 miles, and then turn east on M-134. The town of Hessel is about a fifteen-minute drive, and Cedarville is another five minutes.

Transportation: All but one of the thirty-six islands have privately owned land. Individuals own houses and lots on many islands and, in some cases, are the sole owners of entire islands. The single public island is Government, which is part of the Hiawatha National Forest. It has hiking paths and two campgrounds.

You can drive to two of the islands—Hill Island and Island No. 8. Take the turnoff from M-134 east of Cedarville.

To get out among the islands, you need a boat. You can bring your own; Hessel and Cedarville have public launches. Les Cheneaux Islands Welcome Center (call 888-364-7526, 9–5 weekdays) has a list of places that rent motorboats, outboards, sailboats, canoes, paddleboats, and other craft.

Tours and Fishing: Two boat operators will take you on guided tours of the islands or on fishing trips. I went with James Shutt of Dream Seaker Charters and Tours. Call 888-634-3419. Also you can call Norm Perkins, captain of the twenty-seven-foot *Sea Hawk*, of Les Cheneaux Island Water

Tours and Charter Service. Call 906-484-3776 or 866-322-3776. For kayak tours, biking tours, hiking tours, and birding tours, contact Jessie Hadley, Woods & Water Ecotours at 906-484-4157.

Things to Do: The Les Cheneaux Maritime Museum is on M-134 in Cedarville, four blocks east of the traffic light. The Les Cheneaux Historical Museum is in Cedarville, just south of the traffic light on M-134. During summer, both museums are open 10–5 Monday–Saturday, 1–5 Sunday. For either, call 906-484-2821.

Golf: The area has two golf courses. The older is the Les Cheneaux Club Golf Links, a nine-hole, par-35 course of Scottish design. It has been in use since 1898. The course is just off Four Mile Block Road, which runs south off M-134 just west of the Cedarville traffic light. It is a private club, but it is open to the public. Open 8–8 daily. Call 906-484-3606. The newer 18-hole, par-70 Hessel Ridge Golf Course is a wooded course set on rolling hills just north of the light in Hessel. Open 8–8 daily. Call 888-660-9166.

Gambling: Kewadin Casino at Hessel is a small place with about a hundred slot machines. It's on Three Mile Road, three miles north of the Hessel traffic light. During the warm months, it is open 9 AM to midnight Sunday–Thursday; 9 AM to 1 AM, Friday and Saturday. It closes somewhat earlier during the cold months. Call 906-484-2903.

Lodging: The area has about two dozen places to stay, including cottages and resorts. Contact the Les Cheneaux Welcome Center at 888-364-7526.

Dining: Eating out is generally good, but do not expect gourmet fare. A big plus is that the lake fish are fresh.

Hessel Bay Inn Restaurant is the best of the local places for any meal, with first-rate whitefish. Open for all meals during the warm months. Call 906-484-2460.

Got a craving for a latte or a cappuccino? The only place to get one is Pammi's Restaurant on M-134 in Cedarville. It also serves terrific salads, homemade soups, and fish dinners. Open for lunch and dinner. Call 906-484-7844.

A local favorite, which serves Italian, is Ang-Gios Family Restaurant on M-134 in Cedarville. Open for all meals daily. Call 906-484-3301.

For lunch and dinner with pizza, burgers, jalapeno poppers, and soft-serve ice cream try Jamie's Lakeside Deli in Cedarville. Open 7 AM to 11 PM daily. Call 906-484-2500.

Sink your teeth into a fine charbroiled prime rib, steak, or seafood at Cattails Cove in Cedarville. Lunch and dinner, daily from 11 AM to 10 PM The lounge is open until midnight. Call 906-484-2995.

You can pick up some yummy pastries at Hessel Home Bakery. It is on

M-134, just east of the traffic light in Hessel. Open 6:30 AM to 3 PM Monday–Saturday. Call 906-484-3412.

Information: Contact the Les Cheneaux Welcome Center on M-134 just west of the light in Cedarville. Call 888-364-7526, 9–5 weekdays.

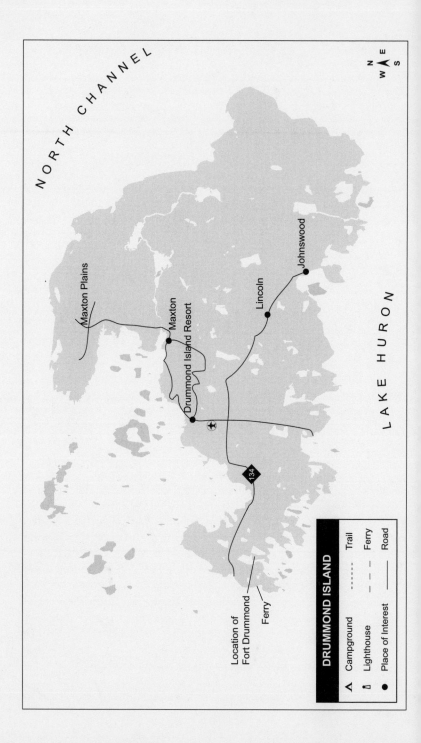

NORTH CHANNEL

Maxton Plains

Maxton

Drummond Island Resort

Lincoln

Johnswood

Location of
Fort Drummond

134

Ferry

LAKE HURON

N
W E
S

DRUMMOND ISLAND

▲ Campground   ⋯⋯ Trail

🏠 Lighthouse   – – – Ferry

● Place of Interest   —— Road

Drummond Island

Every hour a ferry crosses from the village of De Tour to pump cars and trucks into the arteries of Drummond Island. Every hour, the ferry pulls aboard another line of vehicles from the island so they can be returned to the mainland.

In and out they go. In and out. The islanders call it "the pulse."

It's not a heavy pulse. Drummond Island is an out-of-the-way place. When most travelers cross the Mackinac Bridge from Lower Michigan, they tend to head north toward Tauquamenon Falls and Sault Ste. Marie or west toward Marquette and the Keweenaw Peninsula.

Drummond Island lies to the east.

The good thing is that the island has been able, in some respects, to maintain its quiet solitude. It's a good place to spend a week or so fishing, hiking, kayaking, bird-watching, golfing, and, in winter, snowmobiling.

The island also boasts a fascinating history. You can find a few remains of a fort built here by a British commander who fought off an American attack on Mackinac Island during the War of 1812. Islanders can speak with pride of three smart, strong-willed women who helped form the very essence of what the island is today. And then there's Tom Monaghan, the pizza king, who put Drummond Island on the world map in the 1980s.

Drummond, an island shaped something like a Maine lobster, covers 136 square miles. It is the largest American island in the Great Lakes with a year-round population. Isle Royale on Lake Superior is larger, but people—mostly national park service staff—live there only during the warmer months.

Drummond is a natural wonderland. Sixty-one percent of the island is state forest. It hosts uncountable migratory birds, plus deer and other animals, flowers, and, most notably, the remarkable alvar plains, a rare limestone geological feature left from the Ice Age.

And there's more. Resorts range from economical mom-and-pop fishing camps to the upscale Drummond Island Resort, with a bowling alley, pool, harbor front, haute cuisine restaurant, and the Rock, one of the best golf courses in Michigan's Upper Peninsula.

Then there are the islanders themselves. They are friendly, but like islanders everywhere, they are happy to be marching to the beat of their own drum. Between 1,000 and 1,200 people live here. The island pace is slow. Islanders can be clannish. They might dislike some of their longtime neighbors, but they still trust them more than mainlanders.

They also share a willingness to be a bit quirky and accept quirkiness in others. Many people appreciate the semi-isolation of island life because it puts some distance between them and the mainland hustle, bustle, and bureaucracy. But for whatever reason, they love the island.

As islander Buster B. Bailey writes: *This is a gem of an island, a perfect jewel in the sea, / Surrounded by the waters of Huron, it is the world to me.*

The Fort of Last Resort

Drummond Island has always attracted strong, independent people.

Among the first was British Lieutenant Colonel Robert McDouall.

His story begins with the War of 1812. The British had acted quickly after the Americans declared war in June of that year. Within weeks, McDouall marshaled troops and Indian allies at the British fort on St. Joseph Island in the St. Mary's River for a surprise attack on the Mackinac Island fort. The British landed on the north side of the island and marched south to hit the fort on its most vulnerable side. The American troops, who had not even heard that war had been declared, surrendered without a shot. Two years later, with the war still raging, Lieutenant General Sir Gordon Drummond, commander of the British forces in Canada, put McDouall in charge of the Mackinac fort. Within weeks of his arrival in the spring of 1814, McDouall managed to beat back an American attack from both the water and land.

But then his world turned upside down at year's end. The peace treaty, signed on Christmas eve in Ghent, gave Mackinac back to the Americans. The boundary dividing the United States and Canada would remain the same. McDouall did not want to leave. He felt that the island was the Gibraltar of North America, located between lakes Huron and Michigan. It was a key spot, both for the fur trade with the Indians and for military reasons.

Staying was not an option. So McDouall had to find an alternative that would serve almost as well. He chose Drummond Island. Located in the St. Mary's passage, it was a good location for controlling boat travel—the most common form of transportation in that day—between Lakes Superior and Huron and linking up to much of the fur trade to the north. In July of 1815,

McDouall and some 350 troops and families sailed to Drummond. There, based on archaeological digs, the British constructed at least seventy-six buildings on the island's west end near the De Tour passage. The fort quickly became a gathering point for French trappers, Germans, Spanish, and Indians.

McDouall believed deeply in the importance of the Dummond Island fort, which was named after Lieutenant General Drummond. But back in London, the government was losing interest in the Americas. The demand for beaver skins was dropping. The war had sapped more funds than Britain could afford.

The Great Lakes started to seem like more bother than they were worth. As a result, even though McDouall pleaded for construction money, it never came. His soldiers suffered and died of scurvy. Drunkenness became a scourge.

Then, in 1828, McDouall's second fort was taken from him. And once again, he had been deposed by a politically solid but invisible line. This time, it was based on a revised drawing of the border between the United States and Canada.

To make a final determination of the border, an international boundary commission sailed up through the lakes in 1822 to decide which lands would go to the British and which to the United States. It had been agreed that the stretch between Lakes Huron and Superior would be divided based on the ship passage route. To the south and west would be American, to the north and east would be Canadian. Logicially Drummond should have been marked off as Canadian. After all, the standard ship passage went up the De Tour Channel, just to the island's west. But as one story goes, the American commissioner aboard the survey ship got the British commissioner drunk. And while he was still in his cups, the ship sailed through False De Tour Channel on the island's east side. So Drummond officially became American.

The British and McDouall were in no rush to leave Drummond Island. So it was six years later that the remnants of the British garrison—seven officers, forty men, fifteen women, twenty-six children, and three servants—boarded a ship to Penetanguishene on the British side of Lake Huron.

Visitors today can see very little of the fort's remains: a chimney and some grassy mounds where houses once stood. They are located almost within sight of the open pit dolomite mine. Islanders have found bits of nineteenth-century porcelain, buttons, and other artifacts.

Betsy Seaman: Pioneer Woman

Over the years, three strong, strong-willed, and intelligent women have put their mark on Drummond Island.

The first was Betsy Seaman.

Betsy Seaman can accurately be called a founding mother of Drummond Island. Her husband died ten years after they came to the island in the 1850s and she was left to raise 11 children. She not only raised and schooled them, but with the help of her children brought in money by cutting hay and chopping timber for passing steamboats. Her descendants still live on the island. Courtesy of Drummond Island Museum.

Elizabeth "Besty" Gandy was a schoolteacher born in Canada. Her life began a series of major turns when she married Daniel Seaman, a Mormon minister and a follower of James Jesse Strang. Strang, a charismatic and completely bizarre personality, led a splinter group of Mormons to Beaver Island in Lake Michigan, where they set up a community. Strang within a few years declared himself king of Beaver Island. And more than that, he declared that the Mormons should have dominion over all the Great Lakes.

Seaman had previously been married and his wife had died, leaving him with three children.

The Seamans joined Strang's Beaver Island community in 1850. Seaman came with Betsy, his second wife, and three children from the previous marriage. But they did not stay.

At least two reasons have been given for why the Seamans left Beaver Island. According to one, the Seamans became disillusioned with Strang and their lives on the island. They wanted to get away. So late one night, Seaman grabbed a boat and fled with his family. In the other version, Strang and Seaman had planned together that Seaman would start another Mormon colony on Drummond Island.

Either way, Daniel, Betsy, and the family were among the island's first settlers, finally ending up on the shores of Potagannissing Bay on Drummond Island. Unfortunately, ten years later, Daniel died at the age of fifty-two. That left Betsy alone with eleven children and the challenge of survival.

Basically Betsy Seaman gritted her teeth, set her mind, and put herself and the whole family to work.

A trained schoolteacher, she managed to educate her kids in what today might be called home schooling. One daughter even went on to become a teacher herself.

Betsy, who was capable in the way of many pioneer women, did everything she could to bring in money and put food on the table. She knitted, baked, mended clothes, and cultivated lush gardens of vegetables and flowers. Her plum trees and currant bushes were fat with fruit. She raised a few cattle. She set her boys to cutting wild hay near the mouth of Potagannissing River. Some seasons they would cut as much as twenty-five tons. The boys, with the help of local Indians, cut timber to be used as fuel for passing steamboats. Over time, they cut hundreds of cords of beech, maple, and yellow birch.

Many of Betsy's descendants still live on the island.

Maggie Walz: Finnish Entrepreneur

Back in Finland where she was born, her name was Markaretta Johanna Konttra Niiranan, which even in the old country seemed like a mouthful. So it was shortened to Kreeta Kontra.

But then when she came to America in 1878, her name was changed again. Some say it was immigration officers who simply changed her name to something that was easier to pronounce. They often did that in those days. Others said that it was the young Finnish woman herself who wanted a more American-sounding name. Either way, she became Maggie Johanna Walz.

Walz went first to the copper mining town of Calumet on Michigan's Keweenaw Peninsula, and then moved to nearby Hancock. It was boom time for copper mining. Tens of thousands of Finns were flooding into America. They had been suffering under their Russian overlords who, among other things, were drafting Finnish young men into the Russian army. When Finns learned they could make a dollar a day in the mines, they found a way to raise passage for the first westbound ship they could find. It sure beat staying at home and making a dollar a year.

Maggie first took a job as a maid. But for a woman of sharp intelligence and unstoppable ambition, that was only the beginning. She was married briefly, but her husband was killed in an accident, and she never remarried. She learned English. She went to night school and soon started an employment agency for other Finns. She hired out as an interpreter. She went on to study business at Valparaiso University in Indiana. Gaining steam, Walz started a women's club to help the Finnish needy. She launched a Finnish publication called *Naisten Lehti*, which means Ladies Journal. In it, she wrote

Finns came to Drummond Island in the early part of the twentieth century, settled, and became lumbermen. They were led by Maggie Walz, an activist, who was set on developing a Finnish utopian community on the island at Scammon Cove and Johnswood. Courtesy of Drummond Island Museum.

articles supporting women's suffrage and temperance. She invested in mining stocks, and her money grew.

Walz clearly was fashioning her own version of an up-by-the-bootstraps American success story.

Just after the turn of the twentieth century, she started working on something even more ambitious. She wanted to start a utopian community, a place dedicated to education, equality, and cooperative enterprises. She chose to put it on Scammon Cove on the south side of Drummond Island. She built a home there. And then she advertised for Finnish settlers, culled the applicants, and, in 1905, brought twenty-five to the island. Under the homestead laws, they got 160 acres basically for free, if they worked the land. The town was named Kreetan, after Maggie. A meeting hall was built; a farmers cooperative was set up; and the town soon had its own post office.

More Finns came. By 1908, the Finnish population was approaching 1,000. They worked the land and they found jobs at the Hitchcock Lumbering Company and the Kreetan Lumber Company at Johnswood. They gathered at Finn Hall, put on theater productions, read Finnish newspapers and books, and, unlike many English-speaking settlers, discussed the international labor movement and world affairs.

But over time, rifts developed in this utopia. Yes, Walz had supported cooperatives for farmers and stores. But the island Finns were looking beyond her initial ideas. Some wanted to pursue socialism. Others, who had followed the course of the 1914 Russian Revolution, wanted a communist society.

As a result, Walz ended up moving away. But leaving did not diminish her passion. She went on to help Finnish immigrants, as she had in the past, and to push for equality for women. She marched for women's suffrage in England in 1919, and she started a home and school for Finnish girls in Marquette, Michigan, and another one in Houston, Texas.

By the early 1930s, the island's great utopian experiment had run its

The Finns on Drummond Island worked in all seasons felling and hauling lumber, including with this train at Johnswood. Courtesy of Drummond Island Museum.

course. Many people left when the lumber companies closed in the 1920s. Others split off because of political ideals. And still others, who were making good money, stayed on the island but dropped the whole idea of the socialist-style commune.

Today, a number of descendants of the early Finnish utopians still live on Drummond Island. But the only historical remnant of that optimistic era is a small Finnish cemetery off Johnswood Road, just east of the crossroads at Lincoln.

Leila Seaman: A Tourism Visionary

Leila Seaman, the granddaughter of Betsy Seaman, helped launch Drummond Island's first recorded effort at attracting tourism in 1905.

She, with her sister Emma, and three cousins, who were also sisters, put together a vacation place at Seastone Pointe. They figured that city people could vacation there in a natural setting and avoid steamy and uncomfortable hotels and boarding houses. With the help of local Indians, the women arranged to have built some small but breezy cedar-bark cabins. They also offered rooms and a chance to stay in an authentic Indian wigwam. Seastone Pointe was billed as a pleasure resort.

Later Seaman developed a less rustic tourist haven with a hotel called the O'Mah'Me'Kong Lodge. It featured good food and a broad porch that soon was creaking with rockers as guests watched the summer sunsets. The lodge's rather odd name was tapped from the Indian words *kong*, for village, and O'Mah'Me, for Mormon, forming a connection with her grandparents' religion. It was a mainstay of island tourism for fifty years. Guests came not only from every state, but also from Europe and South America.

Seaman also was a big island promoter, basically a one-person visitors' bureau who constantly sent out brochures and answered inquiries. And over time, tourism began to grow.

The lodge also didn't hurt Seaman's other business—real estate. When people came and fell in love with the island, she was more than ready to sell them some island property. One of the most famous buyers was was L. J. Johnson, of outboard motor fame.

Pizza King

Even today, many people who live in downstate Michigan think that former Domino's Pizza czar Tom Monaghan owns Dummond Island. He never did. But he sure put the island on the map.

Newspapers and TV stations gobbled up the news in 1986 when Monaghan bought 2,000 acres of the island's 87,000 acres and built the lavish $30 million Domino's Resort. Drummond, formerly an island of modest fishing camps, suddenly hit the big time with a property that had a lakefront view, bowling alley, swimming pool, meeting rooms, and a gourmet restaurant. Initially Monaghan did not envision opening up the resort to the public. He built it as a place to bring employees for meetings and to offer a treat to staff who had done especially well.

In 1989, he completed a $5 million 18-hole golf course called the Rock. Some joked that first it was going to be named Pepperoni Links. It's now one of the best in the Upper Peninsula.

Initially, many islanders were pleased with Monaghan. For one thing, his money helped keep the local library open. But their goodwill vanished when he announced a plan to dredge the local bay so that he could bring in his 160-foot schooner. Locals feared the dredging would ruin the fishing, a mainstay of the economy. Monaghan backed off the idea in 1988.

And then in 1990, after just five years on the island, Monaghan disappeared almost as quickly as he had arrived.

He left Domino's Pizza and began dedicating himself to his religious beliefs. Monaghan, one of the country's more peculiar millionaires, once gave a speech at Madonna College saying he found poverty to be "one of the most exciting things in the world."

He seemed to be finding that excitement on Drummond Island. By 1992, he had sold the resort to a group of islanders for ten cents on the dollar. It is now called the Drummond Island Resort & Conference Center. And yes, you can still get a pizza there.

Places to See

Not much is left of Old Fort Drummond. Once you get off the ferry at the west end of the island, follow Channel Road, the island's main drag, to the first right turn, Humms Road. Take that straight back until it comes to a T. Right in that area, adjacent to the dolomite open pit mine, you can find an old chimney from a house in the fort and mounds where other houses were built.

Back on Channel Road, head to the center of the island and look on the left for signs for Drummond Island Township Park. It has a beach and a wonderfully pleasant hiking trail through the woods and along the shore. The whole hike might take an hour.

Back on Channel Road, follow it to Four Corners, where it crosses Townline Road. This is basically downtown Drummond Island—grocery and hardware store, drive-in restaurant, sit-down restaurant, church, sports shop, bakery, the Drummond Island Tourist Association, and so on.

Turn left or north on Townline Road and it takes you past the airport and passes a residential neighborhood. At Maxton Road, turn left and follow it around to the right to reach the Drummond Island Historical Museum, set up in a log cabin.

If you turn right on Maxton Road, it takes you past the Drummond Island Resort and on to Maxton Plains, a significant geological region, at the island's north end.

Maxton Plains looks a bit like an abandoned airstrip with weeds growing up through the cracks in the tarmac. In fact, it is one of the largest and least disturbed alvars in the world. An alvar is a broad, flat area with limestone bedrock on which most of the topsoil has been scraped away, in this case by the glaciers.

It is a harsh place for living things, but it does produce some rare plants, mostly mosses, sedges, and some wildflowers. If trees can grow there at all, they are usually stunted. Since alvars are very delicate, it is best to view the plains from the road rather than walking about and injuring plants that are having a hard enough time surviving.

Speaking of the island's natural assets, Drummond Island is a good place to find pudding stones, cheerful-looking conglomerates of quartzite embedded with jasper pebbles.

Drummond, basically a flat island, is good for easygoing and very pretty mountain biking. Some of the better roads and trails lead out from Maxton Plains. Much of the western part of the island is state forest, laced with hikable, bikeable, and four-wheel driveable roads. Lumber is still being culled from these woods, even though the era of clear-cuts is over.

Back at Four Corners, you can continue east on Johnswood Road, which is basically an extension of Channel Road. It will take you past the old Finnish Cemetery, just past the Meade Island Road on the right. It continues on to Scammon Cove and a swimming beach.

If You Go

Getting There: About a dozen miles north of the Mackinac Bridge on I-75, go east on Highway M-134 and follow it to its end in the village of

De Tour. There you pick up the ferry to Drummond Island. Between April 1 and January 1, it leaves every hour from De Tour at 40 minutes past the hour and from Drummond Island at 10 minutes past the hour. The winter schedule varies. Call: 906-297-8851. The island also has an airport with a 4,000-foot paved runway.

Transportation: You can bring your car onto the ferry, and you should. Bring a bike along if you like, but distances are such that you'll appreciate having a car.

Dining: For breakfast, hit the Bear Track Inn, north of Four Corners on Townline Road. It's a favorite hangout for locals. Or stop by the Island Bakery and Deli at Four Corners. For lunch, try a burger and cone at the Tee-Pee at Four Corners, a sort of island Dairy Queen. Or get a pizza at Pins Bar and Grill at the Drummond Island Resort.

Good for lunch or dinner is the Northwood Restaurant and Bar. Both the whitefish and the steaks are good. Or stop by the Gourmet Galley, just east of Four Corners. It also has European wines, cappuccinos, micro-brewed beer, and old-fashioned ice cream.

For a gourmet meal in a romantic setting by the water, get reservations for a table at Bayside Dining and Lounge at Drummond Island Resort. It's expensive, but worth it. Call 906-493-1014.

Lodging: The island has a range of small fishing resorts, rental cottages, bed-and-breakfasts, and the more lavish Drummond Island Resort. Many are very nice. For the complete vacation package, the best bet probably is the Drummond Island Resort, which along with its north woods–style log buildings offers golf, fishing, a pool, trap shooting, bowling, golf, and its own kayaks and canoes. Open year round, call 800-999-6364; www.drummondisland.com.

Fishing: Lots of fish are caught off Drummond Island, including perch, walleye, salmon, smallmouth bass, northern pike, smelt, and lake herring. Most resorts can arrange for fishing boats or charters.

Hunting: Season after season, deer hunting continues to be good on the island.

Swimming: The island has a couple of public beaches. One is at the township park, the other on the south side of the island at Scammon Cove. Expect the water to be cold.

Nature Tours and Soft Adventure: Hiking, biking, and kayaking tours in summer and snowshoe tours in winter are run by Woods and Water Eco-tours. They offer not only fun but lots of good information on birds, wildlife, and geology. Contact Jessie Hadley in Cedarville at 906-484-4157; www.woodswaterecotours.com.

Biking: Once on the island, pick up a copy of a tiny little paperback called *A Mountain Biker's Guide to Drummond Island,* by Dan Harrison.

You usually can find it at the museum or at Drummond Island Resort. It lists some fun trails.

Snowmobiling: Drummond Island has been a stealth destination for snowmobilers. But bit by bit, it is being discovered. The island has over 100 miles of groomed trails and great views of Lake Huron. Drummond Island Resort and a number of other places are open during the winter. Snowmobilers can also follow a path over the ice from Drummond Island to Canada.

Information: Contact the Drummond Island Chamber of Commerce at 800-737-8666; or go to www.drummond-island.com or www.drummondislandchamber.com.

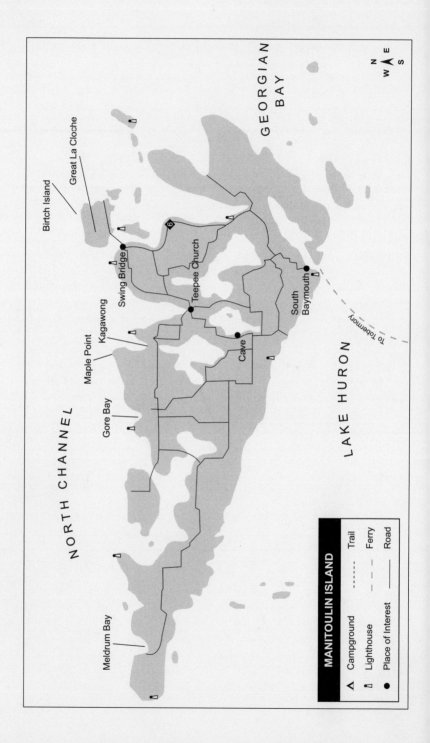

Manitoulin Island

On certain days when the air is heavy and moist, Lake Huron's horizon can simply vanish. To the eye, water and sky are one.

As though in a dream, sailboats glide off into the sky. Swimmers wade and splash among the clouds.

It is magical, mysterious. And for me, this is the very essence of Manitoulin Island, Lake Huron's North Channel, and Georgian Bay.

Manitoulin Island is a place of superlatives. It is the world's largest freshwater island. From tip to tip, it is eighty miles long, almost the distance from Detroit to Lansing. It has 108 inland lakes, including Lake Manitou, which according to the Guinness Book of World Records is "the largest lake within a freshwater island in the world."

No word yet on the largest fish caught in the largest inland lake on the largest freshwater island in the world.

What's not mentioned in these descriptions is that the island has an untrammeled, rural beauty. And it is perhaps this beauty that gives visitors their first, inchoate sense of Manitoulin's magic.

The island has changed little in the last fifty years. It is still an idyll of small farms, quaint villages, bed-and-breakfasts, fishing lodges, and eight reserves for First Nations bands.

There is no glitz. No hustle. Life runs at the leisurely pace of a 7½-horsepower outboard motor. People come with binoculars to search out some 155 breeding bird species. They come for superb fishing, to buy native paintings, to watch the rhythmic swirl of beads and feathers at Indian powwows, to pedal bicycles along quiet lanes, to photograph the gentle waterfalls and fields with split-rail fences, and to gaze out over the endless vistas of the northland's cobalt waters.

Natural beauty, then, is the first and most obvious magic. But Manitoulin and the nearby islands have a more profound magic, one laced with breath-catching intrigue.

The name Manitoulin means "spirit island." For uncounted centuries, the Ojibwa, Ottawa, and Potawatomi people believed that the Great Spirit or *Kitche Manitou* lived in the island's highlands.

Every time I visit, even today, I run into new jaw-dropping, not-en-tirely-explainable stories. Some are as ancient as the Indian legends. Others are quite modern.

They include an ancient rock that rings like a bell, disappearances of airplanes, burning ships that appear in the night, and the strange death of Danny Dodge, heir to the auto fortune.

Manitoulin Triangle

Is it possible that Manitoulin Island is the epicenter of a sort of Bermuda Triangle of the Great Lakes?

Maybe not. But over the years, hundreds of ships and scores of planes have gone down in the waters off Manitoulin Island, says Richard Hammond, an islander and self-styled sleuth of lost planes and ships.

More specifically, by Hammond's estimate, some 300 to 400 ships have sunk off Manitoulin's southern banks, and perhaps an equal number in the North Channel. In addtion, he says, thirty-six airplanes also have disap-peared—some of them permanently—in more recent times.

Hammond suggests a number of not-very-mysterious reasons why these ships might have vanished.

Many got caught in storms, got lost, or simply foundered during one of the island's heavy fogs that settle in during spring and fall. Other ships were so poorly made, they just sank. And still others were probably set afire and sunk so the owners could claim the insurance.

As for the missing thirty-six aircraft, Hammond actually found one of them himself.

In 1999, he salvaged a plane that carried mail for President Franklin D. Roosevelt. It had gone down in August of 1943. At the time, Roosevelt was on a fishing trip in the area. Hammond explained that the incident did not get much publicity because Roosevelt was supposed to be concentrating on winning World War II, not up in Canada catching pickerel.

The plane was a U.S. Army Air Corps Beechcraft UC-43B Traveler Staggerwing that had been sent up from Selfridge Field near Detroit. Dur-ing a takeoff on MacGregor Bay for a return flight to Detroit, an electrical fire broke out. The fuel quickly ignited, and the plane sank in ninety feet of water. The pilot and crew were rescued.

Pieces of that wreck, including the engine, now are on display at the Centennial Museum at Sheguiandah.

As for ships, the wreckage of one famous seventeenth-century ship may have washed up on Manitoulin's western shore. It was the *Griffon*, which belonged to the renowned French explorer René Robert Cavelier, sieur La Salle. Its disappearance is one of the great unsolved mysteries of the lakes.

In the late summer of 1679, the famed explorer La Salle had the sixty-foot ship built at the eastern end of Lake Erie. The *Griffon*, which would be used to transport beaver pelts, was the first commercial vessel on the Great Lakes.

La Salle's plan was to go from his starting point not far from Niagara Falls, across Lake Erie, up Lake Huron, and then down to the foot of Lake Michigan. From there, he hoped to launch an exploratory trip down the Mississippi River to its mouth.

On the way, La Salle made a stop at Green Bay in Lake Michigan, where he filled the *Griffon* with pelts. Since he needed to pay off some debts to the sponsors of his adventure, he sent the *Griffon* back without him. Meanwhile, he and a few members of his crew headed south toward the Mississippi River.

The *Griffon* never reached its destination. It apparently foundered in a terrible September storm.

Exactly two hundred years later, some of the early pioneers on Manitoulin discovered a ship's wreckage at the far west end of the island, on the shore facing the Mississagi Strait. For years, many thought—or perhaps hoped—these broken planks were the wreck of the *Griffon*.

However, more recent theories suggest that the ship never actually made it out of Lake Michigan.

Places to See and a Bit More Magic

For sightseeing around Manitoulin Island, here are a few spots you might want to check out.

If you come to the island using the ferry from Tobermory, Ontario, you land at South Baymouth. From there, head north and think of at least driving through the Indian village of Wikwemicong. Wikwemicong is unique in all Canada; it is the country's only unceded Indian reserve.

In 1836, the Odawa and Ojibwa nations signed a treaty with the Canadian federal government that said that Manitoulin and other islands along the north shore of Lake Huron would be set aside for settlement by native people from all over Upper Canada (basically Ontario). All went fine until 1861, when the government decided it wanted more land for white settlers. The government's idea was to put the native people on Manitoulin in several small reserves and give the rest of the farmland to the settlers.

The people of Wikwemicong would have none of that, and they amounted to 60 percent of the population. But leaders of the other bands

Feet drumming, hoops spinning, this Ojibwa lad dances a hoop dance that portrays the roles and responsibilities in the circles of life. He dances at M'Chigeeng on Manitoulin Island where a pow-pow is held every Labor Day.

eventually agreed to settle for the deal, eventually handing over 80 percent of the island.

Now the 105,000 acres of Wikwemicong land are officially registered as an Unceded Indian Reserve, the only one in the country. Each August many people attend a huge Indian powwow there.

Continuing north, you go through Manitowaning, with its square-frame lighthouse and the wonderful stained glass windows in St. Paul's Church, the oldest Anglican parish church in northern Ontario. It was built between 1845 and 1848.

Still heading north on Highway 6, stop at the Centennial Museum of Sheguiandah. On display are the remains of the Roosevelt Mail Plane and archaeological relics that date back to 9000 B.C.

Heading on north on Highway 6 once more, stop for the view at Ten Mile Point Lookout, which takes in a sweeping view of the North Channel and the La Cloche Mountains. The trading post and gallery there have a good selection of local native art, which is regarded as some of the best in Canada.

Get your camera ready. This is a photo op. The two-lane swing bridge, just on the edge of Little Current, is unique in that it does not lift up so that boats can pass into the harbor. It revolves on a center post, swinging out of the way.

This bridge is the only highway connection between Manitoulin and the outside world. The island's other major connection to the mainland is the ferry that runs to the island town of South Baymouth from Tobermory on Ontario's Bruce Peninsula.

Just on the edge of Little Current, heading west, look for the sign marking McLean's Mountain. Take a steep road to the top and one of the best views on the island. With a single sweep of the eyes you can take in Little Current, West Bay, and the North Channel.

Cup and Saucer Hill is one of the island's best hikes. It goes to Manitoulin's highest point, with a very pretty view. The Cup and Saucer trailhead is about two miles beyond Honora as you travel west from Little Current on Highway 540 (the main east-west road on the north side of the island). At Bidwell Road turn left and go about one-third of a mile to the trailhead. You will see a sign.

This hilltop is the highest point on the island, about 1,150 feet above sea level. The trail to the top is a little more than three miles. You might be a little out of breath when you reach the top, so it's unlikely you'll forget to stop and take in the panorama.

You might be tempted not to stop in the village of M'Chigeeng, which is farther west on Highway 540 at the intersection with Highway 551. But don't just drive through. Here are some nifty art galleries showing paintings and other works by nationally famous Indian artists. Also here is the Ojibway Cultural Foundation, which has a museum and a gallery.

But most fascinating is the twelve-sided Immaculate Conception Church, which is shaped like a teepee. The architecture of this Catholic church (built in 1972 after the original church burned down) represents a unique combination of Christian tradition and native beliefs in the Great Spirit, Kitche Manitou. The idea was to re-create the native tradition of fire pit meetings, where people gathered to talk, listen, and learn about the Great Spirit. So in this church, the altar is in the center of a virtually round building. The shape represents the Creator and the circle of life.

For a short side trip, head south on Highway 551, which takes you past Lake Mindemoya. Look at the lake's island, also called Mindemoya. With the aid of a bit of imagination, the island looks a bit like an old woman on her hands and knees.

As you might guess, this image did not pass unnoticed by the native people, who had their own stories about its formation.

One of a couple of different stories is about the wife of Nanabush, who was the son of a spirit father and a human mother. Apparently his spiritual family connections did not impress his wife, who ran away. Starting somewhere about the middle of what we now know as Ontario, she hied herself up the Bruce Peninsula and from there to Manitoulin Island and then to Lake Mindemoya.

Nanabush followed and, as the story goes, left wonderful hunting grounds wherever he passed. Finally, one day he reached the top of Cup and Saucer Hill, looked down on the lake, and saw his wife kneeling on the island. By this time after so much travel, Nanabush was more than a little tired and irked.

"Well," he said, "you can stay." And she remains to this day.

To the west of the lake is Mindemoya Lake Cave at the Rock Garden Terrace Resort. The cave is about seventy-five feet deep, with a couple of bends and turns. More interesting perhaps than the cave itself is the story that goes with it.

The cave was discovered in 1888 by three Mennonite preachers who were out duck hunting. Inside, they found fifteen skeletons, apparently of Huron warriors who were killed in the mid-seventeenth century by their arch-foes the Iroquois.

Farther west you will hit the pretty hamlet of Kagawong. Hardly big enough to even qualify for village status, it has just a few buildings and a dock. But it's cute. You can get a cup of coffee there, buy an antique, visit a small museum, and see a tiny church designed like a ship.

Also, with just a short walk, you can visit the nearby sixty-five-foot-high Bridal Veil Falls. One lingering look and you will realize why the town was named Kagawong, which is the Ojibwa name for "where the mists rise from falling water."

From Kagawong, you can take the dirt road out to Maple Point where Danny Dodge, heir to the Dodge auto fortune, had a cottage. Young Dodge's death is one of the island's lingering mysteries.

Continuing west on Highway 540, you might want to stop at the Gore Bay Museum, where the curators have displayed some artifacts that some think came from La Salle's ship, the *Griffon*. Going on to the island's west end, you reach the still antique-looking village of Meldrum Bay. From there you can, while driving some less than terrific roads, reach the Mississagi Strait lighthouse, which dates back to 1873. It is here, on this shore, that people believe the remnants of the *Griffon* washed up. Also, in the late nineteenth century, lighthouse keeper William Cullis and his assistant John Holdsworth reported finding four skeletons in a nearby cave. They speculated that these might be the bones of the *Griffon*'s crew. One skull was particularly big, which got Holdsworth to thinking of the *Griffon*'s pilot. He was called Luc the Dane and stood seven feet tall.

Providence Bay is supposed to have one of the most beautiful beaches in northern Ontario. That is arguably true. But given that this is northern Ontario and the very chilly north end of Lake Huron, you can expect that even prolonged wading might induce hypothermia.

One final mystery.

This one, called "the burning boat," was described in *Exploring Manitoulin,* by Shelley J. Pearen.

Apparently this strange phenomenon occurs only at 3 AM on nights with a full moon. To see it, you must stand at the site where a lighthouse once stood near Providence Bay. There, just offshore, you can see a "red, burning mass, often with the outline of a sailing ship." Pearen writes that as many as thirty or forty people have seen it at one time. Could it be just hot gases and reflections? No one is sure. But on this island of mysteries, certainly almost anything is possible.

If You Go

Getting There: From, say, Toronto or Detroit, a fun way to get to Manitoulin Island is to drive up the Bruce Peninsula to Tobermory and then take a ferry to the island.

From Windsor, you follow Highway 401 to Kitchener and then take Highway 6 north to Tobermory at the end of the Bruce Peninsula. From there, you and your car can board a ferry to South Baymouth on Manitoulin Island.

From Toronto, take the 400 north to Barrie and then follow Highway 26 until it connects with Highway 6, just east of Owen Sound. Then head north to Tobermory and the ferry.

Another route is to cross the border at Port Huron, follow Highway 402 to the Highway 21 turnoff, and take that road north along the Lake Huron shore until you reach Highway 6, about thirteen miles past Port Elgin. Then continue on up Highway 6 to Tobermory and the ferry.

For a more roundabout route, approach the island from the north, off Highway 17, which runs east and west across the top of Lake Huron. From the U.S. side, take Interstate 75 north to Sault Ste. Marie, Ontario. Then go east on Highway 17 to Espanola, where you take Highway 6 south to the island. This route takes you over the swinging bridge at Little Current. From the Canadian side, go north to Sudbury on Highway 69, then turn west on Highway 17 to Espanola.

The M.S. *Chi-Cheemaun,* the "big canoe," makes four trips daily between Tobermory and South Baymouth, starting in early May and continuing to mid-October. For sailing times, prices, and reservations, call 800-265-3163; web site: www.chicheemaun.com.

Dining: Manitoulin Island has some truly inspired restaurants. Among them are the the Garden's Gate Restaurant (north of South Baymouth about eight miles on Highway 6 and then west two minutes on Highway 542). Everything is cooked fresh. Do not miss the pecan pie. In Little Current, stop for lunch at the Old English Pantry, an English-style tea room with freshly baked bread for sandwiches. In Providence Bay, expect to get a fine dinner at the School House Restaurant. In Gore Bay, stop by the Bayside Restaurant & Café, for German-Canadian cuisine, wild game dishes, and a view out over the marina.

Lodging: Manitoulin Island has hotels, motels, inns, bed-and-breakfasts, fishing lodges, resorts, and campgrounds. For a list, contact the Manitoulin Tourism Association at 705-368-3021 or go to www.manitoulin-island.com.

Cruising: Manitoulin Island, the North Channel, and Georgian Bay are world-renowned destinations for sailing and yachting. Manitoulin Island has public marinas at the towns of Little Current, Kagawong, Gore Bay, Manitowaning, Wikwemikong, South Baymouth, and Providence Bay.

Island Lingo: Snake fences are the split rail fences found on farmlands throughout the island. A haweater is someone who was born on Manitoulin Island, a true native. Haw are the berries of the hawthorn tree. The story goes that early pioneers once saved themselves from starvation by eating these berries. Little Current celebrates Haweater Weekend on the first weekend of August.

Information: Contact the Manitoulin Tourism Association at 705-368-3021; web site: www.manitoulin-island.com.

The Strange Death
of Danny Dodge

It started as a Cinderella story—the tale of a simple Manitoulin island girl who fell in love and married a prince. But its ending was as dark as that of any Stephen King novel, with a strange, still not fully explained death.

The prince, and I guess we might call him that, was the son of an industrial king—John Dodge of the Dodge Motor Company. His full name was Daniel George Dodge, but everybody called him Danny.

In 1938, at the age of twenty-one, Danny had dark hair, combed straight back, steel-rimmed glasses, and the firm Dodge family jaw. He liked to tinker alone with experiments in his workshop.

At that time, he owned a lodge out on Manitoulin's Maple Point. You can almost see the place from the village docks of Kagawong.

When I first started looking into this story in the late 1980s, a few of the older Kagawong villagers remembered him still.

They recalled that he used to speed about in a flashy red convertible "with lots of horns and lights." Sometimes Dodge would give them rides to the nearby town of Gore Bay. They remembered his dashing speedboat. And they recalled how he used to like to hang around the Kagawong docks with the local kids and wait for the packet boat to bring the mail.

"He was kind of like James Dean," said Austin Hunt, who lived pretty much his whole life in Kagawong. As a boy, Hunt had known Dodge, who was about five years older.

To see the hamlet of Kagawong today is basically to see what it looked like in the 1930s, except that the railroad tracks are gone. It's a quiet, pretty village and just a short walk through the trees to reach Bridal Veil Falls, which gave the town its name. In the Ojibwa language, *kagawong* means "where mists rise from the falling waters."

Dodge owned a lodge on Maple Point, which was about a half hour ride out the bone-jarring peninsula road from Kagawong.

It was a happy day when Daniel Dodge, heir to the auto fortune, married Annie Lorraine MacDonald, a Manitoulin Island telephone operator. Thirteen days later, Danny Dodge would drown under circumstances still shrouded in mystery.

The lodge, which I've visited several times, was no Mackinac Island mansion, but then it was no primitive hunter's cabin either. It was a sprawling ranch-style place with a huge stone fireplace, a pool table, and an electric generator. Outside, young Dodge had a tennis court and a small dock where he kept his mahogany resort boat named MAC.

This was very modest stuff considering that the young man was worth about $11 million back in the days when just $1 million really amounted to something.

As villagers tell the story, Danny fell in love "with an island girl." She was the telephone operator in the nearby town of Gore Bay. Back in those days, you had to speak to an operator every time you made a call. Her name was Annie Lorraine MacDonald. She was nineteen.

Lorraine (whose name was sometimes spelled Laurine in newspaper stories) was tall, athletic, and, in her later years, given to wearing large hats.

When Danny broke the news of his wedding plans, the Dodge family was aghast. His widowed mother Matilda Dodge Wilson apparently pegged Lorraine as a gold digger who only wanted a piece of the family fortune.

But in the end, Danny persevered. The couple was married August 2, 1938, at Meadow Brook Hall in what is now Rochester Hills, Michigan.

Newspapers reported that days later the honeymooners showed up at Danny's lodge on Manitoulin Island's north shore. Lorraine made her presence felt within days. Dodge fired his longtime caretaker and hired three of Lorraine's friends—Frank Valiquette, Lloyd Bryant, and Bryant's wife.

Then, on August 15, disaster struck.

The story gets a little muddled at this point. But apparently Danny and his new helpers were out one day doing stupid kid tricks. Remember that Dodge was only twenty-one. The three men were in the garage literally playing with dynamite. They were laughing and lighting dynamite sticks and throwing them out the window. Lorraine looked on from the door.

At one point, Danny lighted a stick and threw it, but it hit the window ledge and bounced back inside. By some accounts, it set off a pile of dynamite caps on the floor.

The blast was horrendous. Wood splinters and metal fragments flew everywhere.

Newspapers reported that all four were injured and burned. One newspaper quoted doctors as saying Danny Dodge's injuries apparently were so severe that he could not have survived.

Bryant, in fact, lay near death. His body was riddled with splinters and shrapnel. His stomach was cut open and an artery in his arm was slashed.

It's unclear why they chose not to drive. Perhaps the rough road would have been too painful for the injuries. Instead, they decided to use Dodge's boat to get to the town of Little Current.

All four of the wounded, plus Bryant's wife, got into the 250-horsepower Lodge Torpedo speedboat. Lorraine, despite her injuries, took the wheel. Valiquette sat beside her. Danny and the Bryants were in the back, with Bryant's wife desperately trying to stop her husband's bleeding.

If the lake waters had been smooth, Dodge's speedboat could have made the trip to Little Current in about forty minutes. But the North Channel waters were not smooth that day. The boat was battered by waves more than four feet high. After two hours, the boat had only reached Honora Point and was still another forty minutes from Little Current.

At this point, Lorraine finally accepted that she was too injured and too exhausted to continue driving.

"I asked Frank [Valiquette] to take over driving the boat," Lorraine testified later at a coroner's inquest. "My arm hurt so badly."

That's when it happened.

"I then heard Mrs. Bryant scream and when I looked, Dan was going over the side of the boat," she testified. "We turned back and tried to rescue him, but could not. We searched for about ten minutes."

At that point, with the boat still bouncing in the waves, Lorraine and the others made their best guess as to their location and then continued on to Little Current to try to save Bryant's life.

The drowning of Danny Dodge was front-page news in Detroit and across the nation. By some reports, Danny's stepfather, Alfred G. Wilson, offered a $1,500 reward to anyone who could find the body.

Scores of boats, including a two-person submarine, converged on the waters off Honora Point. Days went by, and then weeks. Still, no one found the body. Searchers were giving up hope. But then, twenty-three days later, two fishermen pulled in the remains of young Dodge.

On October 24, 1938, a coroner's jury in Little Current handed down its verdict: "accidental death by drowning."

But was it accidental?

No one really knows except those who were in the boat that day.

Some islanders speculate that the young bride, who might have been casting greedy eyes on the Dodge fortune, planned this apparent accident—or at least took advantage of the bizarre circumstances. One might suspect that the Dodge family—given their misgivings about the wedding in the first place—might have been given to such speculation.

Some agree with the coroner's jury that, in the rough waters, Danny simply slipped and fell.

Others think that Danny Dodge stepped off into the water because he was crazed with the burning pain and was seeking the cool relief of the water.

Lorraine, after a court battle, eventually inherited at least $1.25 million from young Dodge's estate.

In 1991, when I first happened on this story during a visit to Kagawong, two of the survivors were still alive.

One was Lorraine; the other was Lloyd Bryant, the man who everyone thought would die.

Following the accident, Lorraine had a brief marriage to the plastic surgeon who helped her recover. Later she married another doctor, lived in Indiana, and then moved to California. Locals say that from time to time, this island girl would return home for a visit.

As for Bryant, I actually managed to find him after a bit of a search. And it was worth it. He actually put a new slant on those final minutes in the boat.

Then pushing ninety, he had been living in a Gore Bay nursing home. But while there he met and married another resident, and they moved into their own house nearby.

When I knocked on his front door, he and his wife Lillian were just sitting down to lunch in the kitchen.

Bryant invited me in and offered a glass of juice, but said he would not talk about the Dodge incident. He indicated that the Dodge family had put some pressure on him to keep quiet. But Lillian, his wife of two years, urged him to open up a bit.

At that point, Bryant said he did not blame Dodge for the explosion. "I can't say a bad thing about Danny," he said. "He was always good to me. I might have done the same thing.

"But," he went on, "the newspapers had it wrong. They said he would have died anyway. But Danny wasn't hurt hardly at all. There weren't any cuts more than a half-inch long or a half-inch deep.

"I think he was scared," interjected Lillian, speaking of the young man who was responsible for the accident. "He thought Lloyd was going to die. And he just jumped overboard."

Bryant just nodded.

The incident had happened sixty-three years before, but tears were welling up in his eyes.

The cottage owned by Danny Dodge on Maple Point near Kagawong was closed for many years and later was refurbished and turned into a bed-and-breakfast called, appropriately enough, Dodge Lodge. At this writing, it has been open during the summer, but the owners have put it up for sale.

Birch Island: The Legend of Dreamer's Rock

As long as memory holds and stories have been told and retold, Dreamer's Rock has been a place of great power, a place to connect with the mighty spirits.

It is an outcropping of rock, towering some 300 feet above Lake Huron on Birch Island, just a few miles north of the swing bridge to Manitoulin Island.

The view from on top is wide and breathtaking. Its sweep reaches across the North Channel, Lake Huron, Manitoulin Island, and the La Cloche mountains.

From here, the Ojibwa people could look out over the northern cross-roads of Lake Huron and watch history paddle by. First Indians passed here in canoes, later came French voyageurs in search of beaver pelts, then the British; a nearby highway now carries cars and big-shouldered trucks between the mainland and Manitoulin Island.

But the Ojibwa people did not climb to this island high spot just for a pretty view. For centuries it has been a place of great magic and spiritual connection.

Esther Osche is perhaps the best one to tell the story of Dreamer's Rock, a story told to her by her grandfather, who in turn learned it from his elders.

Osche might properly be called a *deh-bah-jeh-mah-jig*, which means "storyteller" in the Ojibwa language. She is one of the few remaining keepers of the oral tradition among the people of her Whitefish River Band.

She has often led people up the stony trail to Dreamer's Rock, a trip that is a special kind of experience. Certainly Osche is quick to smile and joke, but more than that, she offers a profound sense of the miraculousness of this place as she tells the legends of her people.

At its very top, Dreamer's Rock is rather smooth and flat except for one rather interesting indentation. It is a place that has been hollowed out, perhaps by the gods, in the shape of a person lying on his side with his knees slightly bent.

If a person were to stay on top of this rock for a long time, say for days, he or she could lie in this spot and get at least a little protection from the wind.

For as long as the Ojibwa people have been here on this island, young Indians approaching adulthood have climbed up to Dreamer's Rock on vision quests. They would sit on high, exposed to the wind and sun and rain and late night cold. They would eat no food, drink only a little water, and bring perhaps one blanket to protect them from the weather.

In time, the spirits would visit them, bringing insight and direction for their lives.

Sometimes the spirits came in the shape of animals, sometimes in other shapes. Some would speak words of great wisdom.

Dreamer's Rock has not been just for adolescents, Osche said. Adults, too, scramble their way to the top of Dreamer's Rock. They come even today, often seeking guidance for life problems.

But let us, just for a few minutes, sit high on Dreamer's Rock with Ester Osche. We will look out over Lake Huron's blue expanse and listen while she tells the stories of ancient magic.

One legend is of the famous Ojibwa chief Shawonoswe (SHAH-woe-nahs-way), who lived long before the Europeans came to these islands. As a boy and then a very young man, he often climbed to Dreamer's Rock in search of wisdom.

The story goes something like this:

Over many years, Shawonoswe climbed to Dreamer's Rock again and again to fast and to pray.

First he came as a boy, then later as a young man. He would sit for days facing where the sun set over the lake. And as years passed, his people gave him his name, which means "he who faces west."

But despite his many visits, the spirits never came to him. Other boys had visions, but he did not. His friends felt sorry for him. So Shawonoswe felt that he needed to accomplish something with his life. That is when he took up the bow and the lance, and fought his band's enemies without fear.

Years went by. He proved his valor in battle again and again. His fame grew. Then once again he returned to Dreamer's Rock. But on this day, everything was different.

As Shawonoswe sat facing west, a great white thunderbird appeared. He took Shawonoswe on his back and flew off, carrying him east across Lake Huron's waters to the heights of a holy mountain called Nehahupkung.

The thunderbird set Shawonoswe down on the top of a cliff. From there, Shawonoswe looked out and was amazed to see a figure before him, just sitting on a cloud right in midair. What's more, the figure was holding a dish of water in his lap.

"Who are you?" Shawonoswe asked.

"I am your creator," he said. And then he asked Shawonoswe to do something frightening. He asked him to step off the edge of the cliff, come to him, and look at the water in the dish.

Shawonoswe was truly afraid. But still he did as the Creator asked. He stepped off the cliff right into thin air. But to his surprise, Shawonoswe did not fall. Instead, he walked on the air. It felt like his moccasins were stepping on soft, firm moss.

He came to the Creator, and, as he was instructed, Shawonoswe looked into the water. It was swirling in the dish. First he saw animals. And then he realized that he could understand their talk and read their minds.

"Animals are your relatives," the Creator said. "You should not abuse them."

Then he saw the coming of men, fair-skinned men. They were dressed in robes like women. They had hair on their faces. These were the French Jesuits, who would not come until hundreds of years after Shawonoswe had stared into the swirling water.

He saw that wherever the men in robes went, the land was swallowed up and his people fell as in death, speechless and unable to move. He saw his people killed in terrible wars.

The Creator then gave Shawonoswe rules to live by, rules that he was to pass along to his people. These were rules like the Ten Commandments. The rules said that people should share what they have so no one will be in need. The rules said people should be grateful and brave.

Shawonoswe returned to his people and became a great leader and healer. He was a mighty medicine man.

And just as he was told to do by the Creator, Shawonoswe arranged for a celebration of the Creator each spring and fall. And at those celebrations, a great cedar pole was erected. And there, at the base of the pole, the Creator's lessons would be taught.

Years later, when the early French voyageurs came to these islands, they reported joining in a huge gathering of Indian people at a giant cedar pole.

The French said the people were kind, innocent, and tender with one another.

If You Go

This is a sacred place. Understandably, the Whitefish River First Nation does not want it to become a Disney-like tourist destination. No cameras are allowed on top of Dreamer's Rock. Do not go without an escort from the Whitefish River band. You can make arrangements to visit by calling the band office on Birch Island at 705-285-4335.

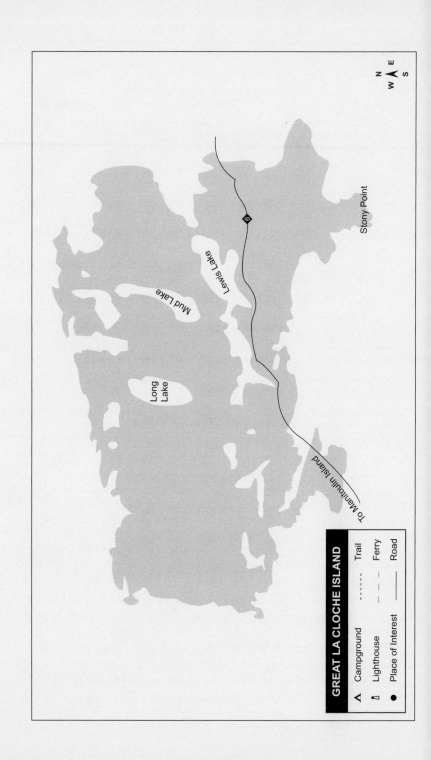

GREAT LA CLOCHE ISLAND

∧ Campground   ······· Trail
⌂ Lighthouse   – – – Ferry
● Place of Interest ——— Road

Long Lake

Mud Lake

Lewis Lake

Stony Point

To Manitoulin Island

N
W ◄► E
S

Great La Cloche Island: Bell Rock

All too often it is easy to dismiss the legends of a people we do not really know.

A story of men who can fly like birds. Impossible. Bringing the dead back to life. Not credible. Walking on water. Unimaginable.

Here on Great La Cloche Island just to the north of Little Current on Manitoulin Island, the Ojibwa people tell the ancient story of the Bell Rock. When you banged it with a stone or tomahawk, it would ring like a bell. What's more, the ringing could be heard tens of miles away. Yes, this legend sounds like a fantasy. But in fact it is true.

In addition to the Ojibwa oral history, the earliest voyageurs reported seeing this rock and hearing its powerful chime.

Today many people doubt such a rock exists, even people who live nearby on Manitoulin. They think that even if such a bell rock did exist, it vanished long ago. One guidebook states that it does exist, but it no longer chimes.

In fact, the Bell Rock *does* exist. It sits in an empty field, just down a dirt service road on Great La Cloche Island. And yes, it still rings.

More than once, I have visited the rock and heard its song with Esther Osche, the Ojibwa storyteller of the Whitefish River band.

She speaks to the rock with the reverence with which one might speak to a wise and elderly priest. She calls it "grandfather." And she makes it offerings of tobacco.

French voyageurs in the 1700s reported stopping at the rock and hitting it with their axes, just to hear its voice. Its ring, they said, could be heard from forty miles away.

The rock was taller than most men, they said. And to reach all the way around it, one needed four men touching fingertip to fingertip.

To the voyageurs, the rock's chime sounded like church bells in their native France. So they named the island for the rock, calling it *La Cloche* or the bell.

To the Ojibwa, the rock sings with the voice of the spirits. It brings them lessons and connects them with their spirit world.

Since Bell Rock could be heard for many miles, the Ojibwa also would bang it to send out warnings. Hearing the chime, warriors would know that their enemy the Iroquois were close. So they would gather to fight.

But even with Bell Rock, sometimes the Iroquois managed to surprise them.

Osche tells of one night long ago when the Iroquois sneaked in and killed many people in the village. Just a few of the Ojibwa villagers escaped. They fled to the shores of Lake Superior.

The Iroquois, of course, knew of the famed Bell Rock. So they settled near it. But to their dismay, the Iroquois could not make the rock ring. They struck it again and again. They hit it with rocks and lances and tomahawks. But the rock never sang.

Then, quite soon, the Iroquois fell prey to a terrible sickness. They suffered a skin disease that had never been seen before, Osche said. And within three days, the Iroquois invaders were all dead.

Sometime later, the Ojibwa villagers returned. They buried the fallen Iroquois and restarted their lives.

Once the Ojibwas returned to their home, the rock began to sing again.

Dire Predictions

Osche also tells of Shawonoswe, the legendary Ojibwa leader and medicine man. Centuries ago, he sought visions to guide his life atop Dreamer's Rock, and, in time, he could foretell the future.

Osche said that Shawonoswe predicted the coming of the Jesuits, whom he called men in black robes. The Jesuits, he said, would disparage the Ojibwa belief in the rock, decry it as idol worship.

His prediction proved true. But despite the Jesuit disapproval, the people secretly continued to worship at the rock and to listen to its song. They continued their worship for hundreds of years.

Then, in the mid-twentieth century, tragedy came. The Ojibwa people found that their great and ancient Bell Rock had been broken into pieces.

No one is quite sure how.

Some people blamed the workers from the nearby aggregate open-pit mine. Others suspected a lightning strike. According to Osche, "A legend says that one day a priest came and blessed the rock. That blessing broke the rock, just as a heart might break." No one is really sure.

Today, Bell Rock is in three hefty-sized fragments. Despite their history and spiritual power, they do not stand in some exalted or pristine place. They can be found—obvious, yet invisible—standing in the midst of an empty field, just a few dozen yards from a dirt road where everyday gravel trucks rumble by, spewing dust into the air.

Leon Jocko, a member of the Birch Island band, uses a stone to bring a soft tone from Bell Rock, a remnant of the original massive stone that had a ring that early voyageurs said could be heard for miles.

No driver stops. None makes an offering of tobacco. Nor would one even be likely to guess that just a few dozen yards from the road is this miracle rock that, Osche says, has yet to be explained by science.

Today, two of the three rocks are silent. But one still rings with the tap of a stone.

Its voice is soft. But be assured, the chime rings as purely as truth itself.

If You Go

This is a sacred place. Understandably the Whitefish River First Nation does not want it to become Disney-like tourist destination. Do not go without an escort from the Whitefish River band. You can make arrangements to visit by calling the band office on Birch Island at 705-285-4335.

Lake Michigan

Mackinaw City

Beaver Island

Rock Island

Washington Island

North Manitou

South Manitou

Traverse City

Green Bay

WISCONSIN

MICHIGAN

LAKE MICHIGAN

Milwaukee

Chicago

ILLINOIS

INDIANA

N
W   E
S

Beaver Island

Nothing quite compares with the sight of a grown man trying to launch a seventeen-pound lake trout into flight.

And for many in the crowd of watchers, it's especially amusing if the man is only slightly sober.

Struggling for a grip on the slippery scales, one Beaver Island local hoists the fish up with both hands, holding it like a wobbly tray. Then he squints his eyes with effort, and with a sweep of his arms he throws the trout backward over his head.

"Nice technique," one observer comments. "But not much distance," says another. Beaver Islanders know good fish tossing when they see it.

For years they have been watching this obscure, and somewhat slippery, art of fish tossing. It is one of the many zany competitions held each St. Patrick's Day outside the Shamrock Bar on this most Irish of the Great Lakes islands.

Most mainlanders, who typically show up in the summer, rarely see such outbursts of zaniness.

For them, Beaver Island is an isolated getaway—quiet, rural, very pretty, and a two-hour ferry ride from Charlevoix.

Visitors love hiking the tranquil woodland trails, touring the Mormon museum, listening to loons on the inland lakes, renting a kayak and paddling along the shore, and doing easy-going stuff like sitting and reading that long-neglected novel, smelling the lake air, and, in the evening, dining on freshly caught whitefish and dancing to live music at one of several pubs.

The island now also has a five-star lodge with six suites on the western shore. Called Deerwood Lodge, it is the most refined of log cabins, with every modern convenience, super service, and meals prepared by a graduate of the esteemed American Culinary Institute.

Veteran visitors to the island also know of its brief and tumultuous

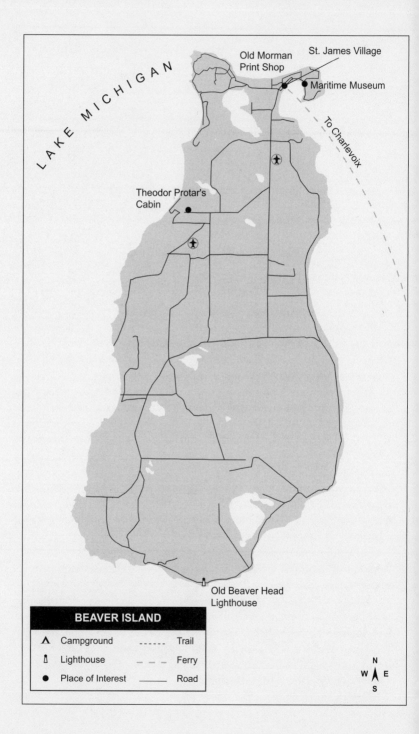

Old Morman Print Shop
St. James Village
Maritime Museum
To Charlevoix
LAKE MICHIGAN
Theodor Protar's Cabin
Old Beaver Head Lighthouse

BEAVER ISLAND

Λ Campground
Ω Lighthouse
● Place of Interest

------ Trail
– – – Ferry
—— Road

N
W E
S

Nice follow-through. The swinging technique is used here to launch a huge lake trout through the air in the annual fish-tossing contest on St. Patrick's Day on Beaver Island.

Mormon history and the famous (or perhaps infamous) story of the Mormon leader James Jesse Strang, who declared himself king of the island in the mid-nineteenth century. In a bizarre display of self-promotion, King Strang ruled Beaver Island Mormons for nine years, until a member of his own flock shot him to death.

Over time, the Mormons dislodged the original Irish islanders. But after Strang's death, the Irish flocked back. Others from Ireland joined them, making for a complete transition from Latter-day Saints to lads from County Donegal.

Today, some Beaver Islanders can trace their families back five generations to immigrants who fled the rock-strewn Irish island of Arranmore during the Great Potato Famine. So St. Patrick's Day is almost as big as Christmas on this island.

With the end of winter in sight, they throw open their arms to welcome spring's warmth. It's a homecoming. Sons and sisters and cousins return from the mainland.

And yes, for this very special occasion, a few islanders might sip a glass of Guinness. Or two. I'm told they quaff a splash to maintain a sense of unity with their friends who are happily tossing fish in front of the Shamrock Bar.

Up go the arms. Whoosh. Up goes the fish. The silver-bellied corpse is lofted into a high, somewhat wobbly arch.

"Whoaaa," the crowd calls admiringly.

"Splat," goes the fish.

Someone in the crowd cracks, "It's a good thing the animal rights people aren't here."

"I'll drink to that," says a second.

Doodlie-Doo

March 17 on Beaver Island is by turns loony, unpredictable, and occasionally profane. And yes, some people—not all, mind you—may drink a glass of Guinness. Or two.

As day wobbles its way into night, the contests continue. Teams, pushing shopping carts, must go from one personally embarrassing activity to another. It ends with a gulp of green beer. In the frozen chicken bowling contest, ten pins are set up in the street, and contestants try to knock them down using pullets fresh from the freezer. It's harder than you might think.

In the bar, a contest proceeds to determine who will be king and queen. Showing up in pairs, the contestants may—one or both—come in drag. Contenders for the throne also are required to perform an Irish jig. There is no music. The audience simply sings out in unison, "Doodlie, doodlie, doodlie, doo." Limericks with predictable profanity are created on the spot and read out loud as the audience howls with laughter.

And out on the street, just about everyone—men, women and children—takes part in the great island tug-of-war. The contest is between the Fish Chokers (traditionally those who live near the water in the village of

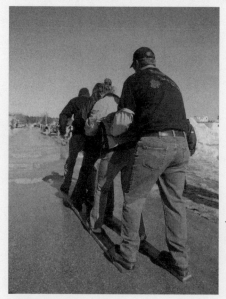

Skiing the hard way, these four Beaver Islanders strapped themselves to two boards for a race for the pull-out-the-stops-and-laugh-a-lot celebration on St. Patrick's Day.

Father Alexander Francis Zugelder, who came as Beaver Island's Catholic priest in 1889, sits down for lunch with some of his parishioners on Beaver Island. Father Zugelder, who stayed until 1905, helped break the monopoly of Irish families on the island by attracting a number of Germans. Courtesy of Beaver Island Historical Society.

St. James) and the Hayseeders (farmers who live on the south part of the island).

In many ways, St. Patrick's Day is emblematic of Beaver Island. It is homegrown fun designed not so much to attract tourists—although it does—but for islanders to amuse themselves.

But certainly this weekend St. Patrick's flurry of good fun is not the Beaver Island that summer visitors see after riding the ferry from Charlevoix.

On all other days, islanders just go about living their lives like the rest of us. The difference is that they live on this wooded island in the middle of one of America's most beautiful lakes.

They buy bread at McDonough's grocery store. Pick up a bag of nails at the Ace Hardware Store. At home, many front doors are left unlocked. Keys are left in cars. Neighbors keep an eye out for everyone's children. Church pews are filled on Sundays. The island's school, grades K–12, has fewer than one hundred kids. Islanders would never consider trading this peacefulness for the mainland's hurry scurry.

But understand, Beaver Island is not Norman Rockwell fantasy either.

Beaver Island is a water-bound small town. So just as families go back decades, so do some of the grudges. Being too successful can be frowned on. The well-to-do are referred to as "lace curtain Irish." But in an emergency, everyone turns out to help—throwing water on a burning house, taking the injured to the hospital.

Good Times, Bad, and Good Again

In the nineteenth century, Beaver Islanders did pretty well for themselves. In those days, the best and easiest way to travel was by boat. Overland travel was rough, slow, and dangerous. So the Great Lakes were the highway to

Motoring in, off the dock at St. James on Beaver Island.

North America's west. And Beaver Island was a major stop along the way.

More boat captains lived on Beaver Island and nearby High Island than any other place in the Great Lakes.

Beaver Island had a natural harbor and protection from westerly gales. Steamboats stopped at the island to take on wood to fuel their engines. Lumbering was big business. The village of St. James grew and prospered as passengers disembarked to stay in hotels, drink in saloons, and see the sights. Fishermen cast their nets for lake trout and whitefish in some of the best fishing grounds anywhere.

But over time, things changed.

The island's trees were shaved down like a Marine recruit's head, leaving few to sell. Ships began using coal and later oil. Lake shipping no longer held the monopoly on east-west travel.

Trains crossed the continent. Cars were built. Highways replaced trails. Trucks carried most of the heavy loads. Fishing stocks thinned and, in the 1950s, were largely killed off by lamprey eels.

Bad economic times came. Once fishing and lumber jobs disappeared, nothing came to replace them. With no work to do, older islanders simply retired. Their children had no choice but to leave the island to find work. By the 1960s, the island's population was so small that every phone number could be listed on a single page.

But the islanders, many of them tenacious Irish, hung on as best they could. Today, times are on the upswing. The new money on the island now jingles in visitors' pockets—and it comes from tourism.

Mainlanders want a little slice of Lake Michigan heaven. So they come for a weekend and want to stay. They want cottages. So lots are being sold for $250,000 and more. Construction workers can put their kids through college by building million-dollar summer homes.

Through all its ups and downs, the island has maintained its Irish base. You can't go anywhere without running into a McCafferty, a Cole, a

McDonough, or a Gillespie. A few locals still play tin flutes and saw on an Irish fiddle. They can sing "The parting glass," dance the jig, and be heard exclaiming in exasperation, "Jesus, Joseph, and Mary."

As a result, St. Patrick's Day is big. "The great day," as the Irish call it. But on the island, it takes on a special character because it also is a homecoming celebration, based in many ways on the fall celebrations in the 1800s held for returning boat captains and crews.

In the street, the fish toss contest continues. Techniques vary. Some use one arm, shoving straight from the shoulder like a shot putter. Some throw the fish like an outsized football.

The spinner technique also is popular. The thrower grabs the fish by its tail with both hands, whirls around to generate speed, and releases. Controlling direction is often difficult for these contestants.

The worst contestant was a man who took the fish by the gills and spun around, only to have its head pop off.

"Oooooh, yuck."

"I'll drink to that," says a man in the crowd. It was one more excuse for a glass of celebratory Guinness. Or maybe two.

Places to See

Locals are known to point out wryly that "there's no such thing as Beaver Island fudge."

They are sticking a needle, of course, into Mackinac Island, the much more famous and touristy island to the east, known for charming horse-drawn carriages, golf courses, the Grand Hotel, scores of ever-so cute shops and restaurants. And yes, Mackinac Island fudge.

Beaver Island is a more homespun place where the Ace Hardware store and the beer-and-a-shot Shamrock Bar & Grill typically get more business

The regulars and bartenders line up in front of C.C. Gallagher's Saloon in 1902 on Beaver Island. Courtesy of Beaver Island Historical Society.

The Mormon Print Shop acts as the island's museum and is a fine place to learn about the reign of James Jesse Strang, who proclaimed himself king of Beaver Island.

than the handful of tourist shops on Main Street. And for the most part, islanders like it that way.

On the other hand, the island has lots to like and plenty to do. Just don't expect summer stock theater, butterfly houses, or even a movie theater.

The Old Mormon Print Shop and the jail are worth an hour. You'll learn about one of the most bizarre figures in Michigan history. James Jesse Strang, a nineteenth-century Mormon leader, declared himself king of the island and was even known to strut about in a paper crown. The Maritime Museum, located in an old fishing shanty, gives a good sense of the time when Beaver Island was at the heart of the best commercial fishing in the lakes.

The island is a great place to drive, especially in October, when the island's dirt roads are draped by fiery colored branches. Make a circle tour with stops at the Old Beaver Head Lighthouse at the south end of the island and at Theodor Protar's cabin on Sloptown Road. For decades, Protar was the island's unofficial, unpaid doctor.

If You Go

Getting There: From Charlevoix, you travel about two hours by ferry to the island's only town, St. James. It is tucked into Paradise Bay at the north end of the island.

The ferry runs Mondays, Wednesdays, and Fridays in April; every day from May through September; and every day but Tuesdays in October. Progressively, Thursdays and Saturdays are dropped in November. And it's a Monday–Wednesday–Friday schedule in December.

Even if it seems warm in Charlevoix before you board the ferry, be sure to take a jacket if you plan to stay on deck during the crossing. It can get cold, even in midsummer.

For information about the ferry, call the Beaver Island Boat Company at 888-446-4095, 8–4 weekdays; Web site: www.bibco.com.

Or you can fly to the island on a nine-passenger, twin-engine aircraft from Charlevoix Airport. The trip takes about fifteen minutes. For information, call Island Airways at 800-524-6895, 8–5 daily; Web site: www.islandairways.com.

Transportation: Bring your car or a bike. Once you leave the village of St. James, the walks are pretty long. Cars can be rented at Beaver Island Car Rental (231-448-2300) or Gordon's Auto Rental (231-448-2438). And there's Beaver Island Taxi (231-448-2339). Bikes, kayaks, and fishing boats can be rented at Lakesports & Paradise Bay Gifts (231-448-2166) near the docks.

Activities: The island trails are great for hiking and camping too. Some 35 percent of Beaver Island is state land. Wait until mid-July, after the black flies disappear.

Swimming from the island's many isolated beaches can be fine. Beaver Island has ten miles of shoreline, but it's best to wait until August when the water warms up. Hunting and fishing can be good. In fall, hunters come for deer and pheasant. The island has some one thousand deer, about twice the human population. And fishing can be good for pike and bass on the inland lakes.

You also can arrange to scuba dive on sunken ships with the Paradise Bay Dive Shop (231-448-3195).

There's horseback riding at Unfinished Farms (231-448-2639). To rent kayaks and take lessons, go to Inland Seas Kayaking (231-448-2221) by the water in St. James village. For golf, hit the nine-hole, par-39 Beaver Island Golf Course (231-448-2294). For a sense of the island's woods and wildlife, try Beaver Island Eco Tours (231-448-2194). To charter a boat for fishing, visiting other islands, or just cruising around, try Island Hopper Charter Service (231-448-2309) or Bonadeo Boat Charters (231-448-2489).

Dining: The restaurants are few, but generally good. For breakfast, hit Dalwhinnic on Main Street. It opens at 7 AM and serves fresh-baked cinnamon rolls. Lunches and dinners are good and moderately priced at the Stoney Acre Grill, which is in an old barn on the edge of town. Don't miss the cheesecake. For dinner, try Nina's at the Beaver Island Lodge for an upscale meal with a fine view of the sunset over the water (231-448-2396). Local's love Nina's.

For authentic local color and good bar food, stop by the Shamrock Bar & Grill on Main Street. As for fudge, you can probably find some. But that's the mainstay of a whole different island.

Lodging: For a luxurious experience and superb dining, try Deerwood Lodge (231-448-3094; www.deerwood.net). Also quite nice with first-rate meals is the Beaver Island Lodge (231-448-2396).

Information: For more details, including specifics on other lodging, contact the Beaver Island Chamber of Commerce at 231-448-2505; www.beaverisland.org.

It's Good to Be King
James Jesse Strang

James Jesse Strang figured out a couple of things early in life.

One, it's good to be king. And two, it's *very good* if your subjects think you have a direct pipeline to God.

For nine years starting in 1847, Mormons dominated Beaver Island. And in turn, they were dominated by a fire-plug-sized con man who declared himself the island's king.

No goal seemed too lofty for Strang, who stood about five feet, six inches—even taller with his handmade crown. He had five wives, a bushy beard, and spellbinding ways that not only got him out of tight spots but also propelled him into the Michigan state legislature.

Nothing seemed to stop, or even slow, his charismatic leadership. Not a trigger-happy sheriff, not the enmity of people on the mainland and neighboring islands, not courtroom trials, not even the threat of a U.S. Navy gunboat. But his reign could not last.

By age nineteen, Strang already was showing signs of unbridled ambition, and further that he would do almost anything to achieve his goals.

Grousing that he was "no more than a farmer," the teenager wrote in his diary in 1832: "I ought to have been a member of the assembly or a brigadier general before this time if I am ever to rival Caesar or Napoleon, which I have sworn to."

Later he wrote revealingly, "I have spent the day trying to contrive some plan of obtaining in marriage the heir of the English crown." He was writing, of course, about the future Queen Victoria, who was then only twelve years old.

Less than twenty years later, Strang would proclaim himself king of an island, although a much smaller one than England.

And just to be sure that he looked the part of an island king, Strang would pull on regal robes. In fact, they were part of a costume left behind by an itinerant Shakespearean actor. As for his crown, he fashioned it from cardboard.

He took being king seriously. And in a Lilliputian version of the lives of his European idols, he took steps to create an empire. In this case, it was a Mormon empire. He saw all of the Great Lakes as his domain. He established Mormon settlements first on neighboring islands and then on the mainland near Charlevoix and Elk Rapids.

Rise to the Throne

Instead of marrying into a royal family, Strang had hooked his ambitions to the Mormon Church, then in its early years.

The pivotal moment came with the death of Joseph Smith, founder of the Mormon Church. This was his chance to grab fortune by the throat. Strang decided he wanted to be more than just *a* leader of the church; he wanted to be *the* leader.

Many of the details of Strang's life presented here were explained by William Cashman, curator of the Mormon Print Shop Museum on the island, and/or described in *The Journal of Beaver Island History: Volume One.*

Smith was killed by a mob in Carthage, Illinois, on June 27, 1844. No more than a few days passed before Strang showed up with a letter that he said had been written by Smith eight days before his death. It read in part,

James Jesse Strang, leader of a Mormon community, declared himself king of Beaver Island. He ruled on the island from 1848 to 1856, sometimes strutting about wearing a cardboard crown and a cape left behind by a Shakespearean actor. He was assassinated by members of his own group. Within weeks of his death, the Mormons were driven from the island. Courtesy of State of Michigan Archives.

Elvira Field was the mistress of James Jesse Strang, leader of the Mormon community of Beaver Island, who was married to another woman. In 1851, Field disguised herself as a man and traveled for weeks with Strang on a speaking tour of the East and Midwest. Strang claimed she was his male secretary, Charlie Douglas. The deception was exposed when the two returned. At that point, Strang made Field his second wife. Courtesy of Beaver Island Historical Society.

"if evil befall me thou shalt lead the flock to pleasant pastures." In other words, Strang apparently was his divinely chosen successor.

Years later, scholars learned that the signature did not match Smith's. And neither did the handwriting.

Strang not only showed guile; he was truly smart. He was a self-styled lawyer, which was common in that day. And he was a good attorney. He also was a silver-tongued charmer.

Strang's campaign for leadership had begun. He capitalized on the counterfeit letter whenever he could, always carrying it with him. But he was in a tough political battle for the leadership with Brigham Young. So he quickly realized that the letter alone would not be enough. He had to do something to solidify his claim.

It was well known that Smith said he had received his revelation from God on gold plates he had found in upstate New York. The plates were covered with writings that only Smith could decipher. Strang apparently figured one buried plate deserved another.

In 1845, he told fellow Mormons that he had gotten a message from God. He and his flock should go out and dig in the ground by an old oak tree. And there, surprise, they discovered several buried plates. Not gold plates, mind you, but brass plates. And each one was inscribed with exotic writing. It turned out that no one but Strang could translate them. And among his translations: Strang would be the new Mormon leader.

Clement Strang, wife, and daughter posed sometime around 1890. Clement was the son of James Jesse and Elvira Strang. Courtesy of Beaver Island Historical Society.

It was later learned that the plates had been pounded out of old brass tea kettles.

Despite this discovery, Brigham Young ended up leading the largest group of Mormons to Utah. Strang stayed in the Midwest with a smaller group.

In 1846, Strang took his believers to Vorhee, Wisconsin. And two years later they moved far out in Lake Michigan to Beaver Island. There Strang and twelve families built houses, constructed roads (the same ones on which islanders drive today), cut timber, set up a sawmill, farmed, and fished.

They prospered. Within a couple of years, the island population had reached 200. By 1865 it had increased to 900, about double today's population.

Passing boats stopped to take on wood, which Strang's lumbermen chopped and hauled to the docks. Chicago fish brokers set up shop on the island.

Brimming with his successes, Strang announced in 1856 that God had told him to take the title of king.

Gentiles, as Mormons called anyone who was not a Mormon, were slowly driven off the island. Strang's power solidified. He got himself elected to the state legislature in 1852 and again in 1854.

While the Mormons on Beaver Island were understandably happy with their success, other residents on nearby Mackinac Island were not. Until the

The 168-foot U.S.S. Michigan, a federal gunboat, sailed the waters of the Great Lakes from 1842 to 1923. A sidewheeler, it could run on either steam power or under sail. It was this gunboat that the Confederates hoped to capture in their effort to free rebel officers imprisoned on Johnson Island in 1864. It also was this same gunboat that King James Jesse Strang of Beaver Island went out to meet when he was assassinated in 1856. The Michigan carried Strang's killers to Mackinac Island, where several days later they were freed. Courtesy of Burton Historical Collection, Detroit Public Library.

Strang takeover, Mackinac Island, situated in the straits between lakes Huron and Michigan, was the major center for fishing and steamship supply. Islanders there felt the sharp jab of competition, and they didn't like it.

Also, people on nearby islands and on the mainland hated and feared Strang, his Mormons, and their polygamous ways. And it made little difference that Strang himself had only one wife.

Non-Mormons throughout the region believed that the Beaver Islanders were little more than a gang of murderers and thieves. Over on Washington and Rock islands near the Wisconsin shore, the Mormons got the blame whenever an unsolved murder or robbery cropped up. It must have been the Mormons, they say, or Mormon defectors, or somehow connected to the Mormons.

Back on Beaver Island, it turned out that Strang's messages from God had not ended.

The most bizarre instance cropped up in 1851 while the Mormon leader was on a prolonged trip to proselytize in the East and Midwest. During the six-month trip, Strang's only companion was private secretary, Charlie Douglas.

Then the scandal broke. It turned out Charlie was, in fact, not a he, but a she. Her real name was Elvira Field, and she was Strang's mistress.

After the two returned to Beaver Island, the people confronted Strang about his promiscuous ways. Brazen as ever, he quickly admitted everything.

"It's true," Strang said. "But," he added, drawing a favorite ace from his sleeve, "I've had a message from God."

Strang declared that God had told him to embrace polygamy. So with that, he married Elvira and subsequently three other women.

Over time, again and again, Strang's life was threatened, and police tried to lock him up. Again and again, he escaped.

He was hauled into court in Detroit and glibly talked his way out of the charges. While he was stopped on a boat trip at Mackinac Island, a deputy sheriff tried to arrest Strang. The officer pulled a pistol and tried to shoot him. When the gun misfired, Strang escaped over the side of the ship, only to appear several weeks later in his seat at the state legislature.

Other Mormons had gun battles with mainlanders who had heard rumors that Strang's people were kidnapping girls to be their wives.

Strang's reign finally ended in 1856.

On June 16, the warship U.S.S. *Michigan* pulled up to the Beaver Island dock. The captain sent a message inviting Strang to come aboard for a visit.

As he made his way to the dock, two disaffected men from his own flock jumped Strang. They hit him with clubs and shot him several times. After finishing their ambush, the assailants then scampered aboard the *Michigan* and sailed away.

Hours later, the *Michigan* dropped the killers off to be jailed on Mackinac Island, which, not incidentally, was a cauldron of hatred for Beaver Island. Their jail sentence lasted two days. After that, they were released to a rousing heroes' welcome.

Strang managed to survive for eleven days.

Soon after his death, a boozed-up crowd of ninety men from Mackinac sailed to Beaver Island. They were joined by men from Washington and Rock islands too. On landing, the thugs went from house to house and warned every family to get out by morning or they would not vouch for their safety.

Ships were lined up in Paradise Bay to carry the Mormons off to Chicago, Wisconsin, and Detroit. No question was left in the minds of the Mormon settlers. Their lives were at stake. Dinners were left on tables, tools in the yards, and crops in the fields.

Within days, the non-Mormons took over the island houses, the fields, the roads, and a ready-made town on an island. By the 1870s, Beaver Island would become the most prominent fishing area in North America.

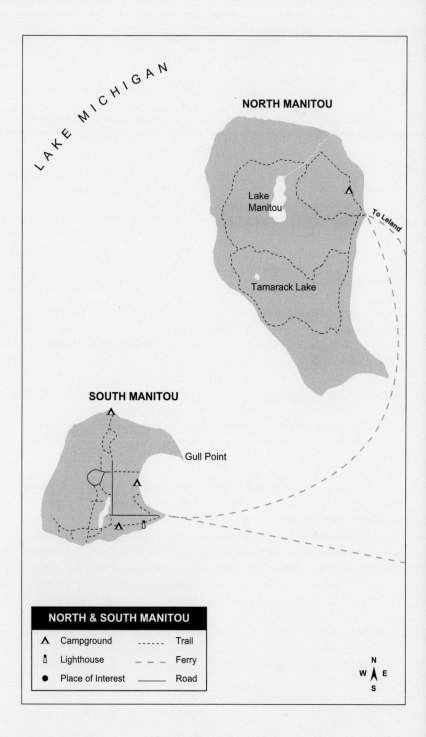

LAKE MICHIGAN

NORTH MANITOU

Lake
Manitou

To Leland

Tamarack Lake

SOUTH MANITOU

Gull Point

NORTH & SOUTH MANITOU

∧ Campground	......	Trail
⌂ Lighthouse	---	Ferry
● Place of Interest	———	Road

N
W ✦ E
S

South Manitou Island

This is one of the bear cub islands.

If you stand on top of Sleeping Bear Dune on the mainland and look out across Lake Michigan's blue, you can see it in the distance—one of two dark, almost furry-looking islands.

These two, North and South Manitou islands, are the symbols of the bear cubs that drowned in the haunting legend of the Sleeping Bear.

But the island has its own story, which on one hand is as cheery as its beaches, but on the other is darker and more haunting than the sleeping bear legend.

A part of Sleeping Bear National Lakeshore, this dark green spot on the lake waters draws day-visiting sightseers and campers on most summer days to enjoy its elegant lighthouse, sunny beaches, historic farmhouses, and woodland trails.

South Manitou Island was not always home to cheerful vacations. Before the white man came, it was the site of a brutal Indian massacre. Later it served as a graveyard for a gruesome mass burial of a ship's passengers who were cholera victims, not all of them dead. Also, like some evil magnet, the island's shoals caused some 150 shipwrecks. Many crewmen and passengers died, but, on the profitable side, quite a few islanders found there was good money in a little midnight salvaging.

In the mid-1800s, South Manitou was a principal stop for steamships sailing between Chicago and the Mackinac Straits. As many as sixty ships might be seen anchored in the crescent-shaped bay. There they picked up food, and passengers knocked back a drink or two at the Center Board Saloon while island lumbermen loaded on freshly chopped cordwood to fuel the ships' engines.

The one hundred-foot-tall lighthouse, built in 1871 and regarded as

A late afternoon calm settles over the docks and the protected bay of South Manitou Island.

one of the most beautiful in the Great Lakes, is an elegant reminder of those days of iron men and wooden ships.

Many of the island's lumbermen, after clearing the trees, bought the land and stayed on to grow apples, cherries, and field crops. And later, in the twentieth century, one farmer raised Hereford cattle, and two others developed a unique strain of rye grain.

But today no one lives on the island, which has national park status. South Manitou, once home to many, is a destination for summer vacationers.

Visitors can board a ferry in Leland to picnic on the island, swim from its beaches, climb the lighthouse stairs, see 300-foot-high sand dunes, gaze out over a protected rookery for hundreds of ring-billed and herring seagulls, and see what could be the world's oldest and largest white cedar tree.

Each year during the warm months, about ten thousand visitors make the crossing to South Manitou Island. Slightly more than half come just for a day; the others bring tents and camp stoves to spend a night or two or maybe even a week on this island that has no greater dangers than stable flies and mosquitoes.

But it was not always that way.

Eerie Stories

Before the Europeans came to the Great Lakes, the local Indians almost never visited the Manitou Islands. Why would they? The crossing was dangerous. And the islands had no deer to hunt.

But according to one Indian legend, groups did come to South Manitou Island a couple of times. And at least once, the outcome was disastrous, according to Robert H. Ruchhoft, author of *Exploring North Manitou, South Manitou, High and Garden Islands in the Lake Michigan Archipelago*.

Apparently a war party from what is now Michigan's Upper Peninsula paddled down and raided a group of Indians living on the mainland not far from the Manitou Islands. The raiders killed all but seven, then crossed over to South Manitou Island to spend the night.

As you might guess, the seven survivors craved revenge. When darkness fell, the seven followed the war party over to the island, sneaked into their camp, and hacked most of them to death in their sleep.

As with the first attack, a few survived. They never saw the seven attackers in the darkness. So they blamed the deaths on evil spirts on the island. From then on, they avoided it.

Brutal times continued after the Europeans arrived in about 1835.

Shipping traffic grew. By the mid-1800s, hundreds of ships passed through the dangerous Manitou Straits. There, just east of the island, safe passage was only one mile wide.

Islanders recalled times when ships ran aground in the bitterly cold winter months. As the boats foundered in these frigid waters, sailors would climb the masts and hope for rescue.

If the winds were cruel and the seas high, which they inevitably were, rescuers would arrive too late. They sometimes were horrified to find the sailors' dead bodies frozen to the masts like so much gory abandoned laundry.

The most ghoulish of all South Manitou's sea tales involved a Chicago-bound ship loaded with Irish and German immigrants, according to Andrea Gutsche and Cindy Bisaillon, writing in *Mysterious Islands: Forgotten Tales of the Great Lakes.*

Cholera broke out on the ship. Passengers first suffered dysentery, then vomiting, cramps, and seizures. And then they died. To protect the crew from the sickness, the captain waited until the dead of night, then pulled the ship into South Manitou and hauled the victims ashore. Most of the afflicted were dead. But some were not, at least not quite dead.

The crew then dug a shallow grave and buried them all, the dead, and the still living. Local stories say that on foggy nights you can still hear the muffled moans and wails of those who lay helplessly as dirt was shoveled over their bodies.

Go to the Mainland? It's Not Worth It

By the 1880s, the island's economic heyday was over. Ships no longer stopped to pick up wood to fire their engines. They used coal instead. And even those ships were less numerous as railroad lines stretched across the country and up into Michigan.

But even if the wood-burners had continued to sail, South Manitou was out of business anyway. After years of lumbering, few trees were left. Many of the lumbermen wandered off to find other jobs in other places. Others, although not many, stayed to farm on the island.

Almost a century passed, and in 1970, South Manitou Island and its sister to the north became part of a newly designated national lakeshore—a national park with no permanent human residents.

It should be said that the islanders, who stayed on over the decades, loved South Manitou dearly. They endured much hardship and deprivation to keep their island homes.

Some would rarely leave.

The story is told of Bertha Peth, called Queen of the Island. She set the record for uninterrupted island residence—twenty-two years.

One time, she did go to the mainland, only to quickly return. It should be noted that Peth was regarded as somewhat "demented" following the death of one of her children. But still her faculties were clear enough to evaluate that trip to the mainland. Her comment: It wasn't really worth it.

Go to the Island? Well Worth It

Each year from late May to early October, visitors board ferries at the shore village of Leland for the trip to South Manitou Island.

Along with strolling the shores, taking a swim, and exploring the island, some visitors bring their kayaks to poke around the shore, and others don scuba gear to explore the broken ribs and battered boilers of sunken ships.

Places to See

One hundred feet tall, the graceful white lighthouse built in 1871 stands at the southern tip of Crescent Bay.

It was abandoned in 1958. The light no longer shines. But park rangers willingly lead people up the 117 steps to the top. It has a terrific view of the island, the Manitou Straits, and the Sleeping Bear Dunes.

For ships' captains plying the straits during the middle and late 1800s,

Construction of the first lighthouse on Manitou Island began in 1839 with a $5,000 congressional appropriation. The current lighthouse was built in 1871.

the lighthouse was literally a lifesaver. It guided them up the narrow straits on their north and south passages on the lake from Chicago to the Straits of Mackinac.

The lakes served as a sort of Interstate 80 of the time. They were the most important east-west route of the northern region. The numbers of passing ships are almost unimaginable today. In the 1870s, from 100 to 300 ships would pass through the straits *each day*. And many would stop at South Manitou to take on wood for fuel.

The lighthouse you see today is actually the island's third. The first was built in 1839. It was replaced in 1858 by the building just behind the lighthouse, which served as the keeper's house and had a small light tower on top. When the present lighthouse was built thirteen years later, a passageway was built to the keeper's home.

Yes, even though the island's population never grew larger than ninety-eight, South Manitou did have a school house. It was built in 1899 near the middle of the island. At one point, thirty children attended classes there. Today, you can't get in. The door is locked. But the South Manitou Memorial Society is slowly renovating the building and hopes to turn it into a small museum.

If nothing else, a visit to the old farms gives you a sense of how tough and isolated island life was in past years. Over the years, the National Park Service has done work to restore and maintain virtually all of the standing buildings.

The August Beck farm was built about 140 years ago. Take a close look at the barn. It's unique. Instead of using rocks or bricks for the walls, the builders packed mortar around big pieces of rot-resistant cedar logs.

A bit of scientific innovation is the main calling card for the 1860 Hutzler farm according to *Exploring North Manitou, South Manitou, High and Garden Islands of the Lake Michigan Archipelago*, by Robert H. Ruchhoft.

In the first half of the twentieth century, scientists at Michigan State University developed a new prize-winning variety of rye seed, called Rosen Rye, and a new pea-bean variety called Michelite.

These beans were grown and tested right on the island by the descendants of the original Hutzler family, George and his son Louis. The special strain of rye became world famous because it yielded five times as much grain as ordinary rye plants. By the mid-1940s, it was estimated that 80 percent of the pea-bean crops in the United States had descended from the Hutzlers' plants.

Why develop it on the island? Simply because South Manitou Island was a very laboratory-like setting, pure and impossible to taint with cross fertilization from other fields, which were eight miles away on the mainland.

You may wonder why the windows are boarded up on the Hutzler house. Ghosts, says Matt Wiberg, twenty-two, who led a recent island tour. He explained that island legend had it that hikers and other people had seen a ghost in one of the windows.

Sailing from Chicago in November of 1960, the captain of the Liberian freighter *Morazon* grossly miscalculated his position when he turned his ship east to pass north of North Fox Island and head on up toward the Straits of Mackinac.

He was actually about thirty-five miles south of that turning point. As a result, he ran the 246-foot freighter aground just off South Manitou Island. All thirteen crew members were saved.

The wreck remains there to this day, high out of the water, covered in rust, and streaked with bird droppings. Each year the wreck deteriorates a bit more. One day—but probably not any time soon—it will disappear entirely.

As with most old cemeteries, a visit to the South Manitou Island Cemetery gives a picture of the lives of the old and prominent families of the place. But it also speaks to a more modern tragedy, one connected to the *Morazon* wreck.

One cross marks the grave of sixteen-year-old Ronald Riker. In August of 1967, he drowned doing the kinds of things that teenagers do. He had swum out to explore the *Morazon* wreck and never made it back.

On the island's south shore, not far from the *Morazon* wreck, is a grove of old-growth white cedar trees, of which one appears to be a record setter.

One tree among the giants is thought to be the world's largest and oldest. It stands 80 feet tall, its trunk is 17.5 feet around and it's estimated to be 500 years old. One might guess that it was just lucky that nineteenth-century lumbermen somehow missed these trees.

The captain of the 246-foot freighter Francisco Morazon *made a miscalculation in November 1960, and the boat ran aground at the south end of South Manitou Island. The decaying hulk has been there ever since, a roosting place for seagulls.*

But George Michael Grosvenor, whose family has run the island ferry for almost ninety years, said the true reason was probably that as the trees grew up in the dunes area, a lot of sand got infused into the bark and wood. That sandy wood could quickly dull the cutters' saw blades. And since it took half a day to resharpen a blade, the lumbermen just gave it up as a bad idea.

So you might say that the dunes saved these trees.

Sandy Gull Point at the north end of Crescent Bay is a rookery for some 900 ring-billed gulls and 250 herring gulls. They are protected. You can see them, but hikers are told not to venture too close. Kayakers and other boaters are warned to stay well offshore.

Many people just love sand dunes. Sitting on top of them. Sliding down the sides. Basking in the sun. If you're a dune lover, the whole west side of the island is like a strip of the Sahara. Some dunes stand as high as 300 feet with a great view of the lake.

If You Go

Getting There: To get to South Manitou Island, you have to take the ferry from Leland, Michigan. To get to Leland, drive first to Traverse City, then take M-22 up the west side of Traverse Bay to the village of Suttons Bay. Just past the village center turn left on M-204, follow that road west until it ends at M-22, and then go north. Yes, that's right, you hit M-22 twice; it follows the shoreline of the Leelanau Peninsula.

The Manitou Island Transit ferry runs daily from Leland to South Manitou at 10 AM and returns in the afternoon, leaving at 4:30 PM. The ride lasts about one and a half hours. For the crossing, try to arrive by 9:15 AM. If severe weather crops up, this schedule is subject to change or cancellation. Reservations are advised. Call 231-256-9061 or go to: www.leelanau.com/manitou.

The ferry runs from May to October, with an abbreviated schedule in spring and fall. It runs daily from June 15 to mid-August.

The crossings can be chilly and bumpy. Keep a jacket or sweater handy, even on the warmest days. And if you are subject to motion sickness, bring your pills or patch.

Day Trips: Somewhat more than half the visitors go just for the day, spending about five hours on the island. This gives you time to visit the old lighthouse, go for a swim, take the island tour, and eat a picnic lunch. Bring your own lunch. The island has no concessions. All you can get is water. The island does have restrooms.

Tour: The one-and-a-half-hour tour fills you in on much of the history. You are taken around in old Ford trucks with beds that have been filled up with seats. You visit the island cemetery, the schoolhouse, farms, and an inland lake. Tours are run by the Manitou Island Transit Company. You sign up during the crossing to the island.

Camping: The island has no lodging. If you want to stay the night, or several nights, you must camp out. The island has three campgrounds. Bay Campground is a short walk from the dock. If you have a heavy pack or a kayak, this one might be good for you. Weather Station Campground, on the island's south side, is a longer walk from the dock, more isolated and set up on a bluff. Popple Campground, on the island's north side, is the longest hike of all. The sites are available on a first-come, first-served basis. Sign up at the park office at the ferry dock in Leland. The park has an entrance fee and a small, per-night camping fee. For details, call the park service at 231-326-5134; Web site: www.nps.gov/slbe.

Caution: Poison ivy. The island has lots of it. If you stick to the trails and roads, the three-leaf itchers are no problem. Once you're off the trail, be careful. Biting flies seem to be particularly brutal around the lighthouse. Bring insect repellent.

Information: Write to Sleeping Bear National Lakeshore, 9922 Front St., Highway M-72, Empire, MI 49630–0277. Call 231-326-5134 or go to www.nps.gov/slbe.

The gentle streams of Bridal Veil Falls plummet 65 feet near the tiny, lakeside village of Kagawong on Manitoulin Island. In Ojibwa, the name Kagawong means "where mists rise from falling waters."

The rocky shore of Isle Royale carries the memory of higher waters in Lake Superior. Isle Royale is the most isolated and least visited of all the national parks in the 48 contiguous states.

Canoeists just off Toronto Island have the joy of rural paddling but in the shadow of the CN Tower and downtown Toronto. In summer, children can take canoeing classes on the island.

As morning mists rise, a sailboat ghosts along under a soft breeze in Lake Superior's Apostle Islands. This pristine national lakeshore is a magnet for sailors and kayakers from all over the country.

With a fair wind, students in a sailing class on Toronto Island head out under a warm sun for a morning lesson.

Sailboats rest in the evening light at the Little Current Marina on Manitoulin Island. Nearby Georgian Bay offers yachters some of the world's best sailing.

Looking to catch the big one, this lad casts a line out into a boat channel at the Fishtown Harbor at Leland, Michigan. From here, the ferries carry passengers over to North and South Manitou islands.

Nancy Frantz, seated at the loom, teaches the fine art of weaving at the Sievers School of Fiber Arts on Washington Island.

Rolf Peterson, the internationally known wolf and moose expert, listens for the beep-beep of wolves with radio collars while standing atop a fire lookout tower on Isle Royale's Greenstone Ridge. Peterson's wolf research project on Isle Royale is the world's most important and longest running.

This lad has saddled up on a somewhat surprised looking ostrich on the 1905 carousel at Centreville Amusement Park on Toronto Island. The carousel has 51 other animals to ride, including horses, rabbits, a lion, a tiger, a giraffe, and even a pig.

It's hard to tell who is having more fun, the Siberian Huskies or the musher, who is John MacCafferty of McCafferty's Unfinished Farm on Beaver Island. Locals and visitors know the McCafferty farm best as the place to go horseback riding.

Not a footprint, not a boat in sight on this lonely dock on Beaver Island in winter.

The Stavkirke or Stave Church on Washington Island, still smelling inside of freshly cut pine, was built from a design that dates back to the eleventh century. Inside, look up at the roof and you can see that the church is built like an old Viking ship. The church's symbols are both Christian and Norse with crosses and stylized dragons sweeping off the roof.

The Icelandic horse is small and, in winter, as shaggy as a sheep dog, with the mild manners of a golden retriever. Riders especially love to saddle up on these horses which have four or five gaits. One of these gaits is the quick-stepping tolt, similar to that of a Tennessee walker. It's like riding a rocking chair across the fields. You can ride this one or one of a dozen more at Field Wood Farm on Washington Island.

Winds blow. The old wooden blades creak and turn. And water rises from the depths. This windmill stands outside a pioneer log cabin at the Washington Island Farm Museum, where summer flowers abound.

The Rock Harbor Lighthouse on Isle Royale is a welcome sight to visitors making the ferry crossing from Michigan's Keweenaw Peninsula. The oldest lighthouse on the island, it was built in 1855, served for 22 years, and now houses a small museum.

This snake fence, of split rails, meanders down a long slope toward the blue, blue waters of the Georgian Bay to the east of Manitoulin Island.

A cheerful June arrival on Isle Royale, these brilliant marsh marigolds can flower as easily under the swift waters of this stream as above it.

A quiet road on scenic Beaver Island where you often hear loons or spot whitetail deer crossing the roads.

The Legend of Sleeping Bear

Once, long, long ago, a mother black bear and her two playful cubs lived in the woods on the west side of Lake Michigan, in a place we now call Wisconsin.

One day a terrible fire broke out. Crackling, roaring, licking at the tall trees with its great yellow tongues, the blaze swept through the woods with frightening speed.

The mother bear knew the smell of smoke. She feared the yellow fire. And she feared for the lives of her two cubs. She knew that somehow, some way, they must escape. So she led the cubs to the shore of the big lake.

Other frightened animals were there, too: the wolverine, the mink, the white-tailed deer, the chipmunk, and the playful otters who were not feeling so playful.

"The fire is coming fast," the mother bear told her cubs. "We must swim to the other side of the lake. We'll be safe there."

The lake seemed very big to the little cubs. If there was another side, they could not see it. They were afraid.

But the mother bear growled. So they splashed into the cold, choppy waters and started to swim. They swam and swam. Still, they could not see the far shore. And so they swam some more.

The mother bear led the way. She often looked back to be sure that her cubs were following. But after many hours, darkness came. She could not see the cubs. She could only hope they still followed her.

Much later, the mother bear finally reached the far shore. She clambered up on the land. She turned and looked back across the broad blue waters. She could not see her cubs. She did not know, but in the black of night, the weary cubs had slipped beneath the surface.

The mother bear still held a hope her cubs would come. So she lay down on the shore to wait. Days passed, and then weeks. Eventually she slept.

And there she stayed, never having given up hope. More weeks passed, and then seasons came and went. The mother bear still waited. After some time, the blowing sands eventually covered the mother bear.

Thus was created the Sleeping Bear Dunes near Glen Arbor, Michigan, which to anyone with imagination look very much like a dozing bear.

Because the mother bear was so loyal, the Great Spirit Manitou created two islands in the lake, just where the cubs had drowned. And if you stand on the shoulder of the Sleeping Bear, you can see the islands in the distance. Floating on the water, they seem small and dark as little bear cubs.

We know these islands as North and South Manitou.

North Manitou Island

You've heard of attack dogs. Well, North Manitou Island has attack chipmunks.

Yes, they're cute. But also they are as toothy and aggressive as a Doberman when you happen to be holding his personal bone.

But that should come as no surprise. Wild, dangerous animals (even the likes of Chip 'n' Dale) should be expected in the backcountry. And the National Park Service considers North Manitou Island a backcountry area, part of the Sleeping Bear National Lakeshore.

As it turns out, the chipmunks are perhaps the fiercest of the island mammals. So visitors can relax and do those soul-soothing things that can only be done where civilization is held at bay. Walk woodland trails in solitude, set up camp wherever they want, cook and eat disgusting freeze-dried dinners, skip stones from the beach, and, if they're lucky, spot a ten-point buck. That's a special sight anywhere. But here on North Manitou, such a deer is a token of a remarkable period in the island's history.

It also should be noted that North Manitou, even with its backcountry status, still shows signs of the original islanders—though they are fading. By the dock stands one of the oldest existing lifesaving stations in the Great Lakes.

Nearby, in what is called Cottage Row, is a house that allegedly was designed by Frank Lloyd Wright and a 1930's wood-frame house that was built from a Sears kit. And on the island's western shore, a few remains linger from an old lumber town.

The island is perhaps best known for its role in the Indian legend of the sleeping bear. It is the symbol for one of the mother bear's lost cubs.

Indians certainly visited the island over the centuries. But man's biggest impact came around 1820, when the Europeans began to arrive. For the next 170 years, the island had at least some full-time residents. First came lumbermen and fishermen, followed by settlers, farmers, lifesaving teams, hunters, summer cottage people, and shopkeepers.

North Manitou is now part of the Sleeping Bear National Lakeshore. The Lakeshore was officially established in 1970, but the government did not finalize payment and possession until 1984. Over time, the last of the island residents and property owners moved off.

The Park Service now is determined to save some of the historic buildings but to tear others down or let them simply rot. So as years pass, man's traces are disappearing and the island is returning to the sort of wilderness the first settlers found in the early 1800s.

Now, even with its handful of buildings, North Manitou is probably the only place in Michigan below the Mackinac Straits that might qualify as true, public-owned backcountry of the kind that can be found on Isle Royale in Lake Superior.

For campers and hikers, the island is a slice of nirvana. They come to the island in the warmer months, taking the small, once-a-day ferry that putters over from the village of Leland.

Just a few hundred yards from the island dock, they can stroll down leafy woodland trails, revel in a quiet deep enough that you can hear the squirrels chortle, find an isolated glen to set up camp, loll on beaches of almost Caribbean whiteness or by a green inland lake, and perhaps even spot an endangered piping plover.

For those who like their primeval forests layered with a bit of human history, you can visit the old lifesaving station and wander among the remaining summer cottages not far from the dock.

Saving Lives

What probably is the oldest lifesaving station in the Great Lakes is here. It dates back to 1854. Buildings include the large keeper's house, a smaller house, and the boathouse. They are among the island's most historic structures.

Bill Herd, park historian for the Sleeping Bear Lakeshore, said the complex of lifesaving buildings is designated a National Historic Landmark, which is "the highest historic designation, just like Independence Hall."

Initially the lifesaving station was run like a volunteer fire department, said George Michael Grosvenor, whose family has run the ferry service from the mainland for almost ninety years.

An alarm would go up, he said, and local farmers, fishermen, and lumbermen would rush out to help a ship that had run aground. Estimates vary, but perhaps as many as one hundred ships ran afoul of the shoals or sank in the Manitou Passage that runs between the islands and the mainland.

The island's volunteer lifesaving station was organized and running seventeen years before the federal government established the U.S. Life-

Yep, hikers will actually have to pick up these backpacks and carry them. Camping is the only way you can stay overnight on North Manitou Island. The buildings beyond were part of the island's nineteenth-century lifesaving station and now are headquarters for the island's park rangers.

Saving Service in 1871. That service was incorporated into the U.S. Coast Guard when it was officially formed in 1915.

The oldest original building looks a bit like an old garage with double doors. But it is the old boathouse, which historians think dates back to 1854. It is the oldest remnant of a lifesaving station in the Great Lakes and is the park's oldest building on the national historic register.

What is now the park ranger headquarters was the commander's home, crew's dormitory, and headquarters for the Life-Saving Service operation. It was originally built in 1887. Just to the south is a small, one-story building that was probably a sort of rec room for the crew, a place where they could get out from underfoot of the commander's family and play cards and be to themselves.

Initially a crew of six or seven manned the Coast Guard Station. That number was cut to two in 1933 during the Great Depression, and the operation was finally shut down after World War II.

Storied Houses

One North Manitou house, called Monte Carlo, was most probably designed by Frank Lloyd Wright, said Rita Hadra Rusco, a longtime resident who wrote a book on the island called *North Manitou Island*. She was the last person to actually live on the island after the park service takeover.

Monte Carlo was built in 1895, she said. And it got that name because college boys who came for summer jobs used to play a lot cards there.

Just to the south of Monte Carlo is the Hollister house. According to Rusco, "It's a Sears kit house, built in the late 1930s. It cost $800." Yet a few steps farther south is the tree house, where people actually lived. To get in, they had to climb a ladder. That house is now collapsing. And next door is the Summer Hotel, built in 1895, which had eight rooms and a gazebo out front. "The woman owner was very short and stocky," Rusco said, "so the steps up to the porch were made very short for her."

On the island's west side, you can find some remnants of Crescent City, sort of an ambitious name for a woodcutters' hamlet with a population that never grew larger than 300.

But for a time, it boasted a sawmill, a bunkhouse, a general store, and even a standard-gauge railroad used to haul hardwood to the dock.

Gazing on these old buildings and hardscrabble farm fields, one can get a sense of the hang-by-your nails tenacity needed to survive on the island. In July or August, when most visitors come, it's easy to think of the island as a lush and balmy place. But February was, and is, a different matter. Harsh winds roar in from the west. Waves gnash at the shore. No boats could cross from the mainland. And for islanders, the isolation could be brutal and run-of-the-mill appendicitis could kill.

Summer Dream

But these days, visitors can come only in the summery months. And their delight is pure.

"It was the best," said Michelle Fehrenback, who recently went backpacking on the island with her seven-year-old son, Austin.

"We sat on the bluff and watched the sunset. We heard coyotes in the distance."

And then hiking back to the island dock, she said, "We looked up and there was a ten-point buck. He was beautiful."

Kara Nygren and Jason Haas, both Michigan State University students, glowed about their western shore campsite near the old Crescent City docks.

"We could hear the waves all night long," Nygren said.

"The sweet thing is just getting away for a little quiet time and being out on the island where the glow of city lights can't dim the stars," said Holly Wallace, of Northville, Michigan, who was camping with Aaron Dresner of Ann Arbor.

"We were just totally by ourselves," Wallace said. "I liked the first night. We watched the sunset and then we watched the stars. It was so clear I could see the Milky Way."

Wilderness Is as Wilderness Does

But life in the North Manitou backcountry is not all sunsets and starry nights.

One needs to be wary, even in the most benign settings—not of bears and wolves, which don't live on the island, but of much smaller things.

You look out over the sandy beaches, for example. They glare white enough in the afternoon sun to make you squint. A perfect place, you think. You toss down a blanket. Your plan is no more elaborate than to sit, stare at the waves for a while, and maybe take a nap. After all, you have the beach all to yourself. But you ask yourself "Why?" Why am I the only one on this gorgeous beach? And just as that thought strikes, so does something else.

Stable flies.

They storm at you buzzing, buzzing, fat as bumblebees, but not nearly so good-natured. They are the island's Luftwaffe. They target any bare piece of skin. Just behind the ear. An exposed wrist. An ankle.

Your defense is simple, but you dare not forget it. Slather yourself with DEET insect repellent. Swab it on even before you put on sunscreen, even before sitting down.

Happily, stable flies rarely show up in the wooded swamps. There, it's mosquitoes. They come in hordes as thick as morning mist.

"In the swamp we got into a swarm of mosquitoes," Fehrenback said. "There must have been a hundred of them on us. You just keep spraying that bug spray, and keep on spraying," she said. "But I think they liked it. They were getting high on it."

But if you don't linger in the swamps (rarely a temptation, anyway), and you use the bug goo with lots of DEET, you should be fine.

Wallace, the woman who loved the starry nights, admitted she did not like the mosquitoes, nor running into spider webs as she walked. And frankly, she's no longer a chipmunk lover.

She had a close encounter with the feared *Attack Chipmunk*.

The couple spent their last night on the island at the campsite near the dock.

What they could not know was that year after year, campers—thinking of themselves as kindly—have fed the cute little chipmunks. For the chipmunks, it was gourmet fare needing far less work than actually hunting for food. Pieces broken off from sandwiches. Chocolate chip cookies. Bits of gorp. Carrot sticks. Remnants of Power Bars. Unfortunately all this largesse created some bad chipmunk habits. They almost entirely lost their fear of man. They got greedy, and very, very demanding.

Three, four, or even half a dozen chipmunks might gather at a campsite, scolding campers in their chirping voices and darting in and out to steal any neglected morsel.

"At first I thought they were cute," Wallace said. "And then one jumped up and bit me on my shorts.

"Ouch."

She explained that, while eating, she had gotten some peanut butter on her hand and then wiped it off on her hiking shorts. "He went after it."

"At that moment," she said, "I went from being a chipmunk lover to a chipmunk hater."

Early Islanders

Historically, North Manitou can boast the oldest Indian artifact found on any of the islands in the Lake Michigan archipelago. It is a large copper awl dated to 3000 B.C. Archeologists have explored seven sites on the island, finding artifacts dating from 2000 and 1000 B.C.

Researchers found that Indians certainly visited the island, but how much time they spent there is not clear.

On the Watery Highway

The island's largely unsullied solitude ended when the Erie Canal was finished in 1825.

Lakes Erie, Huron, and Michigan became the watery highway west through the wilderness. Of course the lakes long had served as the road west, first for Indians in canoes, then for voyageurs and later settlers. But the lake traffic amounted to little more than an occasional canoe or boat.

With the opening of the canal and the advent of steamships, suddenly the lakes seemed to be gunwale-to-gunwale with watercraft.

In 1846, ships commissioned to sail on the Great Lakes included "67 steamships, 26 propellers, 340 schooners, 64 brigs and three barks," writes Rusco. And important stops along the way were Lake Michigan's North Manitou Island, along with South Manitou and Beaver islands.

These islands were basically the nineteenth century equivalent of today's freeway exits. But instead of fueling up at gas stations, the steamships loaded on freshly hewn wood to power their boilers. And in some places, like South Manitou Island and Beaver Island, entrepreneurs served passengers glasses of beer and whiskey, home-cooked meals, and room to sleep for the night. All for a price, of course.

Unfortunately, North Manitou Island—unlike its sister island, South Manitou—did not have a good deepwater harbor on the east side, away

The ferry Mishe Mokwa *waits patiently in a boat channel at Fishtown in Leland, Michigan, to carry passengers to the Manitou Islands.*

from the prevailing west winds. So while on the South Island entrepreneurs opened a restaurant and hotel and offered amenities, the north island served simply as a refueling stop.

Farmers and Fishermen

Soon Europeans came to settle on both islands.

Certainly they were not seeking a Robinson Crusoe sort of isolation. They came to make a living. They would have well understood the advice of today's real estate people about "location, location, location." The island was good not because it was far away from things, but because it was right on the major east-west throughway—a place where they could sell lumber, fish, apples, and whatever else they could produce.

Farmers and fishermen prospered on the island. They had their predictable income. But occasionally islanders managed to grab onto some windfall profits.

There's a story—that may or may not be true—about Vessel Point, a lump on the island's northeast shoulder. Many ships were wrecked near there while trying to navigate the narrow and dangerous Manitou Straits.

In *North Manitou Island* Rusco writes ever so diplomatically:

"There are stories of lighted lanterns set out to lure vessels ashore. It's hard to imagine any islander would engage in such a deed, but it is known that salvaged material and goods were always welcome on the island."

Historian Herd questions that midnight supply story, noting that South Manitou Island had a lighthouse by 1836, so "It is unlikely that ships were lured to their doom by false lights on North Manitou shoals or on the mainland."

Once, No One Knew the Word Ecology

Through the 1800s and much of the 1900s, many people believed that nature was there to serve man, to be tamed.

Lumbermen were the first wilderness tamers. In the nineteenth century they sheared the island's trees like so many Danish sheep. Their wood fueled the steamships. Towering white pines were reduced to fields of stumps.

After a time, most of the timber was cut. But by then, little profit was left to be made. The era of the steamships had passed. They were replaced by ships with oil- and coal-burning engines. Then boat travel just went out of style entirely after paved highways allowed automobiles to quickly go almost anywhere.

But axemen were not entirely finished with island trees. They continued to cull hardwoods up to the 1970s. Perhaps a million board feet a year were shipped to Leland sawmills, and much was sent on to Grand Rapids to be fashioned into chairs, desks, and bed frames.

Rich Man's Deer Camp

It was in the 1920s that North Manitou began to trade in its rough-hewn character for something with a bit more sheen.

The island caught the eyes of some big-dollar executives from Detroit and Chicago. They began to buy it up, until they owned almost the entire island.

They did maintain the farms and cherry and apple orchards. But most of all, they wanted the island as a private hunting and fishing preserve, open just to them and their friends.

The island's new patron was a Detroiter, William R. Angell, former president of Continental Motors, an engine maker. Under his direction, nine white-tailed deer were shipped to the island. While the island probably once had had some native deer that likely crossed from the mainland on winter ice, these whitetails had long since been hunted to extinction by the early pioneers.

But once the immigrant deer showed up, they loved the island and multiplied like crazy. No wonder. Food was plentiful. And the deer had no natural enemies like bears or wolves. Twelve-point bucks were soon as common as stable flies. Not many years passed before the original nine imports—five does and four bucks—numbered 1,500.

For hunters, they were easy pickings.

So each fall for decades, big city swells flew in to bag a stag or two with their high-powered rifles. Even the famous came to North Manitou Island. In 1951, Arthur Godfrey, one of the biggest TV celebrities of the time, flew in to fire off a few shots. As the story goes, locals shone their car lights on the island landing strip so Godfrey's plane could land at night.

These were upscale hunts. The city slickers suffered few more rigors than if they had stayed behind their mahogany desks. And they had more guarantees of killing a deer than of making a killing in the stock market. They spent their island nights in lodges or cabins, not in tents. Local guides took them to some spot in the woods and then went off to drive the deer past their waiting guns. For many, North Manitou provided less a hunting experience than a shooting gallery.

George Michael Grosvenor's father was a hunting guide on the island during those days. He said the fat cats often would just sit around, play cards, drink, and pay the guide to go shoot a buck for them, which they undoubtedly claimed as their own kill during bragging sessions over cocktails in Chicago.

But despite the seasonal blaze of high-priced firearms, the deer herd grew too big for the island. The natural vegetation could not support them. The deer ended up eating every flower, low shrub, and poplar branch in sight. But since a small herd might mean more rigorous hunting, Angell's staff maintained the high deer numbers by feeding them loads of hay, oats, and apples grown on the island.

And each year Angell arranged to have deer feed flown in. Fifty tons of it. Without the Angell handouts, the deer would have starved to death by the hundreds. Grosvenor remembers that as a boy he would earn money by lugging fifty-pound sacks of Kellogg's deer feed off the ferry to the island. "I remember it was in little pellets and tasted like Grape Nuts cereal, but with a little bit more fiber than that."

While this artificial feeding does not fit in with modern concepts of wilderness management, it turned out to be a boon for today's hikers and backpackers—at least temporarily.

North Manitou had a very different look from South Manitou, its sister island. The north island, where deer had cleared all the underbrush, had a fine open feel, very unlike the tangled woods of the south island. Hikers loved North Manitou because they could easily wander off a trail and never get lost. And further, they could pitch a tent almost anywhere.

All this has been changing since the U.S. Park Service took over in 1970. During the next fourteen years, the Park Service and the Angells' Manitou Island Association haggled over the exact price for the island, Grosvenor recalled.

During that time, neither the Park Service nor the association fed the deer. Each winter the deer died by the hundreds. Their carcasses just lay and rotted. Scavenging birds could not keep up with the feast.

The Park Service now has a policy of not feeding the deer, and the island is home to perhaps 150 deer, a tenth of its onetime high. Hunters still come to the island in fall, but, Grosvenor said, they may hunt for five days and never spot a deer.

Another change is that the flowers, hardwood trees, and underbrush are starting to grow back.

Hikers today might complain about knees scratched by branches and brambles. But then again, if they want true wilderness that is what North Manitou is becoming—with scratching bushes and, of course, the feared attack chipmunks.

If You Go

Getting There: Getting to North Manitou Island means you first must get to Leland, Michigan, where you pick up the ferry. Leland is on highway M-22, on the west side of the Leelanau Peninsula, about forty-five minutes from Traverse City.

The ferry is run by the Manitou Island Transit Company. It has daily service to the island from July 1 to mid-August. In June schedules run from three times a week in the early part of the month to five times a week in the later part. From mid-August to September 15, it typically runs three days a week. In the fall, the ferry makes crossings on Fridays and Sundays for bow hunters and campers. Parking is $1 a day. Reservations are recommended. Boats often fill up in summer, especially for weekends. Call 231-256-9061; Web site: www.leelanau.com/manitou.

The boat leaves Leland at 10 AM. Check in at the ticket office on the Leland dock before 9:15 AM. The ferry arrives at North Manitou at about 11:10 AM and leaves as soon as the passengers go ashore and the returning people get on board.

Be prepared for the crossing. Even though it may be a warm day at Leland, the trip across to the island can get chilly. Have a jacket handy. Also remember that the crossing can be bumpy. If you are subject to motion sickness, take your pills, use your patch, or wear the bracelet. The ferry makes one visit to North Manitou each day. So, if you want to actually see the island, you must spend the night.

National Park Passes: To go to North Manitou, you must get a park pass that allows you to stay seven days for a small fee. If you have a national park pass or a Golden Eagle Pass, you can use that. Also, Sleeping Bear Dunes National Lakeshore offers a modestly priced one-year pass.

You also must pay a campsite fee for each night that you stay on the island. Except for a few restrictions, you can camp anywhere on the island. For example, you can camp no closer than 300 feet to any water. That includes Lake Michigan's high-water marks, island lakes, streams, and ponds. An organized campground with eight campsites is located just north of the docks. You can pick up the passes and pay the fees at the Manitou Island Transit Co. office at the Leland dock.

For further information on Sleeping Bear Dunes National Lakeshore, call: 231-326-5134 or go to the website: www.nps.gov/slbe/.

Lodging: On North Manitou Island: Bring your own, a tent. In Leland: Because you must catch the morning ferry to the island, you may want to spend the night before in or near Leland. For information on lodging and campsites, contact the Leelanau Chamber of Commerce at 231-271-9895; Web sites: www.leelanau.com and www.leelanauchamber.com.

Dining: The island has no restaurants, no candy machines, no snack bars. You must bring your own food, typically something you are willing to carry in a backpack for a few miles. Drinkable water is available near the ranger station. Elsewhere you have to filter your water. No fires are allowed, so cooking requires a small propane or gas camp stove. All scraps and leftovers must be packed out. In Leland: My favorite and, I think, one of the better restaurants in Northern Michigan is the Riverside Inn. Dinners are superb. The wine list is long. And you will love eating dinner outdoors on the deck by the water. The Bluebird, a locals' favorite, serves great whitefish, burgers, and other north country favorites. For breakfast, hit the Early Bird Restaurant.

Shopping: Leland has loads of cute little shops. Be sure to stop at Leelanau Books for reading on North Manitou and the other islands and sites in the area. Hit Stone House Bread, just a few blocks south of the main intersection, for freshly baked yummies. And take a few minutes to stroll around Main Street Gallery, the one with all the sculptured animals out front. It's a nice dose of art that's also entertaining.

Ferry Crossings by George

It was a rough ferry crossing to North Manitou Island.

Lake Michigan's wind was a hacksaw. The waves, packed as tight as British colonial regiments, came in hard, angry-green, and flecked with foam.

The fifty-two-foot ferry felt every thump. Passengers were being rattled and bounced like chipped ice in a bartender's blender. They could not stand without staggering. So they sat and tried to find something to hang on to.

"It's real snotty," said Captain George Michael Grosvenor. He kept both hands on the wheel, stared fixedly through the wave-splashed windshield, and didn't smile.

Snotty, maybe. But not particularly dangerous if the pilot is named George Grosvenor. Men of the Grosvenor (pronounced in the English way, GROVE- ner) family—every one of them named George—have been safely carrying passengers between the mainland and the Manitou Islands for almost ninety years.

In his mid-thirties, Michael, as he is called, is the fourth generation of Grosvenor ferry captains.

The first was Michael's great-grandfather, George Tracy. Then came his son, George Firestone (the only one actually called George), now in his eighties, followed by George Michael, in his fifties, who is called Mike and is Michael's dad.

The family jokes that Michael's son, a preschooler, might carry on the family tradition of captaining a ferry boat. His name is George Tracy, after his great-great-grandfather.

Why are they all named George? Just a family tradition say the Grosvenors; then they smile and shrug.

These days, Michael Jr. usually pilots the smaller *Manitou Isle*. His dad captains the sixty-five-foot *Mishe-Mokwa*, "Mother Bear" in Ojibwa.

Through the generations, the Grosvenors have seen it all—icy weather that froze the captain to the wheel, winter mail deliveries, and the stormy sea conditions peculiar to the Great Lakes.

As Mike Sr. tells it, the Grosvenors got into the Manitou Island ferry business as much by accident as on purpose.

Tracy Grosvenor, who lived on North Manitou Island, started back in 1917 with a small boat carrying mail, groceries, supplies, and people back and forth to Leland.

Just to the south another man, Paul Humphrey, held the contract for delivering mail between South Manitou Island and the shore town of South Haven, using an almost new boat.

But one day misfortune blindsided Humphrey. As he usually did, Humphrey motored over to Glen Haven to drop off the mail. He tied up his boat, and, instead of heading back, he went on to visit the nearby town of Empire. While he was gone, a storm came up. By the time Humphrey got back to the dock, his boat had disappeared.

"All that was left was a hawser," a heavy rope used to tie the boat to the dock, Mike Sr. said. "The boat was just gone. No one ever saw it again."

With no boat, Humphrey lost his mail contract. So Tracy Grosvenor, who was in partnership with his cousin, John Paetschow, picked it up and moved the South Manitou mail service operation to Leland.

The early days of sailing were rough, Mike Sr. said. Tracy had to go back and forth in an open-cockpit boat. According to one family story, on rough winter days he'd get soaked with the spray. When he got back to the dock, someone would have to chip his ice-coated body loose from the wheel. Maybe this story is true. Maybe it isn't. The Grosvenors tell it with a smile and a shrug. But no matter; certain of Tracy's adventures need no embellishment.

As a young man Tracy fell for a girl who lived in between Lake Leelanau and Suttons Bay on the Leelanau Peninsula, about seven miles from Leland. That was a big geographic problem, since he lived on North Manitou Island.

But true love was not so easily stopped. Come winter when the boats could not run, Tracy still managed to court her despite the bitter cold. First he would walk the twelve miles over the lake ice from his village on North Manitou to Leland, and then he walked another seven miles to her house. That girl became Mike Sr.'s grandmother.

Adventures did not stop with the first generation. Mike Sr. tells of one time that he walked out from the mainland onto the lake ice with his father, so they could do a mail exchange with the islands.

"I was probably twelve or thirteen years old," he said. "We had to walk about five or six miles out. All the way my dad complained because I was listening to my transistor radio.

They are all named George Grosvenor and all but the littlest one has been or is captain of the ferry that connects Leland, Michigan, with North and South Manitou islands. Left to right, George Michael Grosvenor (called Michael), his grandfather, George Firestone Grosvenor (called George), and his father George Michael Grosvenor (called Mike). In front on the rail is the recently minted captain-to-be little George Tracy. He was named after his great-great-grandfather who started the Manitou Island Transit Company in 1917.

"But on the way home, a storm came up. We couldn't see anything. So I used the transistor radio to home in on the broadcast tower on Sleeping Bear Dune.

"That's how we got back."

Mike Sr. was smiling by this point in his story. "He never complained about that radio again."

As for sailing into danger, the Grosvenors just never do it.

"I don't like to be adventurous," Michael Jr. said. "I'd like it to be calm every day."

The Grosvenors carefully examine weather conditions every day. If the winds are too strong or from the wrong direction, their ferries do not run.

Like many sailors on the Great Lakes, the Grosvenors talk about the Three Sisters. These are lake waves that come in groups of three, unlike ocean waves, which seem to travel in groups of seven.

"Frankly, I'd rather sail in the ocean," Michael Jr. said.

"I've sat and fished in twelve-foot seas in the ocean. A twelve-foot sea on Lake Michigan will kill you," he said. "Waves in the ocean come every ten or twelve seconds. Here they come in half that time."

Inevitably, today as yesterday, the Grosvenors face challenges of storms and high water. But in the rough times, Mike Sr. said he often thinks of his grandfather Tracy enduring the weather in an open boat.

"When you start to complain," he said, "you have to remember."

Washington Island

Although the world hardly noticed, people were fleeing Iceland.

It was somewhat like the Irish escaping the potato famine. In the 1870s, living was hard in Iceland. The island was volcanic, with only a precious few acres to farm. And because it is so far north, what little did grow was stunted—and still is today.

Jeannie Hutchins, a Washington Islander, tells a joke: "If you get lost in an Icelandic forest, just stand up."

So, following to a degree in the tradition of Eric the Red, who left Iceland to start up life in Greenland, the Icelanders began a diaspora. And one of the rare places that actually noticed their flight was Washington Island in Wisconsin.

Today, part of the island's fame is that it is home to America's oldest Icelandic community. You can see Icelandic names right there in the phone book. But it must be said that Washington Island has little to show that actually smacks of Icelandic culture, with a couple of exceptions including some Icelandic riding horses and an Icelandic pancake breakfast.

But no matter, this island of 600 people just off the north end of Wisconsin's Door Peninsula, is a fine and laid-back place. Once you're off the ferry in Detroit harbor, it's hard not to enjoy the unique beaches, the hundred miles of quiet country roads for bicycling, good sport fishing, several unique museums, an ostrich farm, good restaurants, and a fish that's a watery lawyer joke. Also, the island has a storied history that dates back to the Indian legend of Death's Door, the often dicey six-mile passage between the island and the peninsula.

Over the years, Washington Island—and adjacent Rock Island—have attracted the famous and managed a little infamy of their own. The renowned French explorer Robert La Salle stopped by. The social critic Thorstein Veblen, inventor of the term "conspicuous consumption," did much

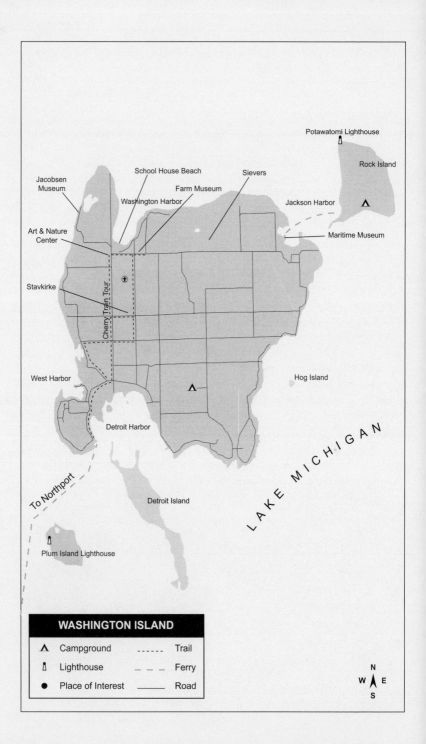

Potawatomi Lighthouse

Rock Island

Jacobsen
Museum

School House Beach

Sievers

Farm Museum

Washington Harbor

Jackson Harbor

Art & Nature
Center

Maritime Museum

Stavkirke

Cherry Train Tour

West Harbor

Hog Island

Detroit Harbor

To Northport

Detroit Island

LAKE MICHIGAN

Plum Island Lighthouse

WASHINGTON ISLAND

⋀	Campground	------	Trail
⌂	Lighthouse	– – –	Ferry
●	Place of Interest	———	Road

N
W   E
S

of his writing on the island. And Chester Thordarson—a brilliant inventor of Thomas Edison's caliber—sank part of his considerable fortune into Rock Island and a monumental stone boat garage–cum–Viking Valhalla.

Angostura Fame

Let's not forget Nelsen's Hall, a saloon on Main Road. To this day, tourists with a thirst to play a bit part in history flock to its bar stools. Built in 1899 by Tom Nelsen, the Hall is the oldest legal, continuously operated bar in Wisconsin, and one of the oldest in America. The key word here is *continuously*. That means it stayed open right through Prohibition.

Nelsen pulled off this trick by getting a pharmacist's license and then serving his customers Angostura bitters as a stomach remedy. Officialdom considered bitters medicinal. And that was fine with customers, who thought the 90-proof stuff to be "good for what ails you." So Nelsen's doors swung wide throughout the nation's dry spell. And neither Elliott Ness nor any of his ilk could touch the saloon keeper–pharmacist.

The story goes that Nelsen himself used to drink half a pint of bitters a day, and he lived to be ninety. Today, the tradition continues. People come and order a shot of bitters, drink it down—"Bleech"—and are then are eligible to join the Nelsen's Hall Bitters Club. Just sign your name, and you get an official, wallet-sized club certificate. It's a big moneymaker. Nelsen's issues about ten thousand certificates a year. And the little saloon on faraway Washington Island is in the Guiness Book of World Records as the largest single purveyor of Angostura bitters.

My suggestion: follow it with a chaser of light beer or something else to kill the taste.

Death's Door

The Indian legend, and there are several versions of it, tells of the peaceful Potawatomi Indians.

They lived on what now is known as the Door Peninsula. Things went fine until the nasty Winnebagos showed up. The Potawatomi people offered to share the land, but the Winnebagos said no. They wanted it all and proceeded to attack the Potawatomis, who were too few to really resist. Eventually, the Potawatomis were forced to retreat to the islands to the north—Washington and Rock.

But even with the waters for protection, the Winnebagos still were a threat. Figuring that perhaps the best defense was a good offense, the Potawatomis decided to make a nighttime sneak attack across the waters.

They sent three spies ahead. Their job was to light fires that would show the Potawatomis where to land their canoes.

Unfortunately for the Potawatomis, the spies got caught and tortured, eventually giving away the planned night attack. So the Winnebagos fashioned a counteroffensive. On the night set for the Potawatomi attack, the Winnebagos cleverly lighted a fire by a rocky bluff where the lightweight bark canoes would be battered to pieces. At the same time, the Winnebagos sent their own warriors out in canoes to circle around and attack the Potawatomi camp on the island.

With all this planning going on, neither side took full account of one factor—the weather. The night was dark. Heavy winds tortured the water of the passage. But, as expected, the Potawatomis crossed the passage and sped toward the false signal lights. It was a disaster. Their canoes were dashed. Many warriors drowned, and others who actually made it ashore were tomahawked to death by the waiting Winnebagos.

But the night went equally badly for the Winnebagos. The storm caught their canoes in open water. Their boats swamped, and the struggling warriors drowned in the violent waters. A day later, their crushed canoes and dead bodies started to wash up on shore.

This was an omen. The tribes would never again try to cross at Death's Door. French explorers later translated the Indian name for the passage as *porte des morts*. And the name stuck.

As years passed, the water gap that connected Lake Michigan with Green Bay proved again and again that its reputation was deserved.

The lighthouse keeper's diary on Plum Island, in the passage, said that ships would wreck at an average rate of two a week for the years between 1872 and 1889. During one week in 1872, nearly a hundred ships were lost or seriously damaged in the passage. Then on a single day, October 15, 1880, thirty vessels were run aground in one of Lake Michigan's worst storms.

Today, boat travel across the passage is simple and safe. The ferries, which run every half hour during the summer, have never lost a tourist's car.

La Salle and the *Griffon*

Robert La Salle, the famed French explorer, built the *Griffon* (sometimes spelled Griffin) near Niagara Falls in 1679. It was the first commercial sailing ship to go out onto Lakes Erie, Huron, and Michigan. La Salle and his crew sailed it west basically as an efficient way to transport furs.

After a stop at Mackinac Island, the *Griffon* went on to Green Bay, making a stop at Washington Island's Detroit Harbor. The crew loaded piles of furs on board, and on September 18, 1679, La Salle sent the ship and a crew of thirty back without him. The furs were to be a payoff for some of his creditors.

The *Griffon* was never seen again.

However, many stories have cropped up about the ship's fate. On Lake Huron's Manitoulin Island, some think the *Griffon* crashed on the western shore. Others believe it went down in Death's Door. In the summer of 2004, a Great Lakes treasure hunter named Steven Libert, of Virginia, said he had found the wreck three and a half miles west of Poverty Island, which is north of Washington Island. Other scholars are skeptical. Finally, some people believe the *Griffon* has become a ghost ship that still sails the waters of Lake Michigan, trying to return home.

Fishing and "Lawyers"

For more than a century and a half, Washington Island life has centered on commercial fishing—whitefish, pickerel, lake trout, perch, chubs. But burbot, a sort of freshwater cod, is not only the locals' favorite dish, but their favorite joke.

They call them lawyers. A sign in front of the K.K. Fiske Restaurant reads: "Fresh Lawyers." Why lawyers? It seems the fish's heart is located right by its anal cavity.

Fishermen were the first Europeans to settle in the islands in the 1830s. In 1850, the township of Washington was established on Rock Island at a village on the east side. The township included Rock, Washington, and Detroit islands. Soon after, however, a log schoolhouse was built at the south end of Washington Island. That marked the beginning of the end of Rock Island's prominence. The larger Washington Island's population continued to grow as the Rock Island village was abandoned house by house.

Washington Island commercial fishermen return from a good day on the water in 1923. Courtesy of the Washington Island Historical Archives.

Over time, fishing changed, says Jake Ellefson, son of a Washington Island fisherman who, now in his seventies, is one of the last of the breed. The island now has only two commercial fishing boats. In some of the better years from 1910 to 1940, as many as three dozen fishing boats sailed from Washington Island.

Fishing has always been hard. The early fishermen on the island went out in small open boats. Ellefson explains that they had to make their own cotton nets, which had a thousand meshes every ten feet. And once soaked and loaded with fish, they were extremely heavy to haul by hand.

Things got a little better when steam-powered boats showed up in the 1870s, Ellefson says. These boats were huge in order to accommodate the big wood-burning engines. Some were seventy feet long. Then, about 1906, semi-diesel engines showed up, and with them mechanical net lifters. This was a major advance. The gas-powered engines came next. They cut the size of the boats by two-thirds compared with the steamboats and allowed the fishermen to go farther out and fish as deep as 500 or 600 feet.

Over time, stocks of fish went up and down. Fish prices went up and down. Politics played a role, and so did alien creatures that sneaked in from the Atlantic Ocean. Lamprey eels virtually wiped out the lake trout. In the 1930s, the lake trout catch was three to five million pounds, Ellefson recalls. By 1947, it had dropped to one thousand pounds. After the lampreys' numbers were cut, efforts were made to restock lake trout from Lake Superior, but they never were able to reproduce.

"It's been sixty years since there was a decent lake trout catch," Ellefson says. The island's two commercial fishing boats are docked at the northeast corner of the island at Jackson Harbor.

Black Islanders

Uniquely, it appears, among Great Lakes islands, Washington actually had a small black community in the 1850s, not long before the Civil War. Some believe that it might even have been the state's largest black community at the time.

In 1854, local chroniclers noted that perhaps nine black families were living on the west side of Detroit Harbor. They made their living by building boats and fishing. The speculation was that they were runaway slaves.

Writings of the day referred to the leader only as Negro Bennett. He apparently was a rousing preacher who often attracted large crowds of white people. It was said that Bennett had been the "coloured cabin boy" to Oliver Hazard Perry during the Battle of Lake Erie in the War of 1812.

The black community, which arrived with little notice, then left the same way—apparently after a local sheriff started nosing around.

Icelanders: Pancakes and Ponies

Jeannie Hutchins calls William Wickman "the island's first PR man."

He was a Dane who initially worked in a mercantile house in Eyrarbakki, Iceland, where he learned to speak Icelandic. In his late twenties, he headed to America and eventually to Washington Island. His letters back to the office would have made any real estate agent proud. Lake Michigan's waters were "a gold mine for fishermen," he wrote. "Land can be had for homesteading and you can let your hogs run wild and catch them in the fall, fat." It was out-and-out exaggeration. But four young bachelors from Iceland bought it and showed up in 1870. They were the first Icelanders to actually settle on the island.

Initially life was hard. None spoke English; their skills were few. Locals had to teach them how to work with lumber, which, along with fishing, was the long-term source of island jobs. Fishing jobs initially were out. While Icelanders do fish in the ocean, they knew little of lake fishing. And more important, they could not afford the substantial expense of getting a boat, nets, and other equipment. But they survived.

In the early years, the four stayed in a huge barn of a building with no insulation that eventually was dubbed "The Castle." It was torn down many years ago.

Over the years more Icelanders came, but not a lot more despite newspaper speculation at the time that thousands of Icelanders were headed to the island. By the turn of the century, the total number of adult male immigrant Icelanders was about twenty. Women and children might have raised the total to a hundred.

Today Washington Island, while it still touts its Icelandic heritage, shows little evidence of Icelandic culture beyond some names in the tiny local phone book. No one speaks Icelandic, which is essentially eighth-century Norse. No restaurant specializes in *thorramatur,* the traditional Icelandic cuisine that includes singed sheep's head. Perhaps that's just as well.

However, the Sunset Resort does serve Icelandic pancakes at its charming bay-view restaurant. The pancakes are as thin as crepes, rolled and topped with powdered sugar. And they are addictively delicious.

The other bit of Iceland on the Washington Island is the collection of small, long-haired Icelandic horses at Field Wood Farm. Visitors can take them out for trail rides.

Laurie Veness, the ebullient owner who claims Irish (not Icelandic) heritage, adores these unique horses, which have been bred for a thousand years for intelligence, sweet disposition, and an extremely smooth ride.

They have four and often five gaits, which include the silky, four-beat *tolt,* Veness explains. Riders compare the *tolt* to the gaits of a Tennessee walker or *paso fino*. It is an armchair ride compared to the thumpity-thump saddle bounce on a trotting horse.

In winter, the Icelandics' hairy coats can grow from four to six inches long. Veness, who brought the horses to the island in 1965, says that in the spring the horses groom each other, scraping at loose hair with their teeth. It comes off in cigar-shaped rolls which they understandably spit out on the ground. This may be the only unattractive quality of these sweet horses.

Veblen's Cabin and Quill

Thorstein Veblen. Perhaps you remember the name from a college course in economics. He was the brilliant and wildly eccentric social and economic critic who wrote *The Theory of the Leisure Class*. He also coined the term "conspicuous consumption."

This brilliant thinker—who was never really accepted in his lifetime—first came to the island because he wanted to learn to speak Icelandic. So he moved in with a local Icelandic family, and before long he was speaking the language. He came to love the island, and in 1915 he bought some land in the northwest corner, between the shore of Green Bay and Little Lake. First he put up a tent, and later he built a one-room cabin. Before long, the ferry was hauling trunkloads of his books from the mainland.

Locals say Veblen, unlike most visitors, did not come to the island to relax; he came to work and to think. He wrote using a quill pen which he carved himself. His wife typed the manuscripts for his several books. Inevi-

Thorstein Veblen, the famous and famously eccentric social economist who coined the term "conspicuous consumption," had a small cabin in the northeast corner of Washington Island. The author of The Theory of the Leisure Class *used the cabin as a getaway to think and write. Courtesy of the Washington Island Historical Archives.*

Proud island farmers about 1915 or '16 stand with their threshing machine. Washington islanders farmed on the island for many decades, particularly on the eastern side. Most notably they raised potatoes and had a prosperous dairy for many years. Most of those farms are now gone. Courtesy of Washington Island Historical Archives.

tably, living on this island with Viking descendants did, at least to a degree, shape some of his thinking. At one point, he wrote that the early Viking practice of seeking national gain "by force and fraud at the cost of the party of the second part" resembled the national policies pursued by statesmen of the present time.

Sweet Cream, Taters, and Tourists

In meandering about the island, many people notice that land on much of the eastern part is wide open or consists of slightly overgrown fields. That was farmland during the first eighty years or so of the twentieth century.

Starting in about 1910, much of the island was devoted to dairy herds. Cheesemaker Andy Justinger opened a creamery in 1925 and turned out milk, cream, butter, and wonderful cheddar and Colby cheeses. The creamery lasted about fifty years and then shut down after the state demanded expensive new milking and sterilization equipment.

About that time, in the late 1950s, the farmers turned to potatoes. And they did wonderfully well. Washington Island quickly became Wisconsin's biggest producer of russets until about 1964.

"Potatoes employed a lot of people," says islander Howard "Butch" Young, who was the island's volunteer fire chief for many years. What's more, Jeannie Hutchins recalls, "everybody had a cellar full of potatoes for the winter—and they were free."

Edward Anderson, the island's potato king, even bought two used ferries to carry the potatoes to market. The boats, which had gone back and forth across the Mackinac Straits between Michigan's Upper and Lower peninsulas, were the *City of Munising* and the *City of Cheboygan*.

But then the market price for potatoes dropped. By 1971 the potato bonanza was over.

Since then, the island's major sources of income—like most of the other populated islands in the Great Lakes—have come from tourism and construction, mostly of summer cottages.

Places to See

Wherever you wander on Washington Island, you'll find something interesting to stop and take a look at.

At Detroit Harbor, you can sit and watch the ferries putter in and out or get on board the Cherry Train for a ninety-minute island tour.

Take the Main Road north past the Trueblood Performing Arts Center and then to the Deer Run Golf Course, a tough set of nine holes. Grab a left and head west on West Harbor Road. On the right you'll see the Double K-W Ostrich Farm, which—in addition to some nasty-tempered ostriches—has llamas, a potbellied pig, a camel, and other exotics. Go a little farther to Field Wood Farm and a smooth ride on a small Icelandic horse.

Continue north on Main Road, and you pass the town center with a couple of bookstores, a grocery and hardware store, and four saloons. One is the famed Nelsen's Hall, where you can slug down a shot of bitters and join the club. Another is K.K Fiske, which has "fresh lawyers."

Grab a right on Town Line Road and stop at the parking lot across from Trinity Lutheran Church. Take the trail through the woods, and keep to your left. Don't rush. Let the trees bring you a sense of calm. Soon you will arrive at the remarkable Stavkirke, or Stave Church. The church, which smells of sweet pine inside, is a remarkable blend of Viking ship construction and symbols that come from both Christian and Norse traditions. These include stylized dragons that swoop from the roof. The first stave churches were built in Nor-

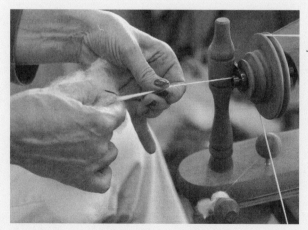

The hands can create a heart's desire on an old-fashioned spinning wheel at the Sievers School of Fiber Arts on Washington Island. The school attracts students from across the country to work on looms and spinning wheels, and even to build rocking chairs.

way at the end of the eleventh century, when Christianity was first being introduced. Thus the stave church represents a blend of old and new religions.

Continue north on Main Road to find the Art & Nature Center, which offers some generally good paintings and photos by local artists and the chance, if you'd like, to pet a snake. Go on farther, take a left on Little Lake Road, and continue to the Jens Jacobsen Museum, which is a small but fascinating collection of everything from ancient arrowheads to historic photos and bits of local history. Note the construction of the nearby Jacobsen log cabin. The logs are not laid horizontally as in a Lincoln cabin but vertically, with the bark still on. This was so the wood would better shed the rain. Thorstein Veblen's cabin was not far away.

Back at the Art & Nature Center, head east along Jackson Harbor Road. A left at the cemetery takes you to Washington Harbor (the docks are long gone) and School House Beach, which is famous because it is covered with small, smooth, and quite rare limestone rocks. Don't even think of taking one home. It's against the law. They are brilliant white in the afternoon sun; they're easy to walk on; and happily they don't act as a breeding ground for biting insects.

Washington Island also has sand beaches, three of them. They are Gislason's Beach on the east shore of Detroit Harbor, Sand Dunes Beach on the south shore, and Percy Johnson Park on the east shore.

Continuing east on Jackson Harbor Road, you can stop at the Farm Museum, which includes an old farmhouse, barn, blacksmith shop, and all the farm tools and such used in the late nineteenth century.

For a side trip with a little heavy breathing, follow Jackson Harbor Road to Mountain Road and turn south where you will find a pull-off and sets of stairs leading to a lookout tower on a high ridge. First you climb 119 stairs to the top of the hill and then another 67 stairs to the top of the tower. Once you catch your breath, you'll discover a pleasant view to the north where you can actually see water at the island's edge, but not much in any other direction. But you can glory in the fine accomplishment of having climbed all those stairs.

Back on Jackson Harbor Road, continue east to Sievers School of Fiber Arts. Look for a large, colorful flag hung by the road. People come from all over the country to take classes in weaving, spinning, basketmaking, embroidery, knitting, quilting, and even making a bent wood willow chair. The Sievers store is a find for anyone who loves these arts and needs materials and tools. In an odd conjunction, Sievers also makes and constructs benches specially designed to hold model trains. (Contact Sievers at 920-847-2264; www.sieversschool.com).

Continue on Jackson Harbor Road until you reach its namesake—Jackson Harbor. There you'll find a tiny fishing village, a small maritime museum, a cart with soft drinks and hot dogs, and docks with actual commercial fishing boats. They are the ones that look like armored personnel carriers. Nearby is the dock for the Karfi, the ferry to Rock Island.

If You Go

Getting There: From Green Bay, Wisconsin, drive north up the Door Peninsula on Wisconsin highway 42. If you are not going to take your car to the island, you can take the Island Clipper ferry (920-854-2972) from Gillis Rock. If you are taking your car or just going as a passenger, take the Washington Island ferry (920-847-2039) from Northport pier. The Washington Island ferry has the most frequent departures and leaves earlier in the morning and later in the evening.

Transportation: The island is bigger than most people think after looking at the map. For example, it is three miles from the ferry dock at Detroit Harbor to the town. This is not really a walkable island. Plan on bringing your car or renting a bicycle at the dock. The island is a terrific place to ride a bike. It has one hundred miles of roads, most of which are paved, and every corner of the island offers some interesting place to stop and see. If you drive, the island does have a gas station.

Tours: Cherry Train Tours of Washington Island (920-847-2039) offers regular ninety-minute scenic and historic tours in an open trolley tram. A similar tour is run by Viking Tour Train, which meets the Island Clipper ferry from Gillis Rock.

Lodging: The island has more than two dozen places to stay, ranging from resorts on the water and a historic hotel to bed-and-breakfasts, motels, and campgrounds. For details, contact the Washington Island Chamber of Commerce at 920-847-2179; Web site: www.washingtonislandchamber.com.

Dining: Fifteen restaurants are scattered around the island. Starting in the morning, stop off at Red Cup Coffee House on Detroit Harbor Road for fine plain coffee or a cappuccino. For breakfast, try the Icelandic pancakes at the Sunset Resort, with a view overlooking Green Bay. Or for a good but more conventional breakfast, try the Cedar Point Inn, with a view of Detroit Harbor, or the locals' favorite, K.K. Fiske, on Main Road. For lunch, try the Albie burger at the Albatross Drive-In at the corner of Main Road and Detroit Harbor Road. For dinner, order the Lawyer fish plate at K.K. Fiske Restaurant. Or on weekends, hit the fish boil. Fiske's fish is fresh. The restaurant has its own commercial fishing boat. A first-rate dinner can be had at the cozy and convivial Sailor's Pub at Shipyard Island Marina on South Shore Drive. Or for a bit of gourmet dining, try the Washington Hotel Restaurant on South Shore Drive, which operates its own culinary school.

Information: Contact the Washington Island Chamber of Commerce at 920-847-2179; Web site: www.washingtonislandchamber.com.

Rock Island

Most of us spend very little time thinking about boathouses. But the one on Rock Island is exceptional.

For one thing, it is very, very big. It is so big, in fact, that the term boathouse conjures an image that is far too small. Boat mansion might be closer. Or perhaps boat castle would capture its magnificence.

It is a huge, big-shouldered building of pale limestone that, in the afternoon light, seems almost to glow from within. From the water side, it is fronted by two great and two small arched boat entries. And above them, three tall, arched windows match the visual theme in the main building. Inside is housed a great hall that the Valkyries could love. The whole thing is topped with a red tile roof that, all by itself, weighs in at fifty tons.

Boathouse? No, that does not quite capture it. This place is more truly a water and stone monument to Chester Thordarson, a man who, though largely forgotten today, was hugely wealthy and an inventor of the caliber of Thomas Edison.

So to take the Karfi ferry from Jackson Harbor on Washington Island over to Rock Island is to come into the thrall of this building, and with it of Thordarson himself.

Rock Island today is a Wisconsin state park which entices visitors to wander its pretty woodland trails, tack down tents in its campsites, wade through its remarkable history, which includes Lake Michigan's third oldest lighthouse, and, of course, take in the Thordarson limestone legacy.

Before the European fur traders showed up, Indians—for the most part Potawatomis—visited and lived on the island. Archaeologists have uncovered some eighty thousand artifacts on the island, left mostly in the 1600s and 1700s.

In terms of non-Indian residents, Rock Island had a year-round population before the larger Washington Island did. In fact, in 1850 it boasted the most residents between Mackinac Island and Green Bay. A fishermen's

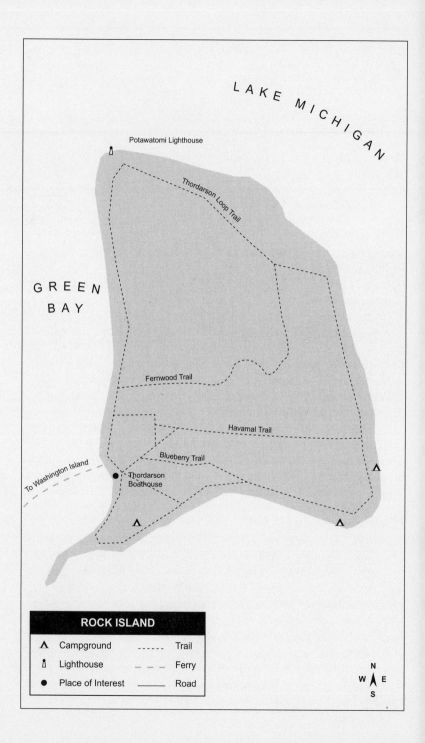

LAKE MICHIGAN

Potawatomi Lighthouse

Thordarson Loop Trail

GREEN BAY

Fernwood Trail

Havamal Trail

Blueberry Trail

To Washington Island

Thordarson Boathouse

ROCK ISLAND

Λ Campground	------	Trail
Lighthouse	— ·· —	Ferry
● Place of Interest	———	Road

N
W E
S

The immense boathouse on Rock Island is more than a garage for boats. It was built as a labor of love by Chester Thordarson, a prominent and wealthy inventor. In the early part the twentieth century, Thordarson bought Rock Island and built the boathouse along with an ancient Viking Hall with a library to hold some 11,000 books.

The huge boat house on Rock Island has room for this boat and many more. Chester Thordarson, a wealthy inventor, built the boat house in the 1920s. It cost some $250,000—a huge amount at the time—and took 20 masons working full time for three years to complete it.

village on the island's east side blossomed briefly, then faded over time. By the late 1890s, the last resident moved off. No remnants of the village are left.

Lighthouse

The single building left from the era of early pioneers is the Pottawatomie Lighthouse, also spelled Potawatomi. It was aptly named for the Indian people there, whose name means "people of the place of fire."

The first light station consisted of a round tower and a small keeper's house. It was built in 1836 and sat about one hundred feet above the water on the island's north bluffs. In 1856, it was rebuilt. Apparently the original workmanship was poor. The lighthouse we see today was solidly constructed of limestone and had quarters for the families of the keeper and his assistant.

The new lighthouse had a fourth-order Fresnel lens. The first light was fueled by lard. Later, in 1880, it was converted to kerosene.

The Icelander Cometh

Chester Thordarson invented the world's first million-volt transformer, which he demonstrated at the St. Louis World's Fair in 1904. Then, in 1915, he invented a transmitter that could send high-voltage electricity over long distances. Eventually he achieved more than one hundred patents for electric innovations we now take for granted—long-distance radio transmission, ignition coils for automobiles, and precipitation of air pollutants from factory smokestacks. In his era, he was considered as great an inventor as Edison.

Not bad for a kid that was born in Iceland. When he was five, his family emigrated to Milwaukee. Thordarson's rags-to-riches story begins with him working at a very young age, first on a farm and then, at age eighteen, in Milwaukee winding armatures in an electric shop for four dollars a week. But his values were strong and his hopes were high. More than anything, he wanted to learn. So he was willing to live poor and even eat badly to educate himself. So he would take a precious one dollar of the four he made each week and use it to buy books.

By 1910, Thordarson was a renowned inventor and massively wealthy. He soon bought up the entirety of Rock Island. He wanted it as a sanctuary where he could follow his passion for botany and wildlife conservation, and as a getaway place where he could bring his famous friends for fishing trips, including his buddy Big Bill Thompson, mayor of Chicago.

He built guest houses. He erected a limestone water tower on the east side of the island where the village used to be. He had plans for a one hundred–room hotel. And, of course, he lavished money on the boathouse in which the great hall had high exposed-beam ceilings, modeled after an ancient Viking hall. His library there held 11,000 books.

The cost was $250,000. That may not seem like very much today. But in the 1920s, a quarter of a million dollars was very big money, big enough to pay twenty masons to work full time for three years and also cover the costs of dredging the harbor.

Inside the great hall, today's visitors can see the specially built rugged, caramel-colored dining tables and chairs, with individual carvings based on Norse myths.

On the back of one chair is a carving of Odin, the most powerful of the Norse gods, with his two brothers. They are getting ready to create the first man from two tree trunks they have found lying on the seashore. On another chair back, Sol drives the chariot of the sun across the sky from east to west. He is pursued by the giant wolf Skoll. And so it goes for a total of twenty-eight chairs.

Speaking of carvings, one of Thordarson's workers apparently did some rock carvings on waterfront ledges near the state campgrounds, just at the east end of the island's south shore beach. These include an Indian's head and an Indian standing in a canoe.

Potawatomi Lighthouse sits high on a 100-foot bluff at the north end of Rock Island. It was originally built in 1836 and then, because of poor workmanship, rebuilt in 1856.

Once, when asked why he lavished so much money on Rock Island, Thordarson said, "If I hadn't spent some of my money this way, I would have gambled on the stock market and probably lost it."

Thordarson died in 1945, leaving his library to the University of Wisconsin. His heirs sold the island to the state in 1965. The price, including all the buildings except the lighthouse, was $175,000.

If You Go

Getting There: Board the Karfi Ferry at Jackson Harbor at Washington Island's northeast corner. The ferry takes just passengers. No cars and no bikes.

Transportation: Rock Island is a Wisconsin State Park, and most of it has been given over to natural woods, so everyone hikes. The trails are wide and well maintained, so walking is easy. Be sure to spend some time in Chester Thordarson's magnificent boathouse and great hall, and follow the Thordarson Loop Trail north along the west shore to the Pottawatomie Lighthouse, which has an old cemetery nearby. If you continue on the Thordarson Loop south along the east shore, you will pass another cemetery near the old, now-razed village, and further on is the limestone water tower.

Lodging: You bring your own, a tent. The island has forty sites, some in groups, others more isolated.

Dining: You bring your own food. The island has no food facilities.

Information: Contact Rock Island State Park at 920-847-2235.

Lake Superior

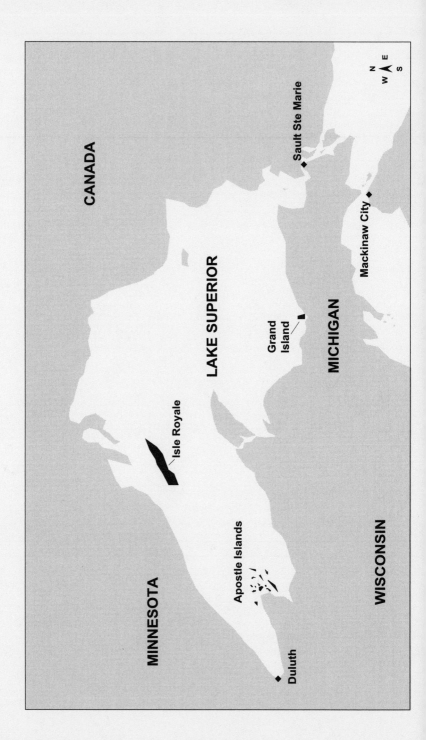

Grand Island

Ojibwa legend says that the Great Spirit Kitchi-Manito created Grand Island.

One day, long, long ago, Kitchi-Manito created several giants just for the fun of it. But because they were so large, he did not enter their bodies to give them life. He was afraid that the giants might be more powerful than he was. Instead he just let them lie on the ground, except for one. Kitchi-Manito thought he had designed that one very badly, worse than the others. So he threw it into the waters of *Giche Gumee*, or what we today call Lake Superior.

Those giants that Kitchi-Manito left lying on the ground now form the hills that surround the town of Munising in Michigan's Upper Peninsula. And the one he tossed into the water, the reject, is Grand Island. As the story goes, the two small islands just to its west—William and Wood—are the giant's hands.

Indeed, Grand Island is big. It is eight miles long and three miles wide at its widest, and its shoreline runs thirty-five miles. It is the largest island off Lake Superior's south shore. The Ojibwas called the island *Kitchi-Minis*, which means great island and is not so different from the name in English.

Today, people find Grand Island just north of Munising, across the blue-black waters of Lake Superior's Munising Bay. It is a U.S. National Recreation Area. From shore, it seems like a formless mound, floating on the water. But from above, the shape is more like a huge left hand laid palm down in the water.

Almost every day during the warmer months, people take the ten-minute ferry ride from Powell Point to the island. There they can find two historic lighthouses, buildings left by nineteenth-century pioneers, sand beaches for those tough enough to brave Lake Superior's refrigerated waters, and a lattice of trails and roads not only for hiking but for some of the very best

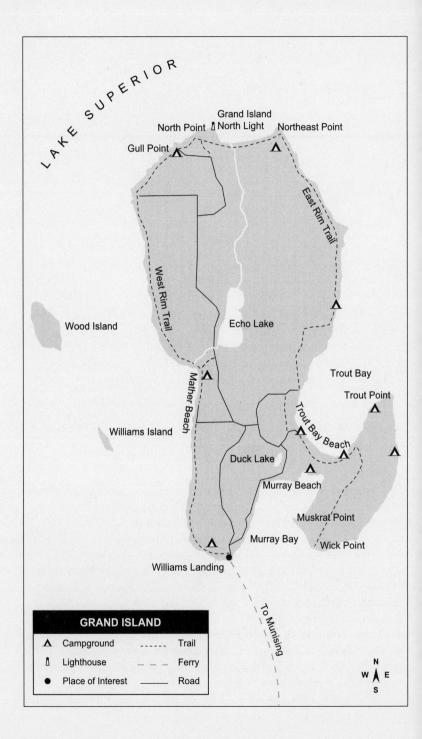

LAKE SUPERIOR

Grand Island
North Point ⓘ North Light   Northeast Point
Gull Point

East Rim Trail

West Rim Trail

Wood Island

Echo Lake

Mather Beach

Trout Bay

Trout Point

Williams Island

Trout Bay Beach

Duck Lake

Murray Beach

Muskrat Point

Murray Bay

Wick Point

Williams Landing

To Munising

GRAND ISLAND

⚠	Campground	-----	Trail
ⓘ	Lighthouse	— —	Ferry
●	Place of Interest	———	Road

N
W ⬆ E
S

The crane on this building, pictured in 1905, was used to haul furs out of Indian canoes. The post first belonged to the British Northwest Company, then to the Hudson Bay Company. Finally in 1814, it was taken over by John Jacob Astor's American Fur Company. Abraham Williams, the island's first resident, took over managing the post in 1840. Courtesy of the Alger County Historical Society.

mountain biking available on any of the islands in this book. Campers can camp, and fishermen can cast lines into the island's internal lakes and into Lake Superior.

In winter when the big lake's ice is solid, snowmobilers skitter out from the mainland to zip about the island trails like so many careening roller coaster cars.

The island's history boasts one of the most engaging Indian tales, and it is truth, not legend. The history also tells of fur traders, pioneers, steadfast conservation efforts, rapacious logging, and an era when the island was filled with exotic animals including caribou, antelopes, and albino deer.

Grand Island harbors some unsolved mysteries as well.

From times uncounted, Indians used Grand Island. Few stayed year round. But many came in the warm months to fish, hunt, and pick berries, often retreating to the mainland during winter's fierce season.

The famed French explorers Radisson and Groselliers were probably the first Europeans to see Grand Island. They apparently passed by, or might even have stopped, in 1658.

Little Duck, Hiawatha, and the End of the Island Ojibwas

The events of what is now the island's most famous Indian story occurred some time before 1820, when it was sung and translated for Michigan Governor Lewis Cass and the explorer-ethnologist Henry R. Schoolcraft. These two men, joined by a full group, were traveling by canoe on an exploratory tour of Lake Superior when they stopped at Grand Island.

An Ojibwa Indian, described by Cass as "a tall and beautiful youth"

Teresa stops to rest a bit after biking up a 300-foot bluff on Grand Island that looks out over Lake Superior. Grand Island is a mountain biker's heaven with scenic lake views that stretch to the horizon and lots of trails and dirt roads to explore.

sang a song of his people's pride and tragedy. His name was Powers-of-the-Air. Today the best and most charming version of that story is in the book *A Face in the Rock: The Tale of a Grand Island Chippewa,* by Loren R. Graham, a Harvard University history professor who for decades has summered on Grand Island.

The story begins with a small group of Ojibwas who lived peacefully on Grand Island, picking berries, hunting game, and living their lives in safety because they were protected by Lake Superior's frigid water moat.

Little Duck, a handsome boy, lived with his family on the island. He was known not only for his sweet nature and good looks, but also for his speed. Every morning he would run along the beach of Trout Bay, which lies where the island's thumb joins the hand. He would run on the sand and in the water, bounding along as quickly as the deer. No one could catch Little Duck.

But trouble was brewing on the mainland. The Ojibwas were at war with the Sioux, who lived to the west. But in the past, when the Ojibwas arranged for war parties, the people on Grand Island always refused to join them. Why go? they said. We are safe on our island. We have no quarrel with the Sioux. But eventually the mainland Ojibwas began to call them cowards. And finally, when a great war party was being gathered, the Grand Island Ojibwas did agree to go. It had become a matter of honor. Their valor had to be proved.

Since the Grand Island group was small, it sent only thirteen warriors. They were later called the Gallant Thirteen. And the youngest was Little Duck.

When the time came, they paddled their canoes to the west end of Lake Superior and there joined with the other Ojibwas to face the Sioux, who had them vastly outnumbered.

As the time for the battle approached, the Ojibwa chiefs agreed that the Grand Island warriors would guard and protect a certain cave. The combat was fierce. The Sioux routed the Ojibwas, killing many and sending the others fleeing. All that remained were the thirteen Ojibwas at the cave. The Sioux offered to spare them. But the Grand Islanders said no. Their honor was at stake. But they did have a sense of history. If they must fight to the death, then they wished to be remembered.

The chief, who was Little Duck's father, arranged for the fleet-footed boy to sneak through the enemy lines, outrun the Sioux warriors, and then, from some vantage point, see the battle and tell the story.

The battle of the cave was brutal and bloody. Eventually, the Sioux killed every one of the Ojibwa warriors, shooting arrows into some, tomahawking others. But the Sioux paid a high price. They lost two warriors for every Ojibwa that they managed to kill.

From his hiding spot on a hill, Little Duck saw his father die. He saw the other men die. He was horrified and heartbroken. But he ran back to the canoes and paddled one toward Grand Island and home. Along the way, Little Duck repeated the words "chemaun poll" and slapped the side of his canoe. Ojibwa legend—and a great tribal secret—held that Mishosha, the magician of the lake, would say these words to make his magic canoe virtually fly through the water.

Little Duck finally returned to tell the story of the brave warriors at the cave. The people, though proud, were stricken by sadness. The news also meant that they could no longer stay on the island, for there were no men— except for Little Duck—to hunt and provide for the women, children, and old people.

When Little Duck returned and they heard his story, the people determined that the boy was now a man. He should no longer be called Little Duck. His new name would be Powers-of-the-Air because he could run fast as the wind, and thus had the powers of the air. And it was he who told the story to Cass and Schoolcraft.

A number of years later, Powers-of-the-Air became a friend of and worked for William Cameron, keeper of the island's North Light. Knowing he would be interested, Cameron one day read Henry W. Longfellow's latest poem to Powers-of-the-Air. It was "Hiawatha." The Indian man listened for a long time without expression. And then Cameron read these words: "Launched his birch-canoe for sailing; / With his palms its side he patted, / Said with glee, 'Cheemaun my darling, / O my birch-canoe! Leap forward.'"

According to Graham, Powers-of-the-Air leaped up and said, "He got it from me! I am the only person who ever told that secret."

And the ones he told the secret to were Cass and Schoolcraft.

It seems that Longfellow, who never set foot on the shores of Lake

Superior, based much of his famous poem on the writings of Henry R. Schoolcraft.

One other enduring memory of Powers-of-the-Air remains. When Cass, Schoolcraft, and their party paddled on west, they camped at the far east end of Au Train Beach. And one of the men carved the face of Powers-of-the-Air into the side of a rock. Today a roadside rest stop is nearby, and you can walk a short distance east along the sand and still see that carving.

Fur Trader to Hotel Man

The island's first permanent white settler was Abraham Williams. He came in 1840 and took over the fur trading post which once had been the British Northwest Fur Company and then the Hudson Bay Company, and then in 1814 was taken over by John Jacob Astor's American Fur Company.

He and his wife, who had twelve children, built solid houses and cottages. Mrs. Williams died in 1856, and Abraham died in 1873. Their gravestones can be found on the island at the Williams Cemetery. Abraham was hugely prominent in his era. Williams Island was named for him. So was Williams Landing. And in 1862, he built a big house that eventually would become the Hotel Williams and the heart of the island's tourist trade for many decades.

In the 1920s, flyers for the Hotel Williams advertised:

Rooms—$3.50, with bath, $5

Breakfast $1.00; Luncheon $1.50; Dinner $2.00

The hotel had cottages and summer people also built vacation cabins on the island.

Over time, tourism faded on the island, and by 1958 the Hotel Williams was closed permanently.

It was during the Williams era that two lighthouses were built on the island.

Hotel Williams, originally built as a log house in 1862, was a mainstay of the tourist business on Grand Island. The Williams family also rented out cabins. In the 1920s, the hotel advertised a room for $3.50, with bath $5. Courtesy of State of Michigan Archives.

In 1855, a forty-foot wooden tower with a light was put up on a cliff at the north end of the island. This light towered a full 204 feet above Lake Superior's waters. In 1867, that wooden tower was replaced with a brick light tower and a brick keeper's house. Keepers kept the light shining until 1941. It is now the summer home of Loren Graham and his wife.

A second lighthouse was built on the island's thumb to help guide ships through the East Channel to Munising in 1868. It operated until 1913. The old wooden lighthouse and keeper's quarters are a tourist attraction. The lighthouse is called either the East Channel Light or, more commonly, the South Light.

Murder at North Light

One of the island's great mysteries developed at the North Light in 1908. The story is spun out in great detail in *Island of Adventure: Tales of Grand Island,* by Marc Weingart.

On a foggy, hand-numbingly cold morning in May of 1908, George Genry was down at the dock in Munising loading up a sailboat with groceries and supplies to be carried out to Grand Island's North Lighthouse. As the keeper, he would be opening the lighthouse and relighting the lamp for the warm-weather sailing season on Lake Superior.

It was a sour day for sailing, but Genry told his wife that he would send her a message or perhaps come back into town within a week.

Sailing out with Genry was his assistant keeper, E. S. Morrison, a thirty-year-old Detroiter. While the two men managed to work together, the upcoming season did not look particularly happy for the lighthouse. Townspeople knew that the two men did not really get along very well. But off they went.

One week went by, and back in Munising, Genry's wife wondered why she had heard nothing from her husband. After two weeks passed with no word, she contacted the sheriff. This was very unlike George, she said.

The sheriff went out to the North Light with a posse of seven men, only to return largely bewildered about what might have happened. The door to the keeper's house was unlocked, but no one was at home. The heavy jackets of the two men, so necessary for the still wintry weather, both were hung on hooks. The groceries and supplies that Genry had loaded into the sailboat were there on a small table—not put away.

The posse searched the light tower and the surrounding area. They found no sign of the men. Then they went down to the beach, where the keeper's sailboat would have been pulled ashore. No sailboat. Where could they have gone? Where was the boat? Why would they go outside without their heavy coats?

Several days later, the sailboat finally appeared. It was up at Au Sable

Beach. Inside was a single dead man, his body battered and bashed almost beyond recognition. But ultimately the corpse was identified as E. S. Morrison. Genry remained missing, and to many he seemed to be the star suspect in what was likely a murder.

But then, some time later, word came that Genry's friend Timothy Dee, keeper of the island's South Light, had discovered the remains of a body on the beach near his light station. Dee said it was Genry's body. But was it? No one else ever saw the body. And many townspeople believed that Dee was simply covering for his friend, who likely fled.

Over the years, a number of theories emerged, most based on slim and largely circumstantial evidence.

One of Genry's daughters, a schoolteacher, suddenly left her classes for several days in 1951. Some believed she had gone to attend her father's funeral. Also in 1951, the Genry family applied for the keeper's pension. Ah, whispered those suspecting conspiracy, the family waited to make an application until George Genry was actually dead.

Finally came a version from the Genry family, who suspected foul play from William G. Mather, the owner of Grand Island. It seems that Genry was not above poaching some of the game living on the island. He liked a little fresh venison on the plate. Mather apparently knew what Genry was up to and was infuriated. The Genry kin believed that Mather hired a couple of thugs, who got to the lighthouse ahead of the keepers and hid inside. After the keeper and Morrison had pulled off their coats and set the groceries down, the thugs leaped out from hiding and killed them. They then put Morrison's body into the sailboat and set it adrift. The body's constant banging as the boat rolled about apparently caused the mutilation. They disposed of Genry's body elsewhere, perhaps burying it.

That theory certainly would answer why the coats still hung on their hooks and the groceries remained on the table.

But the truth is that no one really knows. It is said, however, that George Genry's ghost still lurks around the North Light. And locals joke that when power lawn mowers suddenly start, cars don't start, and refrigerators stop their hum, it's George playing tricks.

All-White Deer, Canadian Caribou, and the Chainsaw

William G. Mather, the man who was cast as the villain in the lighthouse keepers' deaths, was one of the most prominent people in the history of Grand Island.

In 1900, the Cleveland Cliffs Iron Company bought Grand Island. Its objective was to protect the island's natural beauty. Then, in 1901, Mather, who was the president of Cleveland Cliffs, decided to turn the island into a refuge for exotic animals. Exotic, in this sense, meant animals that never had nor could have lived on the island. Some were freaks of nature; others were brought from faraway places.

After building a fence around the island Mather brought in an amazing collection that included albino deer, caribou, moose, elk, antelopes, blacktail and mule deer, mountain goats, grouse, and ring-necked and black-necked pheasants.

One problem Mather did not anticipate was that while people understood that Grand Island was an animal refuge, the timber wolves on the nearby mainland did not. So when winter freezes set in, the wolves just would trot over the ice for a sumptuous dinner of foreign foods.

One wolf apparently was a little too greedy. Alone, it managed to bring down nineteen of Mather's exotic animals. So in late January of 1906, a very upset Mather hired more than twenty-four crack hunters to search out and kill that single wolf. But hunting is not the same thing as killing. And this wolf was sly. It eluded the hunters again and again, hiding in the swamps and ducking through their hunting lines. But on February 11, the hunters finally succeeded. They came back with the body of a female that weighed between seventy-five and eighty pounds.

Given the cost of this army of hunters, the dead exotic animals, and uncounted other expenses, this single wolf probably was the most costly kill in Upper Peninsula history.

Not all the exotics stayed on the island. Over a period running from 1909 to 1935, the company exported some 1,768 animals—mostly deer and elk—to states and parks hoping to build their herds.

Today, no albino deer remain. Nor do any of the exotics. The island has white-tailed deer and black bears, which it always did. Officials with the U.S. Forest Service say that all of the exotic animals were captured and moved off the island. It seems like a difficult task to capture so many deer, caribou, and grouse and pheasant, but perhaps it was done that way.

Considering Cleveland Cliffs' change in attitude toward the island in the 1950s, it would seem difficult for many of the animals to survive anyway. The company began serious logging on Grand Island, and it continued until the mid-1980s. Few forested places were left untouched.

After the company had taken just about every bit of wood worth taking, it sold the island in 1989 to the U.S. Forest Service, which then turned it into a national recreation area.

Sweet Retreat

Grand Island is just a nifty place to get away to for a day, a weekend, or longer.

Hikers will find fine trails. Campers can settle into nearly a dozen camp-

For boat travelers, this weather ravaged dock on Murray Bay leads to Grand Island's only historic building that can be visited by the public. For those who take the ferry, it's a 10-minute bike ride.

sites. And mountain bikers will be thrilled by a route that circles the island and can be managed in just a day visit. The trail runs as a single track or on dirt roads, up and down steep inclines. All but the most sinewy-thighed riders may end up pushing their bikes up some of the hills. As for going downhill, that's often a white-knuckle exercise.

Walk or bike up the road that runs along Murray Bay, and you can visit the old Williams Cemetery and stop by the Old Stone Quarry Cottage. A couple of miles farther on, past Duck Lake, is a steady climb to a fine bluff-top overlook out across Trout Bay.

Unfortunately, both lighthouses are privately owned and cannot be visited. They can, however, be seen from the water.

If You Go

Getting There: The turnoff to the ferry dock for Grand Island is 2.5 miles west of the blinking light in Munising on M-26. Look for the signs to the Grand Island National Recreation Area. At the dock, the ferry can take you and your bikes across to the island. No cars. The ferry runs from Memorial Day to early October. You also may go to the island with your own boat.

Transportation: You can either ride a mountain bike or hike. The island has both roads (for forest service trucks and locals' cars) and trails. You can bring your own bike or rent a junker at the Grand Island dock at Powell Point. For tour bus tickets, call 906-387-4845.

For tour boats, try Shipwreck Tours, with a glass-bottom boat that looks at shipwrecks, lighthouses, and rock formations on the island (June to mid-September).

Lodging: Bring your own, a tent. The island has no hotels or bed-and-breakfasts, but it does have designated campsites. Random camping—not at the designated sites—is allowed with certain restrictions. For day visitors, the nearby town of Munising has a number of motels and bed-and-breakfasts. Contact the Alger County Chamber of Commerce (906-387-2138).

Dining: Bring your own food. The island has no restaurants, not even machines for candy or soft drinks. Munising does have restaurants ranging from fast food to sit-down meals. The Dogpatch, Sydney's, and the Navigator restaurants are popular choices.

Beaches: Swimming is good, if very cold, from Mather Beach along the West Rim Trail, Murray Bay Beach, and Trout Bay Beach.

Bugs: Grand Island has them. Black flies can be bad from mid-May through much of July. Bring bug repellent.

Drinking Water, Toilets: Outhouses and taps with clean drinking water are located in the southern part of the island at Williams Landing, Duck Lake, Trout Bay, and the group campsite on the West Rim Trail.

Fishing and Hunting: Both are allowed on the island. For license information, contact the Michigan Department of Natural Resources at 517-373-1220.

Bears: The island does have black bears, but you'll be lucky if you see one. Do not harass or feed them.

Nearby: Munising actually is most famous for Pictured Rocks National Lakeshore. While it is not an island, it is a wonderful place for hiking and camping. Perhaps the best views of the colorful cliffs along the Lake Superior shore are from a boat. Kayaker tours are available from Northern Waters at 906-387-2323; www.northernwaters.com. Or try Munising Bay Outfitters at 906-387-4400. Another option is the popular boat tour with Pictured Rocks Cruises, Inc. Call 906-387-2379. Cruises run from late May to early October. Scuba divers enjoy Lake Superior's clear but cold waters and dive to many of the wrecks in the area.

Winter: Grand Island and the area around Munising are a snowmobile heaven, with long wooded trails on the mainland and possible visits to the dramatic ice caves that form along the sides of Grand Island. Of course, Lake Superior's ice must be firm enough to hold the sleds.

Information: Stop by the Visitors Center for the Hiawatha National Forest in Munising, just east of the blinking light, or call 906-387-2512 or 387-3700. For information on Munising, contact the Munising Visitors Bureau at 906-387-2138; www.munising.org.

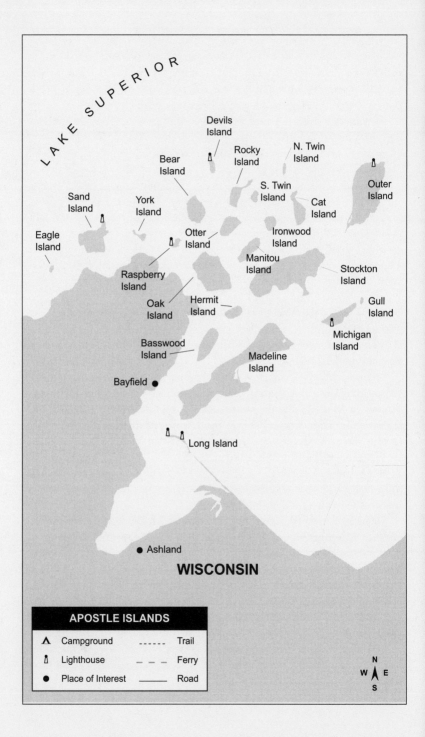

LAKE SUPERIOR

Devils
Island

Rocky
Island

N. Twin
Island

Bear
Island

S. Twin
Island

Outer
Island

Cat
Island

Sand
Island

York
Island

Otter
Island

Ironwood
Island

Eagle
Island

Raspberry
Island

Manitou
Island

Stockton
Island

Oak
Island

Hermit
Island

Gull
Island

Basswood
Island

Madeline
Island

Michigan
Island

Bayfield

Long Island

Ashland

WISCONSIN

APOSTLE ISLANDS

⚑	Campground	------	Trail
🗼	Lighthouse	— — —	Ferry
●	Place of Interest	———	Road

N
W ✦ E
S

Apostle Islands

The Apostle Islands, as the story goes, were named by Jesuit priests who came in birch bark canoes with the earliest voyageurs to the far west end of Lake Superior.

One might guess that the black robes—as the Indians called them—might have been strong on religion, but weak on arithmetic. Either that, or they just didn't care that the Apostle Islands number twenty-two, and the original apostles only twelve.

Another naming story is less well known—and far less saintly.

Legend has it that a band of eighteenth-century pirates kept their head-quarters either on one of the islands or nearby on the mainland. These out-laws would sweep down and hijack passing canoes filled with furs or trade goods. The name of the pirate gang: the Twelve Apostles.

Either way, the Apostle Islands, splayed over 720 square miles of Lake Superior, are one of the most beautifully pristine groups of islands in all the Great Lakes and a paradise for sailors, yachtspeople, kayakers, and hikers.

One visitor in the 1800s said the Apostles "look like a fairy scene; everything about it is enchantment." Not much has changed since then.

What's more, the Apostles are the mother lode for lighthouse lovers. The islands boast seven light stations, six of them built during the nineteenth century. It is the largest such concentration in the Great Lakes. And the stories of their keepers are among the most heroic.

The gateway to the Apostles is Bayfield, Wisconsin, a village of New England charm where the clink-a-clink of hundreds of sailboat riggings fills the evening air; commercial fishing boats mutter into port each day; and the visitor can buy a first-rate piece of art, drink a cappuccino, eat a fine meal, sleep in comfort, and, of course, set out to see the islands.

Of the twenty-two Apostle islands, only one has a year-round popula-

An evening stroll beside the marina at Bayfield, Wisconsin, gateway to the Apostle Islands.

tion. It is the largest, Madeline, and its character ranges from easygoing to downright zany.

The other twenty-one islands and part of the mainland make up the Apostle Islands National Lakeshore, which means they carry the aura of what the islands were like when the first French voyageurs paddled their way across Lake Superior's ferocious waters.

The Lady

Mariners often call Lake Superior "The Lady." It befits this lake's regal status. It is not only the largest of the Great Lakes; it is the largest lake in the world, holding an entire eighth of the world's supply of fresh water. Of the Great Lakes it is the longest (350 miles), the widest (160 miles), the deepest (1,332 feet), and the cleanest. Almost unimaginably in our polluted age, one can still be out on this lake, dip a cup in the water, and safely drink it.

The French called it *Supérieur* because it was the most northerly of the lakes and the highest in elevation; the English kept the name for its superlative qualities.

Some also consider Superior to be the most dangerous of the lakes. Its rap sheet for sinking ships runs long, and the area around the Apostle Islands could be particularly dangerous. Numerous ships have gone down in these waters—along with too many small craft to be counted. More than a hundred larger vessels have been wrecked, including twenty-five major wrecks chronicled in *The Unholy Apostles: Tales of the Chequamagon Shipwrecks*, by James M. Keller.

But where there were tragic wrecks, there also was nearly unimaginable heroism.

A Canadian freighter, a steamship named the *Prussia*, hit a bad storm in September of 1885 while headed from Port Arthur, near Thunder Bay, Ontario, to Duluth. Captain William Anderson tried to seek protection by heading toward Sand Island in the Apostles. That's when the *Prussia's* bad luck really turned sour. About ten miles from the island, a fire broke out near the smokestack. Whipped by the wind, the blaze quickly engulfed the boat. The crew of ten was forced to abandon ship in two lifeboats. They might have all been lost except that Charles Lederlee, the lighthouse keeper, saw the fire break out. He launched his small boat into the fierce waters and managed to retrieve the men from both lifeboats, one of which had lost control entirely and was just drifting through the storm's wrath. Members of the crew later sent a thank-you letter to Lederlee, saying that if he had not come to the rescue "they most certainly would have been lost."

No one was nearby to rescue the ore-carrying schooner *Lucerne* when she went down in a blinding snowstorm with hurricane-force winds on a Sunday in November of 1886. In fact, it was not until the following Friday that a search party found the remains. The *Lucerne's* three masts were still sticking out above the water. And clinging to them were three members of the crew—frozen to death. An Ashland, Wisconsin, newspaper reported that their bodies were covered with from one to six inches of ice.

It went better, but only slightly better when the ore carrier *Pretoria* broke into pieces in a storm about one and a half miles from Outer Island in September of 1905. The ten crew members managed to clamber into a lifeboat and then pulled on the oars for all they were worth against the raging waters. They did well until they were just over a hundred yards from the shore. That's when a gigantic wave smacked the small boat, sending some of the crew flying ten feet into the air. In the next few minutes, five of the crew drowned. The rest somehow managed to cling to the upended boat. At that point, what seemed like a miracle happened. John Irvine, the sixty-year-old lighthouse keeper, rushed into the water and pulled the exhausted sailors ashore one-by-one. A Duluth newspaper called it "a superhuman effort" while "his life was endangered every minute."

Magnificent Six

The first of the six light stations located in the Apostle Islands was a mistake.

In 1857, a Milwaukee construction company used rough stone to build a conical light tower and half-story keeper's house on Michigan Island on the eastern side of the archipelago. Wrong, said the government. The lighthouse was supposed to be built on Long Island at the south end of the Apostle Islands. Oops, said the builder.

Darn right, oops, said the government. Now you can build a lighthouse on the correct island, at your own expense. The La Pointe Light on Long Island was finished the next year, and the Michigan Island mistake was closed down.

Devil's Island Light was the last to be added to the six in the Apostle Islands. The present lighthouse was completed in 1897 and the light itself was added in 1901.

Boat traffic—Great Lakes ships all are called boats—increased steadily. In fact, in 1903, the keeper at the Devils Island Light reported seeing 120 vessels at one time. So over the years, lighthouses were strung around the outside of the Apostle Islands like lights on a Christmas tree.

In 1863, a rectangular lighthouse was built on top of a forty-foot bluff on Raspberry Island to help guide ships sailing between Duluth and Bayfield. Then the government decided that a lighthouse on Michigan Island really was not such a bad idea. So in 1869, it was rebuilt. For eleven years, the original lighthouse had been left to deteriorate while locals scavenged its bricks, windows, and other materials.

In 1874, the Outer Island Lighthouse was built on a forty-foot bluff, with a tower that raised the light another ninety feet above the waterline. This lighthouse, at the island group's far northeast extremity, was a brick structure built in the Italianate style with hooded, arched windows. It was from the top of this lighthouse that the sixty-year-old keeper came to the rescue of the *Pretoria* crew.

Sand Island Lighthouse, at the west end of the island group, is distinctive for a couple of reasons. Built in 1881, the octagonal tower was constructed in a Norman Gothic style and made of brownstone that was quarried on nearby islands. Also, it was the keeper Charles Lederlee (1881–1891) who launched his small boat out in the storm of September 1885 to save the entire crew of the freighter *Prussia*.

In 1895, a second light was added to Long Island, not full light station with associated buildings but simply a tower at Chequamegon Point.

The last light on the Apostles' Christmas tree was the Devils Island lighthouse. Its first version was finished in 1891 with a two-story, Queen Anne–style brick keeper's house and a temporary wooden tower. A permanent eighty-two foot steel tower was completed in 1897 with just one thing missing—the light itself. It took until 1901 for a third-order Fresnel lens to be sent from Paris.

Chequamegon

An Indian legend is the basis of the name Chequamegon (usually pronounced she-QUA-meh-gun), which was given to the nearby bay and also to the entire region.

The name means "soft beaver dam." The Ojibwa story goes that a demigod, Nanabazhoo, built the mainland's Chequamegon Point as a dam that originally formed a connection to Long Island. It seems Nanabazhoo wanted the dam to hold a giant beaver. But eventually the beaver broke through and escaped, creating an opening to Chequamegon Bay.

A related story adds that Nanabazhoo threw huge stones at the beaver as he escaped and these stones became the Apostle Islands.

Madeline Island: Tom's Foolery

Today only Madeline Island among the Apostles has a resident population. It includes about 220 year-rounders and ten times that many who are summer cottagers and tourists. In the warm months, islanders make their living on tourism and construction. In winter, they basically regroup, savor the silence, and, once the ice freezes, drive over to the mainland.

One islander said the ice road, usually marked by cast-off Christmas trees, can be dicey. The water at the halfway point is 150 feet deep. She said she usually leaves the car window open or carries a hammer to break it, just in case the ice caves in and she needs to make a quick escape.

Visitors, who usually come in the summer, typically reach Madeline Island after a twenty-minute ferry ride from Bayfield. Getting off at the La Pointe village dock, they find a first-rate island museum, tranquil places to hike and paddle a canoe or kayak, Lotta's Lakeside Café, a restaurant that would stand out in Chicago, various and predictable art galleries and curio shops, and the zaniest island bar in all the Great Lakes.

Tom's Burned Down Café is just a few steps up Middle Road, past the Island Store, the weavers' shop, and the scooter rental place. You've heard of treats for the eye, but this is more of an assault.

Tom's basically is a wooden platform a few steps up from street level, with a gaudily painted bar and some tables. Instead of a roof, a weather-

Tom's Burned Down Café is a treasure, albeit a weird one, on Madeline Island in the Apostle Islands. When his original café burned down, Tom Nelson had no insurance so he didn't rebuild. He just threw a tent covering over the top and re-opened. It's been that way ever since—a favorite hangout for locals and visitors. Tom's theory: "If you don't rebuild it, they will come." And they did.

beaten striped tent is splayed over the top. Call it *au plein aire* if you are fancy. But this place isn't. The tent is held in place by ropes tied on one side to a battered and rusty Ford truck with the driver's door smashed in and on the other side to an equally rust-riven RV. Apparently tent pegs for a more modern age.

At the foot of the front stairs is a sign: "Sorry, we're open." In fact, everywhere you look are hand-painted sayings that amused owner Tom Nelson. Sayings are daubed on the walls, the floors, the risers on the steps, on the bar, on little signs around the outside. Tom's Café looks, for all the world, like an explosion in an aphorism factory.

"A fool and his money are always welcome at Tom's Burned Down Café." "Red meat is not bad for you; fuzzy greenish-blue meat is bad for you." "What are the long-term effects of instant gratification?" "If a person with multiple personality threatens suicide, is it considered a hostage situation?"

You can't help but laugh. But on the other hand, the timid might fear they are walking into an intellectual freak-out zone.

Owner Tom Nelson is quite smart and not at all crazy, but he certainly might be accurately called a beloved island character.

With a vanishing hairline and a ponytail down his back, at fifty-plus he is the image of the aging hippie. He is from an old, old island family. His grandmother came to Madeline Island in 1896. But staying was never part of Nelson's plan. He intended to grab onto a more rollicking life by spending his days crewing for racing sailboats off Florida and in the Caribbean. And he did that for awhile.

"I thought I would somehow escape the Nelson family curse, workaholism," he says. "But I was wrong."

He came back in 1979 when his father died. He and his brother tried to a make a go of an island golf course, only to discover they were vastly under-capitalized. In 1989, he bought Leona's Bar, a venerable place with a lovable owner where the under-thirty crowd could knock back a few and never get in trouble.

He moved the building from out near the airport into town, but in May of 1992 it burned down. "Arson," says Nelson. He believes he knows who did it. Other islanders say, "Yes, yes, but he's wrong." Unfortunately, Nelson was running so close to his financial limit when bought Leona's that he failed to get insurance. He was crushed. But his friends told him, "You can't give up." And he didn't.

And Tom's Burned Down Café emerged on the somewhat charred floor-boards of what once was Leona's Bar. "And I've been running it as a hole in the ground since 1992," Nelson says.

Now one of his aphoristic favorites is "If you don't rebuild it, they will come." And apparently they have. Tom's Burned Down Café has become an island treasure, if a somewhat weird one.

"Our theme is," he continues, "You gotta be tough, if you're going to be stupid."

Ghosts and Voyageurs

By some estimates, the Ojibwa Indians came in about 1490 to live on Madeline Island, which they called the Home of the Golden-Breasted Woodpecker. They moved onto the island for refuge from the marauding Sioux to the west and Fox Indians to the south.

Why they left is a gorier story, which is told in *La Pointe: Village Out-post on Madeline Island,* by Hamilton Nelson Ross, from which I have drawn much of the islands' history.

Over time, huge numbers of Ojibwas had come to live on the island. Some estimates run as high as 20,000. Whatever the number, problems began when severe winters set in and food ran short. As a solution, Ross wrote, "their medicine men turned to cannibalism, selecting as their victims young children, preferably female."

After a few years, angry tribe members killed the medicine men. By 1610, they all moved away because of fears that the young victims' spirits roamed the islands at night. They were especially afraid of Devils Island. In storms, they could hear eerie noises echoing across the water. We now know the sounds are made when high lake waters wash into the island's shore caves.

The Indians' fears were such that they refused to spend the night on Madeline Island for another two hundred years, unless they were protected by French or British guns.

Many believe that the first European to see and then explore Lake Superior was Etienne Brule, an illiterate young Frenchman with plenty of courage and a knack for Indian languages.

Soon came the development of the fur trade, which lasted until the early 1800s, first under the French, then the English, and finally the Americans.

For almost two hundred years, until the silk top hat came into vogue, Europeans demanded hats made of the fine underhairs pulled from beaver furs. And the Great Lakes region was a gold mine of pelts.

On Madeline Island, the village of La Pointe (still its name) became a major trading post where Indians and European trappers brought furs which were then transported by huge, thirty-six-foot long birch bark canoes back to Montreal. At one point, the English would trade the Indians a gun for two beaver pelts and eight pounds of powder for one.

Among the early and most famous French voyageurs to come to the Apostles were Radisson and Groseilliers (known by some later as Radishes and Gooseberries), who brought back tons of pelts first for the French and later for the English.

For the Love of Madeline

It was during the voyageur era that Madeline Island got its name.

Michel Cadotte (whose family on the island dated back to his father Jean Baptiste and continues to this day) met and fell in love with a young Ojibwa princess whose name was Equaysayway (Traveling Woman). Her father was Chief White Crane, who lived on the mainland not far from what today is Bayfield.

Since no priest was nearby, the couple traveled to Sault Ste. Marie to be married. There, the Indian princess was baptized Madeline. When they returned, Chief White Crane decreed that henceforth and forevermore the island would bear her new name. And so it has.

WhitefishWhite Pine, Brownstone, and Monster Pumpkins

In the 1830s, with the fur business waning, La Pointe and the surrounding area turned to fishing—for whitefish, lake trout, herring, and pickerel.

Numbers of fish caught and sales bounced up and down. Fish were salted, then put in barrels and sent back east. Some shipments never sold and went bad. But by the 1880s and 1890s, fish sales were booming. In 1896, local fishermen caught nearly eight million pounds. The fishing continued into the twentieth century, with profitable years and not-so profitable years. When fishing was good, it was great. Even side businesses like making barrels to hold salted fish were making big money. Prices, however, plunged during the Great Depression. Then, in the 1940s, sea lampreys hit the Great Lakes, decimating the stocks of lake trout. Chemicals eventually brought the lamprey eels under control. Today, for reasons that have as much to do with politics as with fish stocks, Madeline Island is no longer a home for commercial fishing boats. Bayfield, just across the bay, has about six.

Speaking of fish, Ross writes that the planked whitefish dinner, which even today is the beloved dish of the northern lakes, was created in Ashland, Wisconsin, just across the bay from the Apostle Islands.

In the 1880s, it was the specialty of the house at the Hotel Chequamegon, a fancy hostelry where folks who could afford such things stayed to relieve their hay fever.

The major difference between the Hotel Chequamegon's planked fish and today's is that the fish was served only on white pine planks that were never used more than four times. It seems the sap from the fresh pine boards would slightly permeate the fish's skin, giving it a unique flavor. These days, one suspects that the planks under planked whitefish have been used a lot more than four times.

Sand Island was the only one of the Apostles, aside from Madeline, to have a year-round population. People lived there from the end of the nineteenth century until the mid-1940s. Fishing was the economic mainstay. But islanders also did a bit of farming and took in tourists. It had regular phone service to the mainland, a cooperative store, and a one-room school. Locals say that at some point between 1910 and 1930 the permanent population reached one hundred. But a 1920 census counted forty-four.

Loggers hit the islands heavily in the later part of the nineteenth century. White pine logs were typically moved on water. Islands, by definition, were close to lots of water. Sawmills screeched on the mainland.

One might suspect that all that lumber was used to build houses, shops, and other buildings. But in fact, railroad companies—which were growing like crazy—bought vast amounts of lumber.

"It has been estimated that in the last three decades of the nineteenth century, American railroads consumed up to a quarter of the entire timber production of the country," we read in *Historic Logging and Farming in the Apostle Islands,* by Charles Twining, Arnold R. Alanen, and William Tishler. It was used as fuel for steam locomotives and to build bridges, tunnels and train stations, but a lot—by far the greatest amount—was used to make cross ties.

Some 2,700 ties were used for each mile of track, each measuring 9 feet by seven by nine inches for a grand total of 125,000 feet for each mile of track, *Historic Logging* reported. In addition to that, some 400 ties per mile had to be replaced each year.

The islands also enjoyed a brownstone boom. For fifteen years, starting in about 1890, the tightly compressed sandstone was the building block of choice for the famed Fifth Avenue brownstones in New York City, city halls, big stores, houses, and, in the case of the islands, for the Sand Island lighthouse. Quarrymen dug brownstone from pits on Basswood, Stockton, and Hermit Islands, along with two mines on the mainland.

Over the years, islanders made various attempts at farming, some planting fruit trees, others potatoes and other vegetables. Nothing really turned out to be commercially viable. Among other reasons, the growing season was short, and the islanders—by virtue of their location—had trouble getting their products to market.

That said, some islands did produce some mega-vegetables. In the 1870s, for example, Basswood Island's Richard McCloud became famous for growing a squash that weighed seventy pounds. His tomatoes weighed three pounds apiece, and he also produced a four-foot-long snake cucumber and a pumpkin that weighed eighty-one pounds.

The Hermit and the Rich Man's Bride

Two legendary stories evolved on Hermit Island—one about the hermit who gave the island its name and the other about an island mansion built in the name of love.

Hermit Island was named for an actual hermit. He was William Wilson, who lived there for more than twenty years, ending with his death in 1863.

The story of why he ended up on the island often becomes quite vague. But Hamilton Nelson Ross ferreted out the history.

It seems Wilson did not get along with John Bell, a barrel maker of such personal presence that he was variously known as King John, Squire, Judge, and Old Whackum. The two often exchanged snide remarks. Bitterness grew. Then one day Wilson threatened to kick Bell's dog. Tempers flared, and the two finally agreed to fight it out on the streets of Bayfield. They also agreed that the loser would have to leave Madeline Island forever.

Both were big men, and evenly matched. First Wilson would get the edge with a stout hit, then Bell. The battle went on for the better part of one day. Ultimately, Wilson lost. At that point, Wilson moved to what was first called Wilson Island—because he lived there—and then later Hermit Island. He lived on the island alone for many years and developed a fearsome reputation by threatening to shoot any incautious visitor who happened by.

The ironic part of the story came at his death. At his request, Wilson was buried in the cemetery on Madeline Island. So in the end, he flouted Bell and returned.

A second Hermit's Island story is about Frederick Prentice, who had made millions in silver and copper mines in Nevada and had invested in oil.

He also quarried brownstone on both Hermit Island and Houghton Point.

In 1895, soon after he married at age seventy-three, he built a pretentious three story lodge on Hermit Island. It was a remarkable affair. The outside was covered with cedar shingles with the bark still on. It had wooden gingerbread tacked all over, four large fireplaces, at least two of which were carved of solid pieces of brownstone, Romeo and Juliet balconies on the second and third floors, and sweeping vistas of the nearby islands.

The bride came for a visit to Cedar Bark Lodge and immediately decided that she hated it—and never returned. After 1898, no one ever lived in the lodge again. It soon fell into disrepair. Looters scavenged it for whatever could be carried away. And the lodge was finally torn down in the 1930s.

Tourists

One might suspect that tourism was a relatively recent development for the Apostle Islands. Not so.

Certainly the region has polished that reputation since the National Park Service took over management of the islands in 1970. But tourism began more than one hundred years before.

The island got some of its first publicity as a vacation destination on June 26, 1854. The *New York Daily Tribune* reported that the islands were "certainly the most delightful situation on Lake Superior."

The American Fur Company built a hotel with rooms for seventy-five in La Pointe on Madeline Island. It was called Madeline House. The fancy Island View Hotel was built in Bayfield in 1883.

Summer cottages began to crop up on Madeline Island, the most famous of which were on Nebraska Row along the north shore, a development begun by Colonel Frederick Woods of Lincoln, Nebraska.

Some famous people dropped by the islands. Mary Todd Lincoln, with her son Robert Todd, stopped by but declined to stay at the hotel in La Pointe, having heard in Ontonagon, Michigan, that the hotel was "full of knot holes and the men snore something awful."

In 1928, Calvin Coolidge vacationed in the region, paying visits on a friend's yacht to Hermit Island and to La Pointe on Madeline Island.

Today, of course, the Apostle Islands National Lakeshore stands out as one of the truly wonderful places in the Midwest for sailors, kayakers, lighthouse enthusiasts, and people who truly savor the north country.

If You Go

Getting There: Bayfield, Wisconsin, the gateway to the Apostle Islands, is at the west end of Lake Superior, between the Michigan border and Duluth and about 220 miles north of Minneapolis–St. Paul.

Bayfield

Lodging and Information: Bayfield has a range of lodgings—from campsites to bed-and-breakfasts to hotels and motels. For this and most other information, call the Bayfield Chamber of Commerce at 800-447-4094; www.bayfield.org.

Dining: Restaurants range from hot-dog stands to fine dining. For breakfast, the favorite is the Egg Toss Café, a bright and cheery place at 41 Manypenny Ave.; for dinner, Maggie's has good food and a convivial bar scene at 257 Manypenny Ave. For fine dining, try the Wild Rice Restaurant with innovative dishes at 84860 Old San Rd.

On the Water: For narrated cruises of the islands, the lighthouses, and the shipwrecks, contact the Apostle Islands Cruise Service at the Bayfield marina at 800-323-7619; www.apostleisland.com. Every September for a week, the cruise service also makes special tours of the lighthouses during the Apostle Islands Lighthouse Celebration; check www.lighthousecelebration .com. The service also will make water taxi trips between Bayfield and any of the islands.

For Kayaking, Trek & Trail Adventure Outfitters (800-354-8735; www.trek-trail.com), downtown, rents equipment from boats to paddles and wetsuits and does kayaking instruction and guided island tours. Adventures in Perspective, just north in Red Cliff (866-779-9503, www.living adventure.com) does guided island tours.

For sailboat rides, chartering boats, and fishing, a dozen operations will get you on the water. For a list, contact the Bayfield Chamber at the numbers above.

Other Stuff: Bayfield has an afternoon's worth of art galleries. My favorite is Stones Throw at the corner of Manypenny and Second Street. Golfers can fill several hours at the Apostle Highlands Golf Course (877-222-4053; www.golfbayfield.com) for an 18-hole, par-72 course. Nearby, visitors are welcome at fruit orchards and flower farms. Biking is scenic, with designated routes that run from just ten hilly miles through the orchards to twenty-five along the shore. Birding is great for eagles and other raptors, as well as many other sorts of birds during the spring migration. During the summer months, Big Top Chautauqua (888-244-8368; www. bigtop.org) presents live performances of historic musicals and well-known artists under a huge canvas tent.

Apostle Islands National Lakeshore

For just about anything you want to know about the islands, and for campsite reservations if you plan to kayak from island to island, stop at the Park Service's Visitors Center in the old Bayfield County Courthouse in Bayfield. Or contact the center at 715-779-3397; www.nps.gov/apis.

Madeline Island

The Madeline Ferry (715-747-2051; www.madferry.com) leaves about every hour from Bayfield and from La Pointe on Madeline Island during the spring, fall, and early winter. In summer, it runs on the half hour through the heart of the day. Yes, you can bring your car.

Lodging: The village of La Pointe and the island have some fifteen places to stay, ranging from cottages to bed-and-breakfasts to hotel rooms.

Dining: For breakfast, Ella's Island Café is casual and comfortable. Bar food for lunch or a snack is good at the Beach Club & Grill, which has a view of the water. For fine dining that could match most anything in Chicago, try Lotta's Lakeside Café. For an eating and drinking experience to write home about, stop by Tom's Burned Down Café. Tom's motto (or at least one of them) is "We cheat the other guy and pass the savings on to you."

Things to Do: Visit the very nifty Madeline Island Historical Museum (715-747-2415; www.madeline.wisconsinhistory.org), with well-designed displays that go from modern times back to the natives of the pre-European era on the island. Go for a ride on a sailboat, charter one, or go fishing. For a list of operations, check the Madeline Chamber contacts above. Take a two-hour island bus tour; call Madeline Island Bus Tours at 715-747-2051; www.madferry.com. Ride bikes or motorscooters around the island. Both can be rented in town. Kayaks can be rented in town at Apostle Island Kayaks (715-547-3636; www.apostleislandskayaks.com) or at Big Bay Town Park at Bog Lake Outfitters (715-747-2685; www.madelineisland.com/boglake), which also rents canoes. Hit the Scottish-style links course for eighteen holes at the Madeline Island Golf Club (715-747-3212; www.madelineislandgolf.com), designed by Trent Jones. Enjoy the long, sandy beach along Big Bay.

Information: For details on where to stay and other island information, contact the Madeline Island Chamber of Commerce at 888-475-3386; www.madelineisland.com.

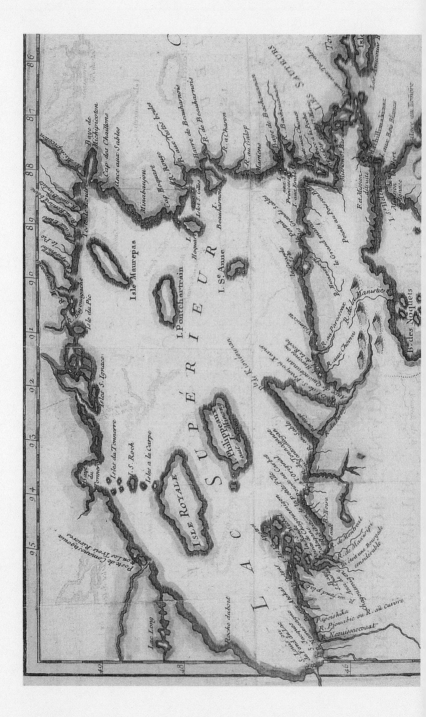

Phantom Islands

You can see them, right there on the map of Lake Superior—phantom islands.

Isle Phillipeaux sits between Isle Royale and the Keweenaw Peninsula. It's huge, almost as big as Isle Royale, and even has a couple of other little islands just to the west.

And over there in the eastern part of the lake are Isle Maurepas, Isle Pontchartrain, and Isle Ste. Anne. Also look close at what is now the Ontario shore and you'll find Isle Hocquart and Isle Beauharnois.

How could that be? These islands don't exist. Yet there they are on a map.

How could maps go so wrong? Robert Karow Jr. explored the question in his article "Lake Superior's Mythic Islands: A Cautionary Tale for Users of Old Maps," in *Michigan History* magazine, January–February 1986.

Early maps of the region can be traced back to a bit of political gamesmanship by an explorer-entrepreneur in the 1730s.

Louis Denys de La Ronde, a French naval captain, was in Montreal when he heard that certain islands in Lake Superior had huge copper deposits. So he made plans to get that copper, big plans. In La Ronde's vision of Lake Superior's future, his ships would carry his copper ore to Sault Ste. Marie, and then other ships that belonged to him would carry it down Lake

Opposite: *Islands that never existed are all over this map drawn in 1744, but every phony island was accepted as true because the map was made by Europe's best map maker, Jacques Bellin. As it turned out, Bellin was fooled by charts made by a Lake Superior explorer, Louis Denys de la Ronde, who simply drew in the ersatz islands and named them after politically powerful men in the French government. These made-up islands included Isle Pontchartrain, Isle Philippeaux, Isle Maurepas, and Isle St. Anne. Courtesy of Clements Library, University of Michigan.*

Huron and across Lake Erie to Niagara, where his barges would pick it up and carry it across Lake Ontario and down the St. Lawrence River to Montreal.

Such a grandiose scheme apparently came naturally to La Ronde. He had earned a reputation as a bit of a scalawag. Earlier in his career, he had been a privateer, basically a licensed pirate; he did a stint as a spy and was known as an enthusiastic self-promoter.

Even so, La Ronde managed to get funding for a scouting expedition to determine the copper mining potential in Lake Superior. So he built a boat on Lake Superior (a forty-ton ship, it was the lake's first sailing vessel) and in 1738 went prospecting with two German miners. Also—and not insignificantly—the government of New France at the same time gave La Ronde a nine-year free lease on the fur trade in Lake Superior. In an era when beaver pelts were like furry gold, such a lease was almost equivalent to being able to print your own francs.

On the prospecting trip, La Ronde found that mining copper was infeasible. But along the way he drew charts and likely a map. Here is where the phantom islands first appeared.

Why would La Ronde intentionally put bogus islands on a map?

At least one clue emerges when you examine the island names. Five of the six islands were named after people who were financially or politically important to La Ronde. He was indulging in a bit of geographic ego massage.

Beauharnois was the governor of New France. He gave La Ronde his first western post and supported his copper mining plans. Hocquart was the Intendant of Justice at Quebec and also La Ronde's friend. Phillipeaux, Maurepas, and Pontchartrain were all names of one man. He was the marine minister, La Ronde's superior officer, and the man who ultimately approved La Ronde's copper-mining venture. His name: Jean-Frederic Phelypaux, Comte de Maurepas et de Pontchartrain.

On his return to Montreal, copies of La Ronde's maps—complete with the fantasy islands—were sent to the archives at the Department of Marine in Paris.

Unfortunately Jacques Bellin, that era's greatest hydrographic surveyor, came upon La Ronde's maps in the archives. It was a sad circumstance. Bellin's reputation for map making was nearly flawless. He was the best. A trained engineer, Bellin always was scrupulous about his sources.

But as most mapmakers do, Bellin had to depend on maps made by others. He might have used a Lake Superior map produced by Jesuit priests in 1671, which when compared to today's maps is remarkably accurate. But Bellin wanted the latest information available—presuming it was the best. Unfortunately the latest on Superior was a figment of La Ronde's imagination.

So in 1744, Bellin produced an error-fraught map. And because he was one of the best, this map became the standard for the next seventy-five years.

Historians call the map drawn in 1755 by John Mitchell the most important map in American history. It was the principal map used by the British and American commissioners to write the peace treaty that ended the American Revolution. Then, in 1820, the boundary commissioners who were figuring the line between the United States and what is now Canada also relied on Mitchell's map, a map influenced by Bellin's and La Ronde's imagination.

Isle Royale

You know they are out there. At night, you have heard their voices. Yips and heartbreaking howls. At times, in the spring or after a rain when dirt on the trail has turned to mud, you have seen their tracks, incredibly large paw prints.

Yes, they are there. They could be watching us. For sure, they have caught our scent as we sweat up the steep, stony trails to the top of Greenstone Ridge or paddle across one of the island's backcountry lakes.

But we need not fear them. Here on Isle Royale, the gray wolves are like woodland ghosts. Their presence is felt, but they are almost never seen—at least not by people.

The moose, on the other hand, should be afraid, and are. For these two—wolf and moose—are the principal actors on the stage that is Isle Royale. They are predator and prey, antagonist and protagonist, the taunter and the taunted. Without both, life's play would have no plot, no tension. They live year by year in a delicate balance. They are what make this island wilderness truly wild.

Isle Royale is a rugged, bony-backed slash of evergreens and lava rock just off the north shore of Lake Superior's cerulean waters. The forty-five-mile-long island, some two hundred additional smaller islands, and the surrounding waters compose Isle Royale National Park, one of the least visited, hardest to reach, and most wondrous parks in the continental forty-eight states.

In any given season—the park is open only for about four months a year—fewer than 20,000 visitors will take the ferries there from either Michigan's Keweenaw Peninsula or from Grand Marais, Minnesota. For comparison's sake, that total is about equal to the number of visitors to Yellowstone National Park on a single summer day.

It's a shame. Because on Isle Royale one can find displayed, as on no other island, a full range of Great Lakes history—open pits left by ancient Indians in search of copper, old fishing shanties, four lighthouses, at least ten major wrecks of ships that foundered in Lake Superior's legendary storms, and the tunnels and debris left by nineteenth-century Cornish hard-rock miners.

And for visitors, wildlife viewing is as easy. Since almost no humans invade the island for eight months a year, the animals treat the place as if they—not we—own it. Moose wander unperturbed, often passing through campgrounds. Silky otters slide and scuttle along the shore. Snowshoe hares dart among the ferns. On the trail, bushy tailed foxes trot past you with all the calm of farm dogs.

In summertime, birders have spotted some 120 different species. In winter, this drops to about 20.

And the island can boast plants that are found almost nowhere else in the region. Robert Janke, Isle Royale's plant expert, has identified 800 different plants on the island. Among these are plants called disjuncts—because they are geographically distant from where they are normally found. Such plants include the spiky Devil's Club, normally found only in the far west, and the crowberry, a kind of stunted evergreen typical of the North American subarctic.

The Ancients: Strawberries and Spear Points

The Indians called Isle Royale "Minong." The word means island or "place where there are good berries."

So clearly, wild strawberries, blueberries, and thimbleberries were part of the attraction that lured the ancients, who had to paddle fifteen miles of dangerous waters from the mainland. But there was more. Good hunting. The island historically had deer, beavers, mink, otters, and perhaps moose. Good fishing for whitefish, lake trout, and sturgeon.

But the biggest reason may have been copper. According to research findings, native people have come to Isle Royale to mine copper for 4,500 years.

Long before the Europeans came with knives and hatchets made of steel, the native people learned to make weapons, tools, and jewelry of copper. The metal could be easily molded. And what's more, the copper weapons lasted longer than those fashioned of stone.

To this day, you can find shallow open pits dug by the native miners. They would use hard stones they found on the beach to hammer loose the precious metal from the surrounding rock. Researchers have discovered that, like the white miners who came later, the Indians would burn away the plants and mosses on top of the rocks to find the ore beneath. When faced with stubborn rock, they would crack it open by setting

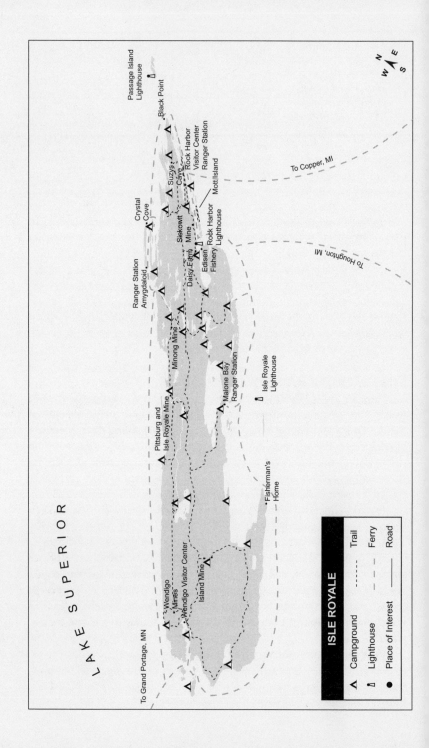

LAKE SUPERIOR

ISLE ROYALE

Campground ⋀
Lighthouse
Place of Interest ●

Trail
Ferry
Road

To Grand Portage, MN

Wendigo
Mines
Wendigo Visitor Center
Island Mine

Pittsburg and
Isle Royale Mine
Minong Mine

Ranger Station
Amygdaloid

Crystal
Cove

Suzy's
Cave
Rock Harbor
Visitor Center
Ranger Station
Mott Island

Siskowit
Mine
Daisy Farm
Edisen
Fishery
Rock Harbor
Lighthouse

Malone Bay
Ranger Station

Isle Royale
Lighthouse

Fisherman's
Home

Passage Island
Lighthouse

Black Point

To Copper, MI

To Houghton, MI

N
W ⋀ E
S

The Ranger III, *a 165-foot, 126-passenger ferry mutters into Isle Royale's Rock Harbor after a six-hour passage from Houghton, Michigan.*

fires, heating the rocks to very high temperature, and then throwing on cold water.

How did they actually find the copper?

Susan R. Martin, in her book *Wonderful Power,* explains that these astute observers of nature noticed the pink veins of copper in the rock, or saw that when hoarfrost formed on plant life in the fall, it did not show up where copper veins were below. The veins gave off heat. Other giveaways were discolored vegetation and stunted trees.

Lady Superior Has Her Way

In important ways, Isle Royale can only be understood by having a sense of where it is—in the midst of the world's largest lake. Lake Superior has been called "The Lady." And at times she can be ladylike indeed. Her sweetness is supreme on summer evenings when the wind is still and a canoe paddle slips through the water like a spoon through cream. But she also can be cantankerous and a heartless killer.

Her profile must be drawn in superlatives—biggest, deepest, cleanest, coldest, and arguably the most dangerous of the Great Lakes. She also can show a magic rarely seen elsewhere.

Three hundred and fifty miles long, 160 miles wide, Lake Superior spreads over 31,700 square miles. This area is bigger than twelve of our states. Stretched end to end, the 2,726-mile shoreline is nearly long enough to reach across the country. Its greatest depth is 1,332 feet. When you put that all together, the lake bed can hold 3,000,000,000,000,000 gallons of water, enough to cover both North and South America with one foot of water.

And the water is cold, very cold. The average temperature is 39 degrees. A person who falls overboard will lapse into unconsciousness in ten minutes. As a sailboat captain told me in Thunder Bay, Ontario, "On Lake Superior, we use life jackets so you can find the body."

Researchers say the lake environment is unusual because it is an extension of subarctic conditions to a southerly extreme. So it's no surprise that subarctic plants actually live here.

Lake Superior also is a place of rare—and to early man often unexplainable—phenomena. It has waterspouts. And its seiches (something also seen in Lake Erie) can be dumbfounding. A seiche occurs when heavy winds force the lake's water to drop suddenly at one end of the lake, leaving anchored boats wallowing in the mud, while at the opposite end of the lake, suddenly rising waters flood over sea walls and wash away docks.

Northern lights come swirling in at night. And during the day, people have seen unimaginable things. In fogs, the island seems to float. And people have seen mirages caused by differences between air and water temperatures. Headlands seem to project from land where none exist. Mountains are turned upside down, with their sharp tops pointed downward toward the water and not up as they should be. And islands can appear to rise up and then disappear.

What's more, Lake Superior has a well-earned reputation as a killer. Over the years, its rap sheet includes some 700 ships, including the famed *Edmund Fitzgerald* that went down on November 10, 1975. Isle Royale has claimed ten major wrecks and countless smaller ones.

On a personal note, I came closer than I would have liked to becoming one of the countless dead claimed by Lake Superior while researching this book. One early September day, I was paddling with a friend around Blake Point at the island's far northeast end. This is open water and catches the full brunt of lake-driven waves. Despite furious paddling, our canoe swamped in a four-foot sea. Getting ashore would not be easy. We faced wave-battered rocks and cliffs known as the Palisades. My friend made it to a rocky outcrop fairly quickly, although battered and scared. I was slower, trying to swim through the waves while pulling an upside-down canoe and hanging onto pieces of floating gear. We survived partly because the late summer day was sunny and relatively warm, and the water temperature had risen to the low 50s. I certainly did not make it to the rocks in ten minutes—the cutoff point for unconsciousness in colder water. We emptied the canoe of water, and I ventured out into the waves twice more to retrieve whatever gear was still floating. On the first of those forays, the canoe flipped again, and once more I had to swim back pulling the canoe.

After we spread out our clothes and gear to dry on the rocks, and when I stopped shaking, I climbed up a cliff for a view of the still churning lake. Not far away, I spotted a buoy. It was only later that I learned the buoy marked the spot where the 140-foot steamer *Monarch* went down on December 6, 1906. Our canoe was just a footnote on the Blake Point rap sheet.

The worst shipwreck off Isle Royale came on November 7, 1885, when the 262-foot steamship *Algoma* got caught in a gale just off Mott Island. Lashed by rain, sleet, and snow, the ship ran aground. Huge waves lifted the ship again and again, each time dropping it onto the rocks. After two hours of this pounding, the steel ship finally broke in two. Three crew members were able to swim to shore, and later a few of those on board got to land in a raft. But the death toll was the worst in the island's history. Of forty-five crew and passengers, only fourteen survived. Local fishermen rescued the survivors a day later.

Four Lighthouses, One Young Ghost

As it did all around the Great Lakes, the government built lighthouses to protect shipping. Isle Royale has four. One—the one seen by visitors as they ride the ferry into Rock Harbor—is the Rock Harbor Lighthouse. It is the island's oldest, built in 1855. Sometimes called "The Old Light," it served for twenty-two years and now has a small museum inside.

The Passage Island Lighthouse, built in 1882, is three and a half miles off Blake Point, at the island's northeast end. Rock of Ages Lighthouse, built in 1908, stands about three miles west of Washington Island at Isle Royale's far southwest end. And Isle Royale Lighthouse, built in 1875, is on Menagerie Island, about three miles offshore to the south about halfway down the length of Isle Royale.

John Malone was the second keeper at the Isle Royale light. He lived there with his wife and thirteen children. They were famous for collecting and eating vast numbers of seagull eggs, which are supposed to taste vile. Sadly, one day one of the Malones' sons slipped on some rocks and died. The story goes that from time to time the boy's ghost still appears.

A U.S. Island?

When you look at a map of Lake Superior, it does not seem logical that Isle Royale would be a part of the United States. And it's perhaps even odder that the island is a part of Michigan.

After all, Isle Royale sits within fifteen or so miles from the Ontario shore. Shouldn't it logically be a Canadian island? Or, if not that, at least a part of nearby Minnesota? Michigan's Upper Peninsula lies far to the south.

A couple of stories have made the rounds. One is that the wily diplomat Benjamin Franklin had heard that the island was rich in copper. So at the 1783 treaty negotiations following the Revolutionary War, he insisted that the border be drawn north of the island. The other story is that the odd borderline was simply a mapmaker's error.

As for how the island ended up as part of Michigan, it seems that in 1837, Michigan territory became the first in the Great Lakes region to be admitted to the union as a state.

Rock Harbor Lighthouse is the most photographed structure on Isle Royale. Sometimes called "The Old Light," it is the oldest of the island's four lighthouses, built in 1855. It now houses a small museum.

Furs and Fish

As on many islands in the Great Lakes, Isle Royale's first Europeans were fur traders and trappers. Beaver pelts were almost the equivalent of gold for more than two centuries, as voyageurs in North America supplied the basic needs of hatters and furriers in Europe.

But by the early 1800s, the island's beaver had been trapped to near extinction.

So over the years, fishing has proved to be the most enduring commercial enterprise on Isle Royale. The Indians, of course, were the first to fish. The Northwest Fur Company sent fishermen along the north shore in the early 1800s. Between 1837 and 1839, John Jacob Astor's American Fur Company set up seven camps around the island. The company eventually folded in 1841, but individual fishermen continued the tradition. They usually stayed in cabins on the island except for winter months, when they returned to ports like La Pointe and Bayfield in Wisconsin so their children could go to school.

Commercial fishing on the island reached its height in the 1880s, with some thirty fishing camps scattered about. While the fishermen hung on as best they could, it was a fading lifestyle that finally died in the middle of the twentieth century. Ultimately the fishermen were done in by a variety of factors including periodic drops in fish prices, vanishing fish stocks, and the arrival of the lamprey eels in the 1940s and early 1950s, which decimated the stocks of lake trout and whitefish.

Visitors can get a sense of a fisherman's life by stopping by the old Edisen fishery with its cabin, docks, and old net dryers. It is near the Rock Harbor Lighthouse. In fact, you can walk a woodland trail between the two.

Copper Hopes

Of course, it's not as precious as gold. But copper is valuable stuff, as Larry Lankton points out in his book *Cradle to Grave*. In the 1800s, people used it as roofing on buildings and as a protective covering for wooden ships. Copper went into pots and pans. It was alloyed with zinc to make brass and with tin to make bronze. Copper also went into weapons, buttons, hardware, decorations, and even candlesticks.

Early mining engineers hoped that Isle Royale might produce as much copper as Michigan's Keweenaw Peninsula, which was the world's biggest copper find. And yes, the island did produce some, but never in the quantities hoped for.

Basically miners tried to pull copper from Isle Royale's rocks during three separate periods in the nineteenth century. Evidence of their work is scattered across the island—ore pits, tunnels, housing plots, slag piles, and even bits of machinery, although most are gone. Virtually every one of today's island campsites was once a mining site.

Miners on Isle Royale were a lot like miners in the rest of America, or anywhere else in the world for that matter. They often rushed in before it was completely legal.

Ownership of the island first had to be wrested from the Chippewa Indians. That did not happen until the Treaty of 1844. But miners hit the island the year before and would stay until 1855. They never got much copper.

Two of the largest operations were within walking distance of present-day Rock Harbor Lodge. One, the Smithson Mine, now basically a hole in the ground with a fence around it, is just fifteen minutes up the Stoll Trail. The other mine is the Siskowit Mine (siskiwit, the usual spelling, is an Indian name for a big lake trout). The old site has tunnels, mounds, trenches,

The Edisen fishery in this photo taken about 1900 differs very little from the fishery where the National Park Service offers a demonstration.

241

Commercial fisherman Pete Edisen, as he did most days, docked his boat and proceeded to clean his catch outside the fishhouse that was just around the bend from the Rock Harbor Lighthouse. Edisen was one of the last commercial fishermen on the island. He and his wife, Laura, lived on the island and fished for nearly 60 years until the 1970s. Today, visitors can still visit the fishery for a demonstration of what a fisherman's life was like in that era. Courtesy of the National Park Service, Isle Royale National Park.

and other artifacts. It can be found off the Rock Harbor Trail between the Three Mile and Daisy Farm campgrounds.

Samuel W. Hill came to Isle Royale and worked as an engineer, surveyor, and superintendent for a number of mining operations. Inner and Outer Hill Islands were named for him. Hill was more than competent, but more than anything else he was famous for having one of the foulest mouths in the Great Lakes. It is said that his garbage mouth was honored, if that's the right word, with the expression "What the Sam Hill!"

During this first period, miners pulled about a hundred tons of refined copper out of holes in Isle Royale. It was hard, brutal work, and the conditions were lousy. Workers wrote of being attacked by so many black flies and mosquitoes that their eyes were swollen shut.

The second rush for copper ran from 1873 to 1881, after copper prices were pushed up by the Civil War. Two relatively large operations were set up on the island. The biggest was the Minong Mine at McCargoe Cove on the island's north side. At the height of its operation, some 150 miners dug two deep shafts and a number of open pits. The men came with their families, so a small town developed with a blacksmith shop, a stamp mill, a dock, and railroad tracks. The second large operation was Indian Mine, in the south central part of the island, inland from Siskiwit Bay. It too developed into a small town.

The last foray for copper was undertaken between 1889 and 1893 at the south end of the island in the area around Windigo, the Indian name for a monster. Even using diamond bit drills, the Wendigo Mine never amounted to much.

Charlie Mott's Last Stand

In 1843 (before the treaty was signed), the Union Company hired Charlie Mott and his Indian wife, Angelique, to spend the winter as caretakers for a mining property.

Cyrus Mendenhall, the mine boss, dropped them off in July on what is now called Mott Island. Mendenhall promised to send supplies soon. They waited, but the supplies never showed up. Basically, Mendenhall had abandoned the couple. Angelique later remembered that all they had to eat was half a barrel of flour, some rancid butter, and some beans.

The Motts did have a canoe. So at first they made do with fishing. But a late summer storm wrecked the canoe, and soon their fish net was too broken to use.

Then winter came. The ground froze solid. They no longer could dig for roots. To survive, they ate bark and a few berries left from pickings in the fall. By Christmas Day, the flour, the butter, and the beans were a memory. Then Charlie died, leaving Angelique with some very big problems. Not only did she need to figure out how to survive alone, but there was a dead man lying in the house. Burying him was out of the question. The ground was too frozen. She stayed with him there in the cabin for three days without lighting a fire. She was afraid he "would spoil." Eventually Angelique solved the dead-body problem by building a second shack and moving in.

She admitted later that she was so hungry that at times she was tempted to carve off a piece of Charlie. But she resisted. Then she saw tracks of snowshoe hares around their cabin. They could be dinner, but she had to catch them first. So cleverly she fashioned snares out of her own hair. The rabbit meat kept her alive. In March, she found and repaired an old canoe and started fishing again.

Finally, in May, a boat showed up. Mendenhall was aboard. According

Windigo, now home for the Park Service at the far west end of Isle Royale, was a company mining town for two years starting in 1890. The town, called Ghyllbank, was the headquarters for the Wendigo Copper Company and had a population of 135 when this picture was taken in 1892. Courtesy of National Park Service, Isle Royale National Park.

to Napier Sheldon in *Superior Wilderness,* quoting Angelique, Mendenhall "said that he had sent off a bateau with provisions. But," she added, "the boys told me it was all a lie."

Fishing, Dining, Critter Watching. And Golf?

Tourists started coming to Isle Royale in the twentieth century. Some built fishing cabins; others came to hike. And still others found a bit of luxury in actual resorts. Lodges were built at Rock Harbor and Tobin Harbor, where the National Park Service now runs its lodges. The Washington Club was built at Windigo. And the Singer Club, complete with a bowling alley and a dance hall, started up operation on Washington Island.

Off the north side of the island, the Belle Harbor Lodge was built on Belle Isle in 1915. It had the only swimming pool in the islands, a first-class dining room, courts for shuffleboard, and a nine-hole pitch-and-putt golf course.

But then efforts materialized to turn Isle Royale into a national park. In 1940, Isle Royale National Park was officially established. It was dedicated, following World War II, in 1946.

Now, although a few cottagers remain, the park is basically open to visitors, who typically stay about four days. Ferries run from Michigan's Keweenaw Peninsula from early June to early September. Ferries from Grand Portage, Minnesota, run a slightly longer season. Lodging, other than your own tent, is available at Rock Harbor from early June through early September.

The Wolves Who Came to Dinner

One of the ongoing fascinations for people coming to Isle Royale is the wolf-moose study being conducted by Rolf Peterson, of the Michigan Technological University in Houghton.

For Peterson, Isle Royale is a hermetically sealed test tube for studying these two creatures that live in a delicate balance on the island.

The research, begun in 1958 by Peterson's predecessor Durward Allen in 1958, is the world's longest-running wolf study. It also is the world's most important, according to Doug Smith, who heads the wolf project at Yellowstone National Park.

Over the years, the islands have seen animals come and go. At one time, Isle Royale had lynxes, caribou, and white-tailed deer. All are gone now. Coyotes used to live on the island, but they could not survive competition with the wolves.

Both moose and wolves are relative latecomers to Isle Royale. The first moose showed up about 1910. Peterson believes they swam over from the mainland. Moose are good swimmers. They can swim as far as 12 miles in two hours. As for the wolves, they came in the late 1940s, walking across the winter ice. Basically the wolves came for dinner, moose meat dinner. And they stayed. Peterson says that the nearly thirty wolves now living on the island, hunting in three separate packs, are all descendants of a single female.

The lives of Isle Royale wolves and moose are intricately linked, and they seem to run in twenty-year cycles. When the moose population trends up, the wolf population tends to drop, and then over the next twenty years the situation is reversed.

For most backpackers and campers, though, just having the wolves on the island is quite special. The campers are safe. The island wolves are deathly afraid of humans.

So it's easy to lie back on a cool evening, pick out the constellations in a dark sky, and, if you are lucky, hear the yip and howl of the gray wolves.

If You Go

Getting There: Four ferries sail to Isle Royale. All can carry passengers, gear, and, for an extra fee, fishing boats, kayaks, and canoes. No bikes, no cars, no pets.

From Michigan: The 126-passenger, 165-foot *Ranger III*, gives the smoothest cross-lake rides. It makes the six-and-a-half-hour crossing from Houghton to Isle Royale's Rock Harbor on Tuesdays and Fridays, and makes the return trip on Saturdays and Wednesdays. Contact Isle Royale National Park at 906-482-0984; www.nps.gov/isro.

The 100-passenger, 81-foot *Isle Royale Queen III*, noted as a rough ride in sour weather, does round trips in a single day. It makes a four-and-a-half-hour crossing between Copper Harbor at the tip of the Keweenaw Peninsula and Rock Harbor, running variously on five-, six-, and seven-day-a-week schedules that change during the summer. Contact the Isle Royale Line at 906-289-4437; www.isleroyale.com.

From Grand Portage, Minnesota: The 149-passenger, 63-foot *Wenonah* makes daily round trips to Windigo at Isle Royale's southwest end. It's three hours one way.

The forty-eight passenger, sixty-foot *Voyageur II* makes a one-and-three-quarter-hour trip to Windigo and goes on for another six hours to Rock Harbor on Mondays, Wednesdays, and Saturdays. It makes the return trip from Rock Harbor on Tuesdays, Thursdays, and Sundays, in the process circumnavigating the island. Contact either Grand Portage ferry at 715-392-2100; www.grand-isle-royale.com.

Also, a seaplane service is available from Houghton. Contact Royale Air Service, Inc., at 877-359-4753.

Transportation: Isle Royale is designed for human power. You walk or

In early June, this moose cow wandered out of the trees. Over the winter, she had rubbed off much of her fur trying to get rid of blood-sucking winter ticks.

you paddle. Also, some may wish to rent or bring motorboats. Rock Harbor Lodge does have a water taxi service that will drop off or pick up campers at various spots on the island. Contact Rock Harbor Lodge at 906-337-4993 from May to September and 270-773-2191 during the rest of the year. The *Voyageur II* (see above) will drop off and pick up as it makes its thrice-weekly circumnavigation of the island. Rock Harbor Lodge runs sightseeing tours on the *M.V. Sandy* to various points of interest on the island.

Lodging: Most visitors—the backpackers and paddlers—stay at organized campsites throughout the island. All have slant-roofed, screened-in shelters that will keep you dry and away from the mosquitoes. It's first come, first served. You should not travel without a tent. Isle Royale can get very cold at night, even in the summer, and the shelters do not hold the heat. Many campers have been known to set up a free-standing tent *inside* the shelter, just for the warmth. The campsites also have outhouses (with toilet paper), picnic tables, and specified places for campfires.

The park charges a small daily backcountry fee for campers.

For noncampers, the Rock Harbor Lodge offers simple lodge rooms and housekeeping cabins. Contact Rock Harbor Lodge at 906-337-4993 from May to September and 270-773-2191 during the rest of the year.

When: Isle Royale can be beautiful any time of year. But the beginning and end of the season in late May and early June and in September are particularly wonderful. The number of visitors is low; the temperatures are cool for hiking and paddling; and you'll hardly notice the bugs.

Dining: Not only do you bring your own food, you bring your own stove and your own pump filter to make sure the water is safe. And you do your own dishes. Whatever garbage you accumulate along the way, you must pack out. Use sand to wash your dishes or biodegradable soap, and not much of that. Do not leave food out where animals can get it. Isle Royale foxes are notorious for raiding campsites. You also can eat at the Lodge or at the snack bar. Remember to drink lots of fluids. Dehydration can be a serious problem.

Buying and Renting Stuff: Park stores are located at Rock Harbor and Windigo. There you'll find replacements for many of the camp supplies you forgot, including gas for camp stoves, snacks, a small selection of freeze-dried meals, aspirin, and some souvenirs.

Fishing boats with motors, canoes, and kayaks can be rented at Rock Harbor Lodge. Call 906-337-4993 from May to September and 270-773-2191 during the rest of the year.

Clothes: Dress for the season and keep in mind that you are in the middle of a very, very cold lake. Midsummer nights can be pleasant. But temperatures can drop at any time of year. Dressing in layers is a good idea. Bring a hat and a waterproof jacket for the sun and rain. If you are camping toward the beginning or end of the season, gloves can be a good idea. Wear sunscreen.

Fishing: Fishing can be good both offshore and on the inland lakes. Unless you are under age seventeen, you will need a Michigan fishing license. It's a good idea to get one before you come to the island. For details, check www.michigan.gov/dnr. For information on the fishing seasons and catch limits, contact Isle Royale National Park at 906-482-0984; www.nps.gov/isro/.

Bugs: Yes, Isle Royale has bugs. Mosquitoes and black flies. In the heart of the summer, they're hard to avoid. Be sure to slather on something with DEET, especially in the evenings and early mornings. Some people have used hats with netting. At night, do not open your tent's mosquito netting with a light on inside. That's just asking for a night of misery.

Guidebook and Map: The best single guidebook is *Isle Royale National Park: Foot Trails & Water Routes,* by Jim DuFresne (Mountaineers Books). The most useful map is the *Isle Royale National Park, Trails Illustrated* map (National Geographic). It is waterproof and tear resistant. Both can be picked up at the Visitors Center in Houghton and at the Rock Harbor gift shop.

Information: Contact Isle Royale National Park at 906-482-0984; www.nps.gov/isro. For Isle Royale weather forecasts, check: www.crh.noaa/mqt in Michigan or www.crh.noaa.gov/dlh in Minnesota.

A Day with Rolf Peterson

The morning air is tart, typical of early June on Isle Royale. The sun spills copper over the evergreens and starts to warm your hair. But still we feel the light-talon touch of every breeze off Lake Superior's gun-metal blue waters.

Fitted out in Gore-Tex and waffle-soled hiking boots, our sinewy-thighed little group is heading out into the backcountry on what many might consider an odd, even ghoulish mission.

We'll be searching for the carcass of a dead moose. If and when we find the moose, its bones will become part of a famous, half-century-long study of the wolves and moose of Isle Royale. Our leader is Rolf Peterson, who for thirty-five years has directed this Isle Royale study. A lean, soft-spoken man with a quick chuckle, Peterson not only is a world expert on wolves and moose, but quite simply knows more about Isle Royale than any other living person.

Our moose carcass search group is composed of a half dozen middle-aged but trail-toughened Earthwatch volunteers who will spend the next week tromping along rocky ridges and through heavy timber in search of moose bones. Also hiking with us are two twenty-ish chatty college coeds who are Peterson's summer research assistants. Candy, Rolf's cheerful and outgoing wife, walks at the back of the line to sweep along any slowpokes.

The hunt will take us from the shoreline at a campground called Daisy Farm, past the remnants of an old copper mine, then up a steep, conifer-shaded trail toward the 1,400-foot-high Greenstone Ridge. This ridge is, in effect, a stony backbone that stretches the length of the forty-five mile-long island.

Isle Royale, the main island, and some 200 adjacent islands are all part of Isle Royale National Park, one of the nation's most stunning and—because of its isolation—least visited national parks in the forty-eight contiguous states.

Rolf Peterson, an internationally recognized expert on wolves and moose, points out details on a moose carcass to a group of Earthwatch volunteers who are helping him gather data for the world's longest, on-going wolf-moose research project on Isle Royale.

Peterson knows approximately where the dead moose should be. Each winter, he does seven weeks of research on the island. That's the only time of year when he actually can watch the wolves, almost always from a low-flying airplane. Last February, he spotted this moose and the blood-spattered snow, a clear sign of a wolf kill.

Wolves and moose of Isle Royale live in an intricate interdependence. Moose are the mainstay of the wolf diet. So basically moose survival means wolf survival. But the island's trees, shrubs, and water plants can support only so many moose. So it's helpful that the wolves keep the number of moose in check, killing off the old, the weak, and the calves.

Peterson explains that moose bones can tell a lot of secrets. They can show the moose's age, injuries, insect infestation, and how it died. In certain years starvation is common; wolf attacks are more rare. Most common of all is death from diseases familiar to many older Americans—osteoporosis, periodontal disease, or hip arthritis.

Perhaps most astounding is that moose teeth and bones can act like monitors of what's going on in Washington, D.C., and other faraway places. For example, carbon-14 has shown up in the teeth of Isle Royale moose. Why? Matter from atomic tests conducted in the 1950s and 1960s in New Mexico, on Pacific Islands, and in Russia has reached even this lonely island in Lake Superior. But there's good news. The carbon-14 levels have been dropping since the nuclear test ban treaty in 1963. Lead, too, shows up in the bones. But those levels too have been dropping since the United States and Canada mandated unleaded gas at the pumps in 1975. And scientists have also found mercury. But Peterson's research has revealed that it too has gone into decline. The reason: air pollution controls enacted in the 1970s.

As talk turns to the wolf packs' movements on the island, Peterson's dry, self-deprecating humor emerges. He has a keen sense of life's absurdities, even when the absurdities are his own.

He starts a sentence saying: "And the wolves do this because they think . . ." And then he stops and chuckles. He finds his own words laughable. "Well," he grins, "who really knows what a wolf thinks?"

Nobody, of course. Many of the mysteries about wolves are still mysteries. But if any human did know or could know, it would probably be Rolf Peterson. He has dedicated his entire professional life to the patient and meticulous study of this island's wolves and moose. He also has been a consultant to most of the world's important wolf studies, in Yellowstone Park, Alaska, and other places.

"Rolf is doing some of the most important wolf research in the world," says Doug Smith, a former student of Peterson's and head of the Wolf Project at Yellowstone National Park.

"The best science is long-term science." Smith says. "The Isle Royale study began in 1958, under Peterson's predecessor, Durward Allen. No other has gone on for so long."

Speaking of wolves, Peterson can spin out some amazing facts. While their eyesight is poor, wolves have an astounding sense of smell. And their endurance is incomparable.

Wolves, walking over a piece of ground, can tell by smell alone that another wolf came that way hours before—and which wolf it was. Moose can be pretty stinky. But a wolf can smell one a full mile away. Wolves also can find the carcass of a dead moose even when it's under more than a foot of snow.

On the other hand, Peterson chuckles, at a point when you might think their super-sensitive noses would send them reeling, "they will also eat a moose that has been dead so long that the stench would drive most people away."

As for physical endurance, Peterson says wolves are ultramarathoners. "They have been known to travel a hundred miles overnight apparently just for the heck of it. And they do this on a routine basis."

Peterson tells of endurance of a different sort with the story of a female wolf that was attacked in mid-February by the island's Middle Pack. She was a stranger. So the eleven-member pack savaged her again and again. They snapped at her throat and her hindquarters, taking off big pieces and driving her into the freezing lake. Peterson, who had been watching from a circling airplane, said she looked dead by the time the pack finally stalked away.

But then one wolf from the Middle Pack came back to her. He had a different idea in mind. The female was in heat. Essentially the male looked after her, even licked her wounds. Five days later, this female wolf that had looked dead now seemed to be recovering.

Peterson, who has yet to get absolute DNA evidence to prove it, believes that this battered female and the attentive male bred offspring that started a brand new pack on the island, known now as the Chippewa Harbor Pack.

The Man and His Island

Peterson, while his fame is connected to wolves and moose, is also the go-to guy on almost every living thing on Isle Royale, including beavers, loons, otters, foxes, snowshoe hares, red squirrels, green frogs, winter ticks, balsam fir trees, and the increasingly powerful impact of global warming.

But Peterson is no posturing braggart. Everyone who knows or ever has met Peterson speaks of his calm, gentle nature. Few, if any at all, have ever heard him even raise his voice. He never even interrupts another's sentence—even if the sentence is ridiculous. Candy says he has some sort of "gene" that makes him calm and gentle. Smith describes him as "egoless."

It should be said, however, that Peterson will speak a truth even if it is self-flattering. "No one," he has said, "knows Isle Royale better than I do." That's not ego talking, that's simple truth.

The island is his passion and, in many ways, his very identity. And he is not alone in his love of the island; almost from the beginning, Peterson's whole family has joined in his passion. In fact, he and Candy first met on the island during their college years.

And now each spring, as she has done for three and a half decades, Candy joins Peterson when he abandons his professor's desk at Michigan Technological University in Houghton and moves lock, stock, and hiking boots to live for three to six months in an age-old fisherman's shack on a spit of land not far from the Rock Harbor Lighthouse.

Accompanied by several outbuildings, their home is remarkable for the more than one hundred moose skulls he has displayed on benches behind the cabin. It sounds eerie, but really most people who see them feel a remarkable sense of peace, almost like the experience of stepping into a Japanese garden.

Many people are surprised that the Petersons managed to raise their two sons, Jeremy and Trevor, in this primitive cabin, far from what many Americans consider necessities—SUVs, television sitcoms, daily newspapers, CD players, 7-Elevens, café lattes, and flush toilets. And the Petersons did not wait around until their kids got older. Candy brought their second son, Trevor, to the island when he was only two weeks old.

Island of Fascinations, Great and Small

As we hike up toward Greenstone Ridge, I can see Peterson's tan baseball cap ahead. Up, up it goes, angling through the dark cedars, past a tea-colored stream where marsh marigolds nod like brilliant bobbleheads. It's spring. Rains have been heavy. So the usually hard-packed trails often sog up, sometimes turning into running stream beds. The toes of our boots turn black in the oozy muck. Soon we top a small ridge, leave the evergreens behind, and strike out into a sun-broiled leafy valley. The tan cap moves on, ever upward toward the high paleness of Greenstone's rocky ledges. He stops periodically. And as the laggards catch up, he points out bits of interest.

On a wooden walkway that bridges a swamp, Peterson notices a tiny green frog. It is so minuscule and motionless that I could hardly find it even when he pointed it out with a stick. For him, animal and plant signs seem as big as billboards. Over there is a pitcher plant. It's a carnivore, a meat-eating plant. It traps bugs, digests them in its gullet. And this is skunk cabbage, which can smell like its name, but its flowers in early spring emit heat and can melt away snow. And over there is the barely visible trail of a snowshoe hare. The dense swamp foliage protects them from owls.

We press on—Peterson floating, the rest of us plodding—mounting the stony flank of the ridge. Then, at a spot Peterson recognizes, we leave the trail and begin a lateral trip across the slope.

After a few hundred yards, Peterson thinks we may be nearing the carcass. The volunteers go into their bone-search formation. They create a loose line, standing ten to fifteen yards apart, and then sweep laterally along the rocky, brush-strewn slope. They carefully look both right and left, like so many police searching a field for missing evidence.

Three or four groups of Earthwatch volunteers have come to Isle Royale to help Peterson by hunting for moose bones every summer for the past sixteen years. Each one spends a week in the field, searching by day and camping at night.

Neither the moose whose bones they seek nor the wolves were among the island's original natives.

The moose first showed up about 1910. Peterson believes they swam from the mainland. But some old-timers think the moose may have been brought in by boat, perhaps for hunting. The wolves did not show up on Isle Royale until the late 1940s. Researchers believe they came in winter, walking across the ice from the mainland. Peterson says that all the wolves on the island today are descendants of a single female.

As of the winter of 2005, thirty wolves lived on the island in three packs—East, Middle, and Chippewa Harbor. Their numbers have been as high as fifty and as low as twelve. A near record low of 540 moose live on the island. There have been as many as 2,400.

What is the future for the wolves? Peterson can only guess.

Some scientists have speculated that the island wolves will die out because of inbreeding. Male wolves are breeding with mothers, sisters, aunts, and cousins. They have perhaps only 50 percent of the genetic variability of mainland wolves.

"If you believe scientific papers, they have no future," Peterson says. "But," he adds with a chuckle, "wolves don't read scientific papers." He says that so far the only physical difference scientists have found between gray wolves on the island and those on the mainland is that a few island wolves have two extra vertebrae, which have not bothered them much.

However the future for the moose is more problematic in some long-term ways.

Moose—animals that eat for twelve hours each day—are finding less and less forage on Isle Royale. Their favorite foods are leafy trees like aspen, mountain ash, and hazelnut, although the hazelnut is almost too twiggy to be chewed by their big mouths.

A couple of major fires, one in the 1850s and another in the 1930s, cleared out enough of the island's evergreens for these first-growth leafy trees to fill in. But steadily the evergreens—spruces and cedars—are taking over. Peterson says 75 percent or more of the moose's prime food in winter now is gone.

"Isle Royale," he says, "is not a great place food-wise for moose."

The island moose, Peterson says, try to make do by eating things that many mainland moose might not even consider. The mainstay of their diet is balsam fir, which is hard to digest. But even that is disappearing on three-quarters of the island. And when food gets really scarce in winter, they eat lichens off the trees.

And that's not all.

Global Warming and Moose

Peterson explains that global warming is now victimizing the island moose. The warm days in fall are running later and later, and spring's melt-off comes sooner. Moose do not do well in heat. They have dark fur, and, like dogs, they don't sweat. And unlike dogs they do not pant. As a result, people in summertime often see them wading in the water to stay cool.

But worse, they suffer from winter ticks. The ticks jump onto the moose from fall foliage, and each one sucks out about one cubic centimeter of blood. That may not seem like much, but a single moose might have 20,000 to 30,000 ticks. They can drain as much as five *gallons* of blood. What's more, they are taking that blood when the moose can least afford to spare it, in winter when food is scarce.

Moose try to scrape off the ticks. They rub against trees and bushes. Peterson estimates they may spend two hours a day "grooming." This is wasted time when the moose should be eating to survive. What's more, the scraping wears away protective hair, leaving many with huge bald spots come spring.

The problem of global warming kicks in when spring arrives. That's when the ticks finally jump off the moose to lay new eggs. If they jump onto snow, they die. But with today's ever-warmer springs, the ticks now tend to land on dry ground—perfect for egg laying. That means the moose must suffer even more ticks the following winter.

Moose numbers are down dramatically, and the future does not look good.

Over the years, Peterson's research equipment has improved. He started with a ten-key calculator, but now he can take advantage of such innovations as radio collars, DNA studies, and computers to speed analysis. But still, much of the research still means doing basic legwork. That usually means hiking for long hours, picking up animal scat, and, as in today's project, searching for the carcass of a dead moose.

A Shout: "Bones!"

Out on the shoulder of Greenstone Ridge, a shout goes up. "Bones." Success! One of the volunteers has found a moose jawbone. Peterson arrives and begins a careful examination of the teeth.

The volunteers start a sweep around the jawbone location, moving in wider and wider circles. Another shout comes within minutes. "Bones. Lots of bones." The shout has come from back in the brush, where a volunteer has discovered a rib cage, backbone, skull, legs, and hooves. The wolves have even chewed away the ends of the bones. They needed the calcium. Later, we'd find the spot just up the hill where the wolves had devoured the innards, eating everything but the fur.

Like a sylvan Sherlock Holmes, Peterson quickly notes that this moose was elderly and well fed, but walked with a limp. How did he know? The teeth were worn down, indicating an age of about twelve years. The bone marrow had lots of fat, so the animal did not starve to death. As for the limp, Peterson noted that the right rear hoof was not as worn down as the left.

Volunteers wrap the bones in plastic and strap them to a backpack. Their week of searching has just begun.

Peterson, Candy, and the two interns will head back to the cabin. As we walk, I ask Peterson about a career so connected to death—bone hunting, searching for dead bodies, the daily battle for survival by the wolves and moose, a backyard filled with skulls. How does it affect him?

"Well," he says, in his practical way "death is a normal part of living. So I am relatively dispassionate about it." Then he adds, with his patented chuckle, "I'm not sure how I'll feel about my own. But I probably won't be surprised."

Islands of the Great Lakes

Island	Lake	State/ Province	Square Miles
Manitoulin Island	Lake Huron	Ontario	1,068
Isle Royale	Lake Superior	Michigan	209
St. Joseph Island	Lake Huron	Ontario	141
Drummond Island	Lake Huron	Michigan	136
St. Ignace Island	Lake Superior	Ontario	106
Michipicoten Island	Lake Superior	Ontario	71
Beaver Island	Lake Michigan	Michigan	56
Cockburn Island	Lake Huron	Ontario	53.5
Sugar Island	St. Mary's River	Michigan	50
Wolfe Island	Lake Ontario	Ontario	48
Great La Cloche	Lake Huron	Ontario	36
Bois Blanc Island	Lake Huron	Michigan	35
Barrie Island	Lake Huron	Ontario	31
Parry Island	Lake Huron	Ontario	30
Simpson Island	Lake Superior	Ontario	28
Amherst Island	Lake Ontario	Ontario	27
Madeline Island	Lake Superior	Wisconsin	24
North Manitou Island	Lake Michigan	Michigan	23
Washington Island	Lake Michigan	Wisconsin	23
Grand Island	Lake Superior	Michigan	21
Neebish Island	St. Mary's River	Michigan	21
Fitzwilliam Island	Lake Huron	Ontario	21
Philip Edward Island	Lake Huron	Ontario	20
Pelee Island	Lake Erie	Ontario	18
Pie Island	Lake Superior	Ontario	18

Bibliography

Apostle Islands

Apostle Islands: Lights of the Apostles. Washington, D.C.: U.S. Department of the Interior.

Holzhueter, John O. *Madeline Island and The Chequamegon Region.* Madison: State Historical Society of Wisconsin, 1986.

Keller, James M. *The 'Unholy' Apostles: Shipwreck Tales of the Apostle Islands.* Chelsea, Mich.: Sheridan Books, 2000.

Ross, Hamilton Nelson. *La Pointe: Village Outpost on Madeline Island.* Madison: State Historical Society of Wisconsin, 2000.

Twining, Charles, Arnold R. Alanen, and William H. Tishler. *Historic Logging and Farming in the Apostle Islands.* Madison: State Historical Society of Wisconsin, 1996.

Battle of Lake Erie

Altoff, Gerard T. *Oliver Hazard Perry and the Battle of Lake Erie.* Put-in-Bay, Ohio: The Perry Group, 1999.

Altoff, Gerard T. *Deep Water Sailors, Shallow Water Soldiers: Manning the United States Fleet on Lake Erie—1813.* Put-in-Bay, Ohio: The Perry Group, 1993.

Altoff, Gerard T. *Among My Best Men: African-Americans and the War of 1812.* Put-in-Bay, Ohio: The Perry Group, 1996.

Gilbert, Bill. "The Battle of Lake Erie." *Smithsonian,* January 1995.

Norris, Walter B. "Oliver Hazard Perry." *Dictionary of American History,* Rev. ed. New York: Charles Scribners Sons, 1976.

"Oliver Hazard Perry." *The Harper Encyclopedia of Military Biography,* New York: Harper-Collins, 1992.

"Oliver Hazard Perry." DISCovering U.S. History, 1997. Reproduced in History Resource Center, http://galenet.galegroup.com/servlet/HistRC/.

Paulin, Oscar. "Oliver Hazard Perry." *Dictionary of American Biography, 1928–1936.* Reproduced in History Resource Center, http://galegroup.com/servlet/HistRC/.

Beaver Island
The Journal of Beaver Island History. Vol. I, Beaver Island: Beaver Island Historical Society, 1976.

A Day with Rolf Peterson
Peterson, Rolf O. *The Wolves of Isle Royale: A Broken Balance.* Minocqua, Wisc.: Willow Creek Press, 1995.

Drummond Island
Ashley, Kathryne Belden. *Islands of the Manitou.* Privately printed, 1978.

Brumwell, Jill Lowe. *Drummond Island History, Folklore and Early People.* Saginaw, Mich.: Black Bear Press, 2003.

Grand Island
Castle, Beatrice Hanscom. *The Grand Island Story.* Marquette, Mich.: The John M. Longyear Research Library, 1987.

Graham, Loren R. *A Face in the Rock: The Tale of a Grand Island Chippewa.* Berkeley: University of California Press, 1998.

Weingart, Marc. *Island of Adventure: Tales of Grand Island.* Philadelphia: Xlibris Corp., 2002.

Isle Royale

DuFresne, Jim. *Isle Royale National Park: Foot Trails and Water Routes.* Seattle: Mountaineer Books, 2002.

Janke, Robert A. *The Wildflowers of Isle Royale.* Houghton, Mich., Isle Royale Natural History Association, 1996.

Lankton, Larry. *Cradle to Grave: Life, Work and Death at the Lake Superior Copper Mines.* New York: Oxford University Press, 1991.

Long, Mega. *Disaster: Great Lakes.* Holt, Mich.: Thunder Bay Press, 2002.

Martin, Susan R. *Wonderful Power: The Story of Ancient Copper Working in the Lake Superior Basin.* Detroit: Wayne State University Press, 1999.

Parratt, Smitty, and Doug Welker. *The Place Names of Isle Royale.* Houghton, Mich.: Isle Royale Natural History Association, 1999.

Shelton, Napier. *Superior Wilderness: Isle Royale National Park.* Houghton, Mich.: Isle Royale Natural History Association, 1997.

Mackinac Island

May, George S. *War of 1812.* Mackinaw City, Mich.: Mackinac State Historic Parks, 1962.

Porter, Phil. *A Desirable Station: Soldier Life at Fort Mckinac 1867–1895.* Mackinaw City, Mich.: Mackinac State Historic Parks, 2003.

Porter, Phil. *Fudge: Mackinac's Sweet Souvenir.* Mackinaw City, Mich.: Mackinac State Historic Parks.

Porter, Phil. *Mackinac: An Island Famous in These Regions.* Mackinaw City, Mich.: Mackinac State Historic Parks, 1998.

Porter, Phil. *View from the Verandah: The History and Architecture of the Summer Cottages on Mackinac Island.* Mackinaw City, Mich.: Mackinac State Historic Parks, 1981.

Straus, Frank, and Brian Leigh Dunnigan. *Walk a Crooked Trail: A Centennial History of Wawashkamo Golf Club.* Mackinac Island, Mich.: Wawashkamo Golf Club, 2003.

North and South Manitou Islands

Gutsche, Andrea, and Cindy Bisaillon. *Mysterious Islands: Forgotten Tales of the Great Lakes.* Toronto: Lynx Images, 1999.

Ruchhoft, Robert H. *Exploring North Manitou, South Manitou, High and Garden Islands of the Lake Michigan Archipelago.* Cincinnati, Ohio: Pucelle Press, 1991.

Rusco, Rita Hadra. *North Manitou Island: Between Sunrise and Sunset.* Chelsea, Mich.: Bookcrafters, 1991.

Pelee Island

Garno, Noah. *The Story of Pelee.* Privately printed, 1954.

Martin, Jessie A. *The Beginnings and Tales of the Lake Erie Islands.* Harlo, 1992.

Segers, Ladislaus. *The Song of Hulda's Rock.* New York: Vantage Press, 1960.

Smith, Thaddeus. *Point au Pelee Island.* Amherstburg, Ontario: Echo Printing Co., 1926; Leamington, Ontario: reprinted by Speedprint Inc., 1996.

Tiessen, Ronald. *A Bicycle Guide to Pelee Island.* Privately printed, 1997.

Phantom Islands

Karow, Robert W., Jr. "Lake Superior's Mythic Islands: A Cautionary Tale for Users of Old Maps." *Michigan History Magazine,* January–February, 1986.

Toronto Islands

Freeman, Bill. *A Magical Place: Toronto Island and Its People.* Toronto: James Lorimer and Co. Ltd., 1999.

Gibson, Sally. *More Than An Island: A History of Toronto Island.* Toronto: Irwin Publishing, 1984.

Toronto Harbour: The Passing Years. Toronto: The Toronto Harbour Commission, 1985.

Washington and Rock Islands

Eaton, Conan Bryant. *Death's Door: The Pursuit of a Legend.* Washington Island, Wisc.: Jackson Harbor Press, 1996.

Eaton, Conan Bryant. *Rock Island*. Washington Island, Wisc.: Jackson Harbor Press, 2002.

Eaton, Conan Bryant. *The Naming: A Part History of Washington Township*. Washington Island, Wisc.: Washington Island Township, 1988.

Eaton, Conan Bryant. *Washington Island: 1836–1876*. Washington Island, Wisc.: Jackson Harbor Press, 1997.

Friends of Rock Island. *Rock Island State Park Guidebook*. Washington Island, Wisc.: Jackson Harbor Press, 2002.

Olson, William H., and Charles J. Olson. *Washington Island Guidebook*. Washington Island, Wisc.: Jackson Harbor Press, 1995.

Whitney, Ann T. *Let's Talk About Washington Island: 1850–1950*. Washington Island, Wisc.: Washington Island Township, 1995.